HE
Kept ME

HE Kept ME

Scripture and prayer guides for your darkest moments.

KAREN M. IZEKOR

XULON PRESS

Xulon Press
2301 Lucien Way #415
Maitland, FL 32751
407.339.4217
www.xulonpress.com

Paperback ISBN-13: 978-1-6628-1476-1
Hard Cover ISBN-13: 978-1-6628-1477-8
Ebook ISBN-13: 978-1-6628-1478-5

Dedication

I WOULD LIKE TO DEDICATE "HE KEPT ME" TO MY GRAND-mother, Ethel Lou Miller. She was a housewife and married for forty-three years. My grandmother bore 12 children, 3 of whom died during birth. Regardless of this, she still named them and spoke to them often. In her eyes, they were in heaven to keep Jesus company. As a young child my grandmother spoke volumes into my life, just through the way she carried herself and lived her life. I noticed Christ in her, and I adopted Him into my life too. She was soft spoken, quiet, and never opinionated. Always serving others and was quick to excuse actions of unruliness. I was a very talkative child with a busy mind. Grandma Ethel Lou never left a question of mine unanswered, and oftentimes would respond from the word of God. She was known for her big heart and forgiveness was something she lived by. Even as a child, I could see many

Mrs. Ethel Lou Harrison Miller
1924-2002

who were not deserving of her kindness. Although, many people around her fell short, my grandmother never missed an opportunity to extend her love to them. Unlike many of her grandchild, I was fortunate enough to attend church alongside her on many different occasions. Because of this I always had a standard of Christianity to go by. Today, I acknowledge my Grandma Ethel Lou Miller and the footprints she left behind in my life and many others.

Table of Contents

Foreword

Karen Izekor will encourage you to live your life to its fullest potential and maximize your seasons. Her story is a powerful testimony of how one becomes a mighty woman of God—being rescued and delivered by the power of God. Her teaching and ministry will draw you into a closer relationship with our loving Heavenly Father. She will share with you the tools to gain freedom from whatever it is that is troubling you

Karen and I first met the week my doctor told me I had cancer. As a minister myself, I knew the scripture and promises of God for my healing, but when I needed a sister to walk it out with me, she was there. I was healed that night at the healing room, where she was serving as one of the intercessors. My healing became fully manifested in the following months after that visit from the healing room.

A group of us women on fire for God traveled to Washington, D.C., in 2017, to join thousands of others around the world for "The Call," a conference held by Lou Eagle. Karen and I, among many others, walked the entire government district area in the cold and rainy weather protesting against same-sex marriages, abortions, and reconciliation between men and women and racial and ethnic groups. This was a week that many lives were changed because of the unity in the body of Christ from 50 states in America in prayer, fasting and marching for the Kingdom of God ... Between protesting, Karen and a few others and I spent time evangelizing throughout the state of D.C. Our mission was to share the gospel and the love of our Lord Jesus Christ which we did ...

I count it a great privilege to know Karen Izekor. Her heart for ministry is massive and her love for our Father is larger than that. Karen is a woman who knows the Word of God, her personal story of deliverance will inspire and encourage you. Pastor Karen Izekor's ministry will leave you wanting more from your walk with God. I count it a great privilege to know her. Karen's character displays a true woman of God. The fruits of the Spirit of God are evident in her life. Her personal story of *HE KELP ME* will give you a new perspective through the eyes and heart of our Heavenly Father.

Evangelist Nancy Mastroeni
A Daughter of Zion!

Preface

"He Kept Me" was written to encourage and inspire those who have lost hope in a life which is surrounded by disappointment, hopelessness, rejection, abandonment, alienation, oppression, depression, abuse, addiction, and chronic illness. Many people have given up hope in God, man, themselves, and even life due to a particular event that they experience. An offence that never received restitution and, or a repeated cycle trauma. My book aims to show you that you are loved, and you are not alone; and more than that you are deserving of all good things that Father God has placed on this earth for his people: they are obtainable. In my life experiences, God has shown me how all things worked together for good for those who love God, and for those who are called according to his purpose (**Romans 8:28**). This biography is my testimony of the goodness of God. May He be glorified in every area of my life. **Isaiah 62:10** was given to me by the Lord and was utilized for the foundation of "He Kept Me". I wrote this entire book using **Isaiah 62:10's** principles as my outline.

Isaiah 62:10 (AMP) reads

"Go through, go through the gates; clear the way for the people; build up, build up the highway, remove the stones, lift up a standard over the people."

Isaiah is called the eagle eye prophet. The eagle is known to have the sharpest eyesight in the animal kingdom. Their eyesight is estimated at 4 to 8 times stronger than the average human's. An eagle is said to be able to spot a mouse from 2 miles away. As well as their speed and accuracy in hunting. Isaiah prophesied thousands of years into the future with sheer accuracy. Jesus fulfilled dozens of Isaiah's messianic prophecies, *and in turn Isaiah became the most quoted prophet. My point is that this verse is still relevant for us today, even though Isaiah said it thousands of years ago. It reads: "Go through, go through the gates." The gates were speaking of the gates of Jerusalem, which was used by the Jews returning from captivity in Babylon. The revelation the Holy Spirit connected me to was that when standing before the gates of hardship, know that it is God who has helped you through it or you out of it. You were never alone, **He kept You**. The next verse says to clear the way for the people. When we go through hard times, we can quickly become narrow-minded and think we are the only ones that have been through something, or even say Jesus does not care because he allowed it. My book will bring glory to the King of all Kings; because I wouldn't be here today if it hadn't been for Him. This is why the name of my biography is, **"He Kept Me"**. No matter what type of predicament I have found myself in, God saw to it that I'd still be standing here today and would be sharing my testimony. Our God has a plan for each one of us and it's not for evil. **Jeremiah 29:11** tells us His plan is to prosper us, not to harm us, and to give us hope and a future. Our free will is the most valuable thing God has given to man. Man lives by the choices he makes. Part of clearing the way is shining the light on the dark lies of the devil by using the Word of God. Then applying the Word of God to your story as a testimony for others. **Revelation 12:11** tells us that we are overcomers by the blood of the Lamb and by the word of our testimony. The next point that **Isaiah 62:10** makes is that we are to build up the way. My book will show that there's good in all bad situations that we go through. Part of building up the way is being able to look and focus on the good. No matter how small it is, find good and build yourself up from there. Your first ray of light is how you made it through. Be encouraged if you haven't yet made it through, knowing it too will pass. What does the Lord say concerning it passing? (**2Cor 4:18**) "So we fix our eyes not on what is seen, but on what is unseen, since what is seen is temporary, but what is unseen is eternal." This verse tells us that everything other than God's word will pass, because the things we see are only for a season. **James 1:2-4** says: "My brethren, count it all joy when you fall into various trials, knowing that the testing of your faith produces patience and completeness, lacking nothing." Meaning, when you fall into various trials; be prepared and not surprised. God is saying no matter what your situation is; His grace is sufficient (**2 Cor 12:9**) and He'll never allow you to be tempted above your means (**1 Cor 10:13**). The next* *point in **Isaiah 62:10** tells us to remove the stones. **God's word** always shines light on our darkness and makes the rocky roads smooth. (**John 1:5**) And the light shines in the darkness, and the darkness has not overcome it. I have placed scripture throughout my book in order to show my readers how the **word of God** is our only road map for a successful life. God is offering everyone who will receive Him and live their life by His word a guarantee of success pertaining to life here on earth as well as life after death. The scriptures that have been placed in this book are in **Bold Print** showing readers that everything we go through will pass or fade away in our life; but **God's word** will outlast the end of time. The word of God gives us principles which we should place in our life in order to make it "successful". That means God supports His word and will not be proved wrong. The final point Isaiah makes is to lift up a standard over the people. That is why we should never walk in a defeated spirit. It's never what we go through, nor the end results, but how we choose to go through our trials that leaves us victorious. Can you speak something positive about the crises you've encountered in your life? If so, then you have won the victory. I challenge you to connect with Abba Father in away that will change you for the better forever. Thank God for the offense and pray a blessing over the offender. Watch God restore you a 100-fold. This book is God inspired, and as you read it you will encounter His Spirit. Before the finishing of this book I went through deliverance, restoration, and now restitution: without the Holy Spirit this would not have been possible. I felt led to equips my readers with prayers that line up with scripture. They are placed at the end of this book to give readers quick access to them. Praying and decreeing Gods word daily is the main ingrediency to freedom from the devils destruction. All honors of this book belong to the Heavenly Father.*

Introduction

IF IT HAD NOT BEEN FOR THE LOVE OF GOD WHERE WOULD I be? There are a lot of ways to respond to that question, but none of them are worth spending time elaborating on. My focus is on my position in Christ Jesus, which gives me a heart of peace and gratefulness, not condonation, judgement or damnation. As you read my story, ask the Holy Spirit about yourself and whether or not you're able to live as a new creation in Christ without letting go of the past hurts and offensives. **_Revelation_ _12:11_ (KJV) "_And they overcame him by the blood of the Lamb, and by the word of their testimony; and they loved not their lives unto the death._"** Yes, our testimony will always be important, it will bear witness of where you came from but, not where you're going. My prayer to everyone after the reading of my story is salvation for many, but for all a new mindset. Your testimony is not to be used as a crutch or handicap to your calling, purpose, or destiny: where we never walk into who God has created us to be. That's why the ending of this scripture says we love not our own life to death. My brothers and sisters if we allow our life unfortunate events and circumstances to consume us; then the blood shed of Jesus was inveigh. Jesus took on our sin and our ancestors' sin and generation curse from the past to the future and forevermore. **_Romans_ _3:23, 24, 25_ (NKJV) "_For all have sinned and fall short of the glory of God, being justified freely by grace through the redemption that is in Christ Jesus. Whom God set forth as a propitiation by His blood, through faith, to demonstrate His righteousness, because in His forbearance God had passed over the sins that were_** *previously committed."* The true factor of this scripture has opened up the door for Christ's testimony to be the new foundation of all humans' lives, as a new creation. Through the death, burial, and resurrection of Jesus Christ. The ending of our story as a victim now will always be victorious because of the finished work of the cross.

Today I have a new walk and a new song. *"My walk is with Jesus and my song says: Victory is mine, Victory is mine, Victory today is mine! I told Satan to "Get thee behind!" Victory today is mines! Joy is mine, Joy is mine, Joy today is mine! I told Satan to "Get thee behind!" Joy today is mines! Peace is mine, Peace is mine, Peace today is mine! I told Satan to "Get thee behind!" Peace today is mines! Healing is mine, Healing is mine, Healing today is mine! I told Satan to "Get thee behind!" Healing today is mines!* My Life is spent sharing and talking about the love of Jesus and how He is worth it all because He first loved me.

Chapter 1
What lies behind your roots?

MY STORY BEGAN IN SPARTANBURG, SOUTH CAROLINA IN the year 1969. It was during a time period where the world was going through a transition of desegregation. For those who may be unaware, the word desegregation is the process of ending the separation of two groups of people: usually in reference to race. Desegregation was supposed to end the discrimination of unfair policies, laws, and actions but instead it was only the beginning of a long process of uncovering the truth of racism to the rest of the nation. Time has allowed change in many areas; however, that spirit of division is still evident in today's world. In 1969, the atmosphere in southern states was totally

different; it's inexplicable how vile people had acted. It is well-known that racism is everywhere. No matter how much a place appears to have unity and community let it be know that racism is much more prominent in certain places compared to others. The generation I was born into accepted division as a way of life, most white communities favored this in order to show their control and power over the black race. The African American people were not respected as equal partners to work alongside the Anglos. Many African American families have experienced push back and increased hostility due to the high tensions raised by the Anglo's refusal to change the American law and amend the Constitution which were practically encouraging racism.

Black communities have still managed to excel in society despite our nation's discriminatory practices. They have created their own businesses and established their own housing communities. My mother's family were farmers, seamstress, builders, and preachers. My father's side of the family were military and entrepreneurs. During the era that I was born in; both sides of my parents' family were hard workers and believed in taking care of their family. However, mom's side of the family lived a more lavish lifestyle in the upper middle-class areas of town. Whereas dad's side of the family lived across the tracks were more conservative color families lived. This part of the town was where the lower middle class and impecunious color families lived. It was clearly evident in Anglo as well as African American people in how the spirit of division displayed itself. My mother's family didn't support her being in a relationship with my father for that reason and many others. They desired her to have someone who could take care of her at the economic level she was raised in. They also wanted her to focus on her education. Their desire was for mom to go to college or a trade school to sustain her status as an upper-middle class African American female. On top of all these reasons mom's parents felt she was too young to get involved and hitched. There had already been a display of acts of less than sound judgment on Mom's part by getting pregnant a year earlier to a guy who had no good intentions. They fear that if mom took this way out it could interfere with her completing high school which was not looked on favorably. Not too long after my parents met, mom did what her parents feared most. Mom and dad finally decided to be a couple. Because mom no longer had the support of her family; leaving high school was the only option. Mom had no one to help with the care of her son and transportation to get back and forth to school. She dropped out of school completely. As an adult, I look back on some of the bad strong-willed decisions I made as a teenager, just like mom. God was there to oversee me and keep me from a permanent destruction. He was also there with mom during her life challenges. God uses hard life lessons to make us stronger and draw us to Him when we wouldn't otherwise have been drawn or strengthened to reflect on God's glory and goodness.

Proverbs 16:9 (NKJV) "*A man's heart plans his way, but the Lord directs his steps."*

Proverbs 19:21 (NKJV), *There are many plans in a man's heart, Nevertheless the Lord's counsel-that will stand.*

I thank God for mom and her strong-willed personality. It's gotten me to where I am today. I have learned a lot from mom. Yes, the path she took was filled with a lot of uncertainty, but God had his own plan. God worked everything out for mom's own good and now He is being glorified. I found this out through my own life detours, away from God's will, into my own will and plan. As we read through this book and here about different testimonies in my life's journey; you will see for yourself how some of my rebelliousness and bad choices caused me to be in situations that looked hopeless. However, God used those same situations to mature me and bring me closer to Him.

Romans 8:28 (NKJV) *And we know that all things work together for good to those who love God, to those who are the called according to His purpose.*

Before I came along, mom had a baby boy who she named Kaleb; he was three years older than me. We have two different biological fathers, but my father adopted Kaleb once mom and dad got married. After my parents had me a year later my sister Tina was born. When I was three years old, dad bought us our first house. Our neighbors were not friendly; they didn't want us to live in "their "neighborhood because of our race. Everyone that spoke to my parents had mean things to say about us living in the area. Mom explained to us that black people usually weren't accepted around white people. Due to our neighbor's dislike for "darker skin people"; mom was always scared that something bad may happen to one of us because we were getting verbally attacked every time, we would leave the house. Finally, my dad put his foot down and said, "No one will run us off. This is our house! We have just as much of a right to be here as any of those other people do."

One night us kids awoke to mom screaming; the noise sounded like it came from the living room. We kids got up and ran into the living room and saw mom standing by the window. We ran by her and looked out of the window: There was a very large cross burning in the middle of our front yard. Dad grabbed his shotgun and stood posted in front of the living room door. He told our mom to get us away from the window and get on the floor and into the corner. He called the police before he headed outside and stood on the porch. He was screaming, "Get off my property!" The men who put the cross there were still outside yelling all kinds of ugly things about our family and us living in the neighborhood. When the police pulled up, mom left us in the house and ran out to meet them. Before she left us, she told us to stay in and sit down on the floor. I looked out the window and the police were standing in front of dad saying, "You brought this on yourself by moving your family here. Why don't you move where your own kind are supposed to be?"

Dad responded, "We have just as much right to live here as anyone else."

"I don't know what you want me to tell you then." My dad sighed in defeat.

"Why don't you gentlemen just head on home, so nobody gets hurt.". No one was arrested or charged for the act of terror they committed against our family. Dad took that cross down immediately and properly disposed of it the next day. A few days later we woke up one morning to all the trees in our front yard being covered in wet toilet paper.

"What is the purpose of having a home if it's not safe enough for my kids to play outside?" my mom said. "A house that feels like a prison can never produce happiness because it's walls are built out of fear."

As a child, I didn't quite understand what she meant but my dad understood because not long after that, we moved.

Leviticus 19: 17-18 (Amplified) "You shall not hate your brother in your heart; you may most certainly rebuke your neighbor but shall not incur sin because of him. You shall not take revenge nor bear any grudge against the sons of your people, but you shall love your neighbor as yourself; I am the Lord."

Dad had some serious choices to make as head of the household. I'm proud that he chose not to bring forth revenge on the men who threatened our family, as he knew it wasn't worth sacrificing our lives. Even he didn't know at the time: his choice aligned with God's word **Lev 19:17-18**. *Things could've gone sideways very quickly and gotten much uglier than they did. Not only with our family, but to the others who brought hate crimes against our family. Selfish choices and decisions can cause God's people to lose sight of the Father's heart.* **Lev 19:18** *tells us to love your neighbor as yourself. This scripture alone tells us that Father God's heart is of love, not division.*

Romans 2:11-12 (KJV) "For there is no respect of persons with God. For as many as have sinned without law shall also perish without law: and as many as have sinned in the law shall be judged by the law. 1Sam 16:7(NKJV) But the Lord said to Samuel, do not look at his appearance or at his physical stature, because I have refused him. For the Lord does not see as man sees; for man looks at the outward appearance, but the Lord looks at the heart. Romans 2:11, 1Sam 16:7" *This stands as proof that God sees every man as equals. Also, God doesn't judge man by the outward appearance of his skin, rather the man's heart is what matters to God. Everyone was relieved that we moved, even mom and us kids but dad: he had to have known that without the support of the law enforcement, he had a losing battle ahead of him.*

Our family kept to themselves from then on. Mom was a stay-at-home-mom and a housewife during the time my parents were married. She took care of Kaleb, Tina, and I, all while overseeing the house. Dad worked a lot, and I would hear mom call him a workaholic, but I did not really understand what that meant. He only ever had Sundays off from work, and during the week he'd leave before we'd even woken up. My mom making sure that we were ready for bed or already in bed was very crucial when it came to keeping peace in the house. Whenever dad got home from work, he required all of our mom's attention. There were times where dad's job cut back hours because they were slow. During these sporadic times, dad was very hard to live with; he yelled and complained about everything. I never did understand why dad was like that; not just with us but with mom too. He was an excessive drinker and smoker. He never had friends over, and never wanted to go anywhere. When mom needed to go to the grocery store or to pay a bill, dad always took her. He treated mom with no consideration; her having no means of transportation as though it was an inconvenience to him. Sometimes that required for him to rearrange his schedule at work or maybe miss his lunch to take us. We were too young to leave at home during this time; so, we would have to go along with them. Car rides were never enjoyable, as my dad was a chain smoker; and he did nothing to eliminate the odor that lingered in his car. When I would get in the car, I'd immediately grab one of the window seats in the back, and wind it down. Even with the window down, my eyes would burn, and I would still have problems controlling my coughing; but at least I could breathe a little. Kaleb and Tina would always say I was over exaggerating. Just because it didn't bother them, did not mean that it didn't bother me. I truly felt as though I was being tortured.

The only thing close to being more tortuous than dad's smoke was his foot odor. Mom had a rule that he could only take off his shoes in their room, in their bathroom, and with their door closed. This ensured that she could immediately dump foot powder into his shoes and socks. Even with the door closed, the whole house would light up with the scent of his stinky feet. You could go out on the porch and still smell Dad's feet; it was like a bomb had gone off. I'm sure everyone agreed with me on this issue. Mom had all kinds of air fresheners to help ward off the stink. She believed in letting all windows down to air out the house regularly.

Most of dad's time at home was spent in his room with the door closed, he never really cared to spend time with the family. Every time mom tried to talk to dad about getting out of the house for a family outing; dad would not even consider it. Mom was persistent even in trying to get him to go to church. Dad said Sunday was his day to rest and he was not going to church to have to put up with "church people". Since he did not allow mom to take us anywhere without him, that meant no one got to go to church. Us kids did not care as much as we suppose our mom did, but that's because she was hands-on during the entire week. It wore her out, never having any kind of break.

During the week mom had us on a regular schedule. Every morning she'd allow us to watch cartoons while she prepared breakfast. After breakfast she'd give us our morning baths. Then got us dressed and combed our hair as though we had someplace to be. She would then place us right in front of the television. We would watch educational shows; while she cleaned the house and got her daily chores out of the way. We had loved watching Rocky and Bullwinkle's show, Sesame Street and Schoolhouse Rock (I'm just a Bill). Mom made sure the programs we watched were balanced between educational programs and cartoons. We weren't allowed too much T.V. though, as after an hour or so we were sent away to have playtime in our rooms. Mom was always on time with lunch, so that we would be on time for our naps. She wanted us in bed by noon so she could watch her sitcoms in peace. The most fun part of our day would be after we woke up from our afternoon nap. Mom had our snack ready for us followed by a walk to the park, if the weather permitted and if she felt up to it. However, if mom did not feel like going to the park, it was no big deal to us. We knew we would still have plenty of games to play at home which could keep us busy: like jumping rope, drawing with chalk on the ground, and the lemon twist, which was a rope tied to my ankle with an artificial lemon on the other end of the rope, you would jump over the rope with your other leg. That was Jack and my favorite game to play. Tina would always fuss over the hula hoop and Kaleb was content with his set of green military soldiers. We were never bored with mom, unless dad was around. Like clockwork Mom would have us back inside with enough time to cook dinner and feed us. After dinner, there was a certain T.V. shows we loved watching with mom: *Family Feud, Wonder Woman, Charlie's Angels,* and *The Incredible Hulk* were just a few of our favorites. Every evening it was a different television show, and mom would act them out with us: it made things so much fun. However, mom loved playing cards. So, she taught us how to play spades. No one could bet mom and even now. Because Kaleb was a sore loser; mom would many times allow him to win just to get him to play with us.

During the times that dad was home, he liked watching *Animal Planet* or *The Wild Kingdom*. If we were in the T.V. room while Dad was in there, we had to stay completely quiet and be still. He would kick us out the room even if we just asked a question pertaining to the show. Dad would often substitute our names with "Dumb Dumb" or "Stupid". He rarely called us by our real names, and it didn't matter whether or not we did something to deserve it; he felt it helped him to get his point across. He also had a habit of hitting us without thinking. He would hit first, then correct the action. Dad had big, heavy, and rough hands. He was quick to snatch me by my arm when I was not doing something, he'd asked me to do, or if I was not doing it fast enough. If you were smart, you knew to never stand close to him. Mom stood up to dad when she saw he was hurting us unnecessarily. Dad was always drinking when he was off of work, sometimes more than others. Mom could tell when he'd been drinking too much. He would become very belligerent and louder than usual.

At one point, Mom said that she had concerns with Kaleb and his nose bleeding. It didn't matter if it was day or night, Kaleb's nose had a tendency to bleed for no apparent reason. When we were outside playing Kaleb nose would bleed and when we were inside playing or watching television Kaleb's nose would bleed. However, during the night mom concerned was his noses bleeding during his sleep. Mom found that if Kaleb's head was laying a certain way while he slept his nose would bleed and could possibly have him choking. One night mom got up to use the bathroom and went to check on Kaleb and his pillow was soaked in blood. From then on mom decided if she were awake, she would start checking on Kaleb first things first. Another concern mom had with Kaleb was him wetting the bed. Mom said that dad made it to be more of a big deal than it really was. She said dad would get angry to the point where he would put Kaleb out on the porch if he had wet himself during the night. Kaleb would be forced to spend the rest of the night out there... All mom's kids had their own problems, and she did not look at us with any less love because of them.

Mom said Tina would get up through the night to come get into bed with her and dad. Because Dad was so uncompassionate, he never allowed it. Mom could not bear to make Tina go back to her room; so, mom would place Tina on the floor next to the side of her bed on a pallet; that way dad would not have a fit. However, before dad would wake up mom would sneak Tina out of the bedroom; so, she would not get discovered.

She also had many worries when it came to me too: I would sleepwalk. Mom said she would hear thumping in her closet or bathroom in the middle of the night and find me in there standing fast sleep. On other nights, mom said she would find me walking around in the house bumping into walls. Mom said she would see me and call my name softly. I would immediately say, "Mom? Why did you get me out of bed and wake me up?" Mom said that they had to start double locking all the doors so I could not go out of them.

There was a day that dad had off from work, and the whole family was able to sit down and have dinner together... On this particular night, Mom had cooked liver for dinner; it was my least favorite food. My parents had this rule that if you did not eat all your dinner, it would be put in the refrigerator for you to finish the next morning for your breakfast. This particular night I was struggling to eat my food because of my strong dislike for liver. Unlike other nights, dad wouldn't allow mom to put my plate in the refrigerator for the next morning. He stood over me threatening me about eating all of my food. That night never ended for me: It started at 6:30pm when we all sat down to eat and went on until around 1am. Kaleb and Tina had gone to bed 5 hours before me. Dad told mom to go to bed and that he'd deal with me. He went to their room and got his thick leather work belt. Mom knew better than to leave me up alone with him. Dad had been drinking all night and he was very angry. He stood over me with that belt and started a 30min countdown: It was to announce that I would get a whipping if I had not finished all my food by the time, he stopped counting. Mom came back into the dining room trying to convince dad to let me eat the food the next day for breakfast but that did not work. Dad already had his mind made up. She knew dad was on one of his rampages, because he was screaming at her; so, she kept her distance and quieted down. He threatened me every 10 minutes to let me know my time was running out. I was so tired during the entire ordeal. I nodded a few times but after he got that belt my eyes got really big. I was looking right at that belt sobbing. I started trying to convince myself in my head to swallow everything all at once really quickly so I wouldn't be able to taste the flavor as it went down. But the thought of it going into my mouth made me nauseous. Dad started yelling at me again, so I got scared and swallowed it right away and started gagging. Dad yanked me by my arm, and I ran to the bathroom.

He was yelling, "You better not! You better not throw it up!" I was choking on my own throw-up right at the entryway of the bathroom. I threw it all back up once I was in the bathroom. It was everywhere. Dad grabbed my arm once again, and this time he started whipping me. I was spinning all around. I didn't have a

9

spot on me that wasn't whipped with bruises. Mom finally grabbed the belt, but it was too late as far as I was concerned. Then they started fighting, and he eventually gave in to Mom's pleas. Mom cleaned me up the best she could: in spite of the bruises, I had endured. That night I could barely stand because my body hurt so badly. It was torture even to lay down or my bed sheets threatened to irritate my open wounds. It took three days for me to be able to tolerate water hitting my skin. Mom had to doctor me for weeks until I was better. I still have permanent scars to this day. After that incident, Mom made sure she arranged for us to eat separately from dad from then on.

I believe mom loved dad at one point, but the drinking and abuse became intolerable. Now that I'm older, I can say dad loved us in the only way he knew how. For many broken fathers and husbands, being a good parent or partner is all about providing and through ruling over the house. However, it's a partial truth which is a whole lie. The bible teaches _1 Tim 3:2-4_ (ESV) *"Therefore an overseer must be above reproach, the husband of one wife, sober-minded, self-controlled, respectable, able to teach, not a drunkard, not violent but gentle, not quarrelsome, not a lover of money. He must manage his own household well, with all dignity keeping his children submissive."* and _Colo 3:21_ (NKJV) *"Father, do not provoke your children, lest they become discouraged."* as well as _Eph 5:21_ (NKJV) *"Wives and Husbands submit yourselves one to another because of your reverence for Christ."* In Genesis, man was created to have dominion and stewardship over God's creation, but not over other men. When God created Eve, she was meant to be there to support Adam, and to walk hand-in-hand with him as she was the weaker vessel.

Mom became unhappy living in what she called a "caged-marriage". She wasn't allowed to go anywhere alone or have any friends. It was hard to see love in their relationship; as well as our own relationship with him. Mom was suppressed in her relationship with dad. In time, she was pressured by dad to accompany Dad when he drank. There were many reasons why she wouldn't even consider it in the beginning: A large part of it was the history of alcoholics in our family. Dad figured that if he got Mom to drink, she would stop trying to make him quit. Mom was consumed with failure and grief so at that time drinking became the only option for her. She never did get over the death of her own mother who died when she was still very young. She began to sink her sorrows into alcohol, just as our father did. That's when their marriage came to a critical breaking point.

Because of the hostility in our home any time my parents would allow me to go see dad's mother, I couldn't help but beg for an extended visit. Grandma was precious to me; to all of us kids. Those times with her were some of the happiest memories in my life. It was between the ages of 4 and 7 years old when we were going often. Kaleb and Tina had no desire to stay or go over to Grandma's because of the roaches and rat infestation that she had. I adored her, and not even those pests could've kept me from spending time with my grandma Ethel Lou. I remember sitting on the couch watching television, and every 5 minutes I'd see something small with a tail run across the floor. At first, I thought I was seeing things, but then I decided to ask Grandma if she saw it too. She said, "Honey don't worry about those rodents. They love playing tag and scurrying around looking for food. I told her that I was scared that they would bite me. Grandma's response was that if you do not mess with them, they will not mess with you. I started to notice that she was right: and that they weren't scared of us. We'd see them sometimes sitting out in the open just stirring at us. I took Grandma's advice to heart and left them alone by giving them the right of way. After that, I had no problems with them. They really were just looking for food and running around playing.

Grandma had a rooster in her backyard that was faithful in waking up at 4a.m. promptly every day including weekends. It would crow for 15min. It was like an alarm clock for me. The whole neighborhood could hear him as far as I knew. The first few times I slept over it startled me, but I got used to it. I would always jump up out of bed and look out the window because the sun was rising, and it was so pretty to watch. I had a few other reasons why I loved going to my Grandma Ethel Lou's: She had this large bush full of hydrangeas that were covered in all types of blue, purple and pink blooms as big as my hand. They cover her complete flower bed in front of her house. They multiplied and grew quickly; every time I went to see her, they seemed to have grown larger and prettier: until I noticed they were covering the whole front portion of her house. They were the prettiest flowers I've ever had the privilege of seeing. Another thing I couldn't wait for was to watch the sun go down to see the lighting bugs come out. They would light up Grandma's yard. It was too much fun, running around and trying to see how many I could catch to put in an empty pickle jar grandma had given me. It was beautiful after I had the jar full. It would light up like a Christmas tree.

Grandma had a big heart. She was such a caring and compassionate person. She treated everyone with respect and honor. Grandma made no difference in how she treated family members nor the love she showed outside of her home. No one was a stranger to grandma. I would hear her say very frequently, "It's not a problem, I would be honored to help."

We did a lot of things together. One year, she bought me this tall doll that was almost as big as I was. We styled the doll's hair and made her clothes. We even played dress up. Grandma and I loved having tea parties too: she would never forget the cookies or pastries. Grandma played hide and seek, if she got tired, I never knew it. Grandma didn't complain once. Grandma's smile would bring me so much joy. I would forget sometimes until she started laughing that she didn't have any teeth. As soon as she mentioned to me about baking, we both would get excited, and I could see grandma's naked smile. We would smile and laugh even harder. Grandma would be right there beside me most of the time. She kept me company as long as no one else required her attention. Anytime grandma was busy taking care of grandad or doing chores in the house: my favorite thing to do was playing in their backyard on the swing set. I spent plenty of time on it every visit.

Grandma didn't know how to drive, so we would walk to the grocery store together. The store didn't seem close to me. She would make a whole day out of our trips to the store. We would go to the park and stop somewhere to have lunch. This would make our travel time feel a lot shorter. One of the many impactful events that happened while at Grandma Ethel Lou's was: I would also go to church on Sundays. She went to a small neighborhood church; it was within walking distance from her house. I loved grandma's church. Whenever we went the people there would always greet us with smiles and hugs. Singing with them was my favorite part. Many of the songs had very few words, and would generally just repeat themselves, which made it easier for me to join in. Together we formed a sound that was heavenly, or at least what I would imagine heaven sounding like. Many of the songs you would hum to with the music or hum with no music at all.

Whenever it became time to leave church, I was already looking forward to the next time I could go back. During the time of my parents' marriage this was the only church experience I had.

There was one visit to grandma's where she noticed I had bruises decorating my skin; it prompted her to speak about my father. Grandma said, "Your father is a good man and he really loves you, and your brother, and sister, and your mom."

I told her that it did not really seem like it. She explained how sometimes people who are treating others mean are not intending to. Grandma went on to say how people can get caught up in their own anger and disappointment with themselves because of the choices they've made in their life. They don't feel deserving of God's love. So instead of receiving God's love, they walk in judgment and resentment of their past. Grandma said many times they fault others for their situation. Their unhappiness comes out in the way they try to connect or deal with people. At the age of 7 you would have thought that I understood; but because of the Holy Spirit in grandmother, I was able to understand most of the things she shared. I was no longer mad at my dad and I forgave. Now I looked at him in a different light. I was able to feel sympathy for him and granddad.

Grandad was a lot like dad when it came to his relationship with Grandma. He'd speak to her impatiently. He used a harsh tone and would be reduced to name calling. I would rarely see him acknowledge my presence when I came to visit. Most of the time, he was tired or preoccupied. To me, it resembled my dad's personality in a nutshell. Grandad wasn't the type to show affection outwardly. He worked hard and long hours. I believed that he showed his love in providing for the family. He owned his own bakery. He was very considerate in bringing home all the leftover baked goods. It never went to waste with my uncle and aunts still living there. I saw how hard grandma worked to please him and the rest of the family. She never looked for a thank you. It was this unspoken love that came out by her attending to everyone's needs. She seemed to be happy enough with being able to help. It hurt my heart to see her cry when Grandad would yell or call her names. She never stopped serving him though, nor my 3 grown aunts, and one uncle who still lived with them. My uncle had down syndrome; Grandma waited on him hand and foot. I didn't understand what special needs were at that time.

I just thought he was spoiled. She never looked at it that way. Grandma saw an opportunity to give her love and nothing more. She had 12 children, and three of them died during childbirth. Grandma raised 9 kids however at that time four were still living at home. Grandma was patient with each and every one of them. She would be excited when the older ones like my dad who had moved away stop by for a short visit. I would see her fussing over them with kisses and hugs. Throughout my visits I recall grandma randomly speaking about her children who passed away because of labor complications. Grandma was very sure that they were being well taken care of in heaven. I would hear her say their names and then grandma would go on to say that she can imagine each one having an enormous amount of fun playing. Grandma said that they were keeping Jesus company and bringing joy to everyone who was there with them. Now that I am grown, I believe that those babies were placed there because God knew how much grandma loved children. God had them there waiting on her. To bring the joy she dreamed of for others with them: she would experience it for herself.

The word "No," was not in her vocabulary. Resting did not seem to be a priority. I never saw her raise her voice up even to her own children. Love was the only thing my Grandma knew how to display. I would definitely say she reflected *1Peter 3:4(NKJV) "Rather let it be the hidden person of the heart, with the incorruptible beauty of a gentle and quiet spirit, which is very precious in the sight of God."* From Grandma alone I learned by her walk that she displayed God's true love. *1Corinthians 13:4-8 (NKJV) "Love suffers long and is kind; love does not envy; love does not parade itself, is not puffed up; does not behave rudely, does not seek its own, is not provoked, thinks no evil; does not rejoice in iniquity, but rejoices in the truth; bears all things, believes all things, hopes all things, endures all things. Love never fails. But whether there are prophecies, they will fail; whether there are tongues, they will cease; whether there is knowledge, it will vanish away."* What I know now is that no one is deserving of God's love, nor can we ever earn it. God's love was given unconditionally to everyone who would receive Him as their savior. That's the love that Grandma showed everyone. She was so forgiven and never sad for any long length of time. I saw it in her eyes, her voice, and her spirit.

I did understand a little bit what my grandma was trying to tell me concerning my dad. However, as a child you expect your parents to be a place of refuge and I felt the opposite. There was nothing but anger and sadness displayed by him. God was good to highlight that he still loved me in spite of that. As I got older, I learned that your parents can only give you what they have. My dad did the best he could with the knowledge and resources he had. I've forgiven dad since my childhood. God kept me; He has been everything to me that my earthly father wasn't and more. My true opinion is that if I was given the world's best dad, it still wouldn't have been a close match to my Heavenly Father. *1 Corinthian 6:18 (NKJV), "I will be a Father to you, and you shall be my sons and daughters Says the Lord Almighty."*

Romans 8:14(NKJV), "For as many are led by the Spirit of God, these are sons of God."

1 John 3:1(NKJV), "Behold what manner of love the Father has bestowed on us, that we should be called children of God."

Matt 7:11 (NKJV) "If you then, being evil, know how to give good gifts to your children, how much more will your Father who is in heaven give good things to those who ask Him!"

Dad always had a job that paid him enough to keep a roof over our heads and food in our refrigerator to eat. Our basic needs were met like shoes, clothing, a nice room with our own beds, and even television, which some people who were less fortunate did not have. I will never lose the value of the things my dad did provide. I know it was the love of the heavenly father that helped dad provide for us. Throughout my life the adoption and revolution of the heavenly father I understand there are many different types of love. I believe that we can only demonstrate what we've been taught or learned throughout our life experiences. Dad's father taught him that providing for the family is loving one's family and the only responsibility he has as a father and husband. Mom on the other hand was full of love and compassion. She displayed it well when she was not consumed with her own pain of loss of love because of the early and unexpected death of her mother.

Isaiah 26:3 (NKJV), "You will keep him in perfect peace, whose mind is stayed on You, Because he trusts in You." Job 30:27 (NKJV), "My heart is in turmoil and cannot rest; Days of affliction confront me." There was truly never a moment of peace between my parents right before they were separated. When they finally did, Mom struggled to take care of us alone. She did everything she knew how to do to get work; to provide for us. It was more than any young African American woman without a high school diploma and no work experience outside of the home could handle on her own. She had been a housewife for nine years, and the only real skills she had were keeping a house. Dad left all the financial burdens on mom. After the separation, I was able to see Grandma Ethel Lou once again; but only briefly. She told me, "Don't ever forget that God loves you. He will never leave you." Grandmother was right. The first year of my parents' divorce we were scarce on food, and truly had no money. Mom still did all she could to give us the bare minimum. There wasn't a day that went by where we didn't have something to eat. **God kept us** from becoming homeless and hungry. However, I never knew the magnitude of how bad off our financial situation really was. Mom was so strong. She hid that from my siblings and I to protect us from worrying; and it worked, most of the time.

2Cor 4:8-9(NKJV) *"We are hard-pressed on every side, yet not crushed; we are perplexed, but not in despair, persecuted, but not forsaken; struck down, but not destroyed."*

Chapter 2
A struggle outside of the norm

Mom drove Kaleb and I to my Aunt Rachel's house. At that time, I was 8 years old, and Kaleb was 11. We weren't aware that mom had asked Aunt Rachel to take us in for a while to live with her. Mom never talked to us about staying with Aunt Rachel for any length of time. On the day she planned to take us we thought we were just going to visit them. Tina had been left with one of mom's friends. We honestly thought we were coming back. Once we arrived Uncle Taylor and Aunt Rachel were standing in the driveway waiting for us. I got out of the car, ran, and gave both of them a hug. I continued towards the house to see my cousins Rayan and Sarah until I noticed Kaleb was not following me. He was still talking to Mom who I then noticed getting stuff out of the car and handing it to Uncle Taylor. I then turned back to go see what was going on. I could hear Kaleb ask Mom if she was going to leave us there. Before I could get back to her, Kaleb started

yelling. "I don't want to stay here!" Mom had already given Uncle Taylor two suit-cases and he laid them down to grab Kaleb. He was hitting mom and crying. I started crying too once I figured out what was happening. Aunt Rachel grabbed me before I could get back to Mom. Mom got back in the car quickly with no explanation, nor did she mention when she was coming back to get us. I asked Aunt Rachel why mom did not take us with her.

She said," Your mother loves both of you. She will be back to get you as soon as she is in a position to take care of you. You're going to be staying with us for a while." Kaleb didn't come down as quickly as I did. He refused to come into the house after Mom left. He stopped struggling with Uncle Taylor though Kaleb told him that he did not want to stay with them.

He went on to say, "I'm going to stay outside until mom came back and get us." I was sad for a while, but after speaking with Aunt Rachel I was encouraged that Mom would be back as soon as she could. I went outside to console Kaleb with the words Aunt Rachel had shared with me. Kaleb said if you believe anything Aunt Rachel or Uncle Taylor said then I was stupider than I look. Then Kaleb went on to say how Mom would not be back and if she did come back it would not be anytime soon.

"Do you really believe that?" I said. "If you do, then why are you sitting outside acting like you're waiting on her to show up?" Then I told Kaleb that he was the stupid one; I left him outside. As I walked away, I thought about my sister Tina and I wondered why mom allowed her to stay. None of these things seemed far to me. I knew Tina was the youngest out of us all. However, she was only a year younger than I.

Aunt Rachel and Uncle Taylor have two children, a daughter that's 11 years old named Sarah: the same age as Kaleb. And a son who is 14 years old named Rayan. When I got back into the house, Uncle Taylor told me to go to my cousin Sarah's room because that's where Aunt Rachel was: Apparently, she was in there making space for me.

I spoke to Sarah and she told me not to talk to her nor to touch anything in her room. I stood back as Aunt Rachel instructed Sarah to take all her clothes out of one of her chester drawers and put her winter stuff in a trunk. Aunt said so, "There would be space for Karen". Then Aunt Rachel started pulling a bunch of clothes out of Sarah's closet. I had never seen anyone with so many clothes. Sarah had more clothes than Tina, Kaleb, and I put together. Aunt Rachel pulled out 10 to 15 beautiful dresses, and just as many fancy shoes to match. I didn't even know Sarah wore dresses because she was such a tomboy around me. Then I noticed a box Aunt Rachel took off the top shelf of Sarah's closet. Aunt Rachel told Sarah to go through the toys in her box and pick out what she wanted to keep; Aunt Rachel said she was putting the rest of the toys away in the attic. I watched as Sarah sorted through the huge box of toys. Most of the toys were still in their original packaging and had never been opened.

Sarah looked up at me with this mean glare and said, "You will never play with any of my stuff."

Aunt Rachel came back into the room after that and pulled another box down that was colorful, but a bit smaller. She opened that one up herself, and I'd never seen so many ribbons and hair bows in all my life. I'd seen rich kids on television, but never in person. Aunt Rachel closed that box back up and then she picked up Sarah's jewelry box off her dresser and rearranged some things in it: It was beautiful. This was the first time I had seen one of those jewelry boxes that have a ballerina spinning around inside while playing music. It was the most precious thing I had ever seen. Aunt Rachel left the top up on it and I was able to see all the earrings and matching necklaces that my cousin Sarah had. I had never owned any jewelry of my own and definitely not a jewelry box. Seeing all Sarah's things was so exciting to me even though she was not going to allow me to touch any of them. Sarah spent the whole time complaining that it wasn't fair that she had to share her room, instead of helping Aunt Rachel make space for me. Aunt Rachel made it clear that everyone was making sacrifices for us to be there because that's what family does. As soon as I was more settled in, she gave me a tour where everything was located throughout their house. As soon as she was finished with her tour, Sarah started following me around micromanaging me. During the first few weeks she acted as a teasing tattletale on everything concerning me. She was trying to get me in trouble and would stop at nothing to do so. When no one else was around, Sarah would bully me. Later on, she found that giving me the cold shoulder and ignoring me completely worked the best. Sarah and I could be in the kitchen with everyone else and she would ask Rayan or Kaleb to give me a message. If I responded, Sarah would look right over my head as though I was not there. I never got used to that, but I never said anything to Aunt or Uncle because I felt it would just make things worse. Plus, there were times when they would be in the same room when Sarah acted like that and they never said a word. It got worse anytime Aunt Rachel or Uncle Taylor did something special for me or with me. Sarah would make my life increasingly taunting. She was a thorn in my side.

Around the same time that we lived there, I began having a recurring dream that lasted around four years; at least in the dream world it did. In this dream, I was a King Cobra Snake. I ruled over all the other snakes who lived in the kingdom. The snake kingdom operated just how an ant colony would, where all other snakes were subject to my laws and pecking order. I had an army that helped me keep order in the community and take territory over all other snakes. All these things never changed but every night I had to deal with a new situation pertaining to discipline or correction in being able to bring order to the snakes who were out of order. The entire snake community looked up to me and honored me as their leader.

During the time I was living with Aunt Rachel, God placed a guardian angel over me. Every night after going to sleep, I would wake up an hour or two later to find an older lady in a rocking chair doing needle point. She would just be looking at me. She was the spitting image of Nancy Green, the African American Woman who was the poster board model for "Aunt Jemima Pancakes". She had on the same headscarf, long sleeve dress, and apron. Her soft smile told me to go back to sleep, and that everything was okay; and so, I listened.

Psalm 91:11(NKJV), "For He shall give His angels charge over you, to keep you in all your ways."

My sleepwalking didn't stop after my parents divorced; it only grew worse. Aunt Rachel and Uncle Taylor said one night the neighbors brought me home in the middle of the night after noticing me walking down the street by myself in my pajamas. Uncle Taylor and Aunt Rachel were very concerned, to say the least. They had tried just about everything that they could to prevent me from getting out, but their only option left was to lock me in the room at night. Uncle Taylor attached a key lock to the bedroom door of Sarah's room where I sleep. I had expected Sarah to complain or at the least make fun of me, but she did not. Sarah slept hard throughout the night and nothing ever woke her. She had told Rayan that it was too bad that anyone brought me back.

Kaleb never did get over being mad at mom for leaving us for almost 3 years. He was always doing stuff to get in trouble. Uncle and Aunt were always looking for an alternative way of handling Kaleb because they didn't want him to continuously be punished or disciplined. They knew Kaleb had only been misbehaving that way because he missed our mom and wanted to be back with her. He was given school assignments to work on and extra chores if he persisted in rebellious behavior. He struggled everyday with anger. It began to consume him. Eventually, he earned his own share of whippings, after persistently not changing his way. We would all be having fun, when out of nowhere Kaleb would say or do something stupid and spoil everyone's time. There were also times when he would separate himself away from everybody. I tried to talk to him a few times, but he called me a traitor and told me I didn't love mom anymore. He also called me a "goody two shoes," and I honestly could not understand where he was coming from. I still loved Mom, and I missed her too, but I did not think about it as often as he did. Aunt Rachel and Uncle Taylor were good to us even when Kaleb was trying to take the fun out of things. Uncle Taylor was fun to be around. Uncle had a beautiful voice, but he would only sing in the shower. so, I used to sit outside of the bathroom during his showers, just to hear him sing. He always sang The Temptations love song. He was always happy, even when he got off from work; he would spend time with us kids every day. It was nice to have a father figure that truly enjoyed being one. He cared about Kaleb and me just as much as his own two kids. He never made a difference between us.

Some of the fun things Uncle Taylor would do for their family was weekend barbecues at their house. This was to give Aunt Rachel a break from cooking and it was a good way for us all to spend family time together. My absolute favorite was his homemade ice cream which he made whenever he would barbeque. I never tasted anything like it before. It had a sweet and salty taste all at the same time. I loved watching him make it while the meat was on the grill. All of us kids had a part to play in the weekend barbecue, whether it was setting the table or the boys helping him grill. Uncle's hamburgers were the best, until this day I haven't found a better beef patty. I would literally make myself sick from eating so much every single time. But once you tasted Uncle's well-seasoned hamburger, there was no turning it down, no matter how hungry you insisted you weren't. The flavor and tenderness of the meat alone had me excited about his weekend barbecues. It was nice to have something to look forward to.

My other favorite thing that Uncle Taylor did for the family was to take us to the drive-in movies on Friday or Saturday nights. It was the only time we got to stay up past 9pm. On top of that, we were able to be under the stars at night while watching movies. It never mattered to me that not once, was I able to stay awake for one entire movie. The excitement of laying on top of the car under the stars at night, with a blanket and eating popcorn and other junk foods was awesome. I would be shoulder to shoulder with Kaleb and Rayan. I felt special. Sarah's comments about not wanting to sit by me did not bother me one bit. I felt like God and His angels were looking down on us every time we went. It was the only time that everyone would be still, quiet, and stay in one spot. I would always glance at my Aunt Rachel while we were sitting there. She would smile at me and wink as though to say I love you; I could tell just how happy she was. When I awoke it was always the next morning? I had no earthly ideal on when and how we had made it back home.

Aunt Rachel was a firm believer in us going outside daily to get exercise. Aunt Rachel and Uncle Taylor's house was big, and it had a lot of property around it; woods, trails and all. My great grandmother and great grandfather lived in the area, a few streets over. She had raised Mom and Aunt Rachel there, as well as my grandma. We didn't spend too much time with them though. They had a garden in the back of their house. My great grandmother would call Aunt Rachel to bring us over to pick all types of vegetables for herself and others in the family that she wanted to bless. My great grandparents would go fishing regularly; getting up as early as 3 am to go. They love big Bass fishing. Aunt Rachel let me go a couple of times. Great grandma had our lunches packed along with some snacks. We would always be there early enough to see the sunrise. We fished from the bank while sitting on blankets that "Greatma" had packeted. She and "Greatpa" didn't care about catching any other type of fish outside of the big Bass. Most of the fish that were caught were tossed back into the water, even if they had been Bass fish. I asked Greatma about that once, and she said that they were not out there to catch just any old fish, only the full-grown big Bass. She went on to say how most of the time they would only be fishing for sport anyways.

I knew they were both up there in age. However, I never understood how two people could be so quiet for such a long period of time and be right next to each other. There was never more than a full sentence between the both of them. In many ways, it was better than all that yelling or disrespect in conversation that dad's side of the family dealt with, even if it was a bit boring sometimes. It felt like I was with two total strangers because neither of them would ever talk or interact with me. Every time I went to bring up a conversation, Greatma would quickly shut me down in the most innocent way she could.

She would say, "Child don't be so busy in your mind; sit still and be quite like a good little girl." It was very obvious they didn't want me to ask them any questions concerning anything. I was puzzled about that because they had so much information about my mom and grandma, seeing as they raised them both.; I had never even had the opportunity to know my grandma, so I was curious. After the second time going fishing, I had made up my mind that it was too boring for my liking. Also, it was too secretive for me to be around Greatma and Greatpa. They were always shushing me even when I would be with them at their house. We could be outside in the garden, the yard, or in the tool shed and they would never say a word to me. Other than a short word to correct me to be quiet.

Uncle Taylor told us repeatedly that he built every square inch of their house with love just for Aunt Rachel. That sounded so loving and caring; I wasn't used to hearing a man being open in front of everyone with his feelings. I hoped one to have a husband who would one day love me as much as my Uncle loved my Aunt.

Their house was in the country with big trees that surrounded it. There were back roads and side roads. We loved the hills and enjoyed going bike riding through them. It was all of our favorite things to do. There were hiking and biking trails that would cover that entire turan; from beginning to ending. Everyone's homes and properties were surrounded by woods. Unless we were told to stay close, we would ride our bikes and be gone for hours. Aunt Rachel had a rule that unless we went together, we couldn't go. When we did go, I had a problem keeping up with everyone. Kaleb would wait for me and still catch up with Rayan and Sarah after we left the wooded paths. At the ending of the wooded path, we would end up on top of a really tall hill. Then Kaleb would leave me and catch back up with the others. I would be fine then. The hill was a 20-minute ride downward at top biking speed. It was well worth the 40-minute hike uphill in the woods. Kaleb was the happiest when we were outside riding bikes. It seemed to me he'd forgotten about being mad at Mom and everyone else. There were many things to do even when we didn't hike or go on bike trails. Rayan and Sarah had a tether ball, ping-pong table, as well as a swing made out of an old tire in their backyard. Kaleb and Sarah enjoyed playing basketball more than anything else. Sarah was a big basketball star at her school. She and Kaleb played daily to help Sarah train. All these things were unfamiliar to Kaleb and me until we came to stay with Aunt and Uncle.

Aunt Rachel was very guarded when it came to us watching television. We could watch television only once or twice a week and it had to be a program of her choosing. Outside of that, Aunt Rachel had us playing board games or reading books when we were inside the house. It was always something to do during the summer, weekend and evenings. During the school year, our choices were narrowed because of homework. It was our first priority and then preparing for school the next day was second. Aunt Rachel was serious about making sure our schoolwork was done and having us read regularly. She would also increase schoolwork if we got in trouble.

Aunt Rachel was a seamstress; she sewed all our clothes. She taught me a lot of nifty things like how to make potholders, rugs and other needle point work. Sarah had no desire to learn any of that, so Aunt Rachel taught me instead because she saw how much I enjoyed it. That also led her to putting me in the Girl Scouts, to be able to do more of those kinds of things and hangout with girls my age. I really enjoyed going to Girl Scout meetings. The new friends I met loved the same things as I did, and they were fun to be around. Plus, unlike Sarah, they actually wanted to be around me.

Aunt Rachel took us to church most Sundays, though Uncle Taylor did not go because he said that was his day to rest, which was exactly what my Dad had said too. Though, on occasion he would accompany us which made Aunt Rachel very happy. It was great when we'd have the whole family in church. The first time I went to my Aunt Rachel's church, it was the largest church I'd ever seen or been to. My Grandmother's church, on my dad's side, was nowhere near as big as this one. At first, I was excited, but then I quickly became nervous. It was nice to see that many people in one place all there to worship God. I was curious to see all the people inside the big church. However, Aunt Rachel took me to the back of the church instead of where the adults were gathered. Kaleb, Sarah, and Rayan went to a different part of the church. Where Aunt Rachel took me was something that was around the size of a school cafeteria. It had other rooms connected to it. When you first walked in, you noticed how it was just a big room filled with chairs with space left open for a stage. Aunt Rachel signed me in and told me she would be back for me after her church service. I wanted to go with her, but it was obvious all the kids my age was brought here. They taught us some songs and took offerings. Then all the kids would be separated by age into their own classrooms. My class had probably 16 kids in it in total. They were all between the ages of 8 and 9 years old. The Sunday School teacher had a Bible worksheet for all the students: It was like a real school but only learning about things in the bible. That first day I learned that there is so much I don't know about the word of God. The other kids in my Sunday School class knew who the son of God was "Jesus". I found out that the entirety of the New Testament was written about Him. The church kids had been taught stories and parables in the Bible and, some of them knew all the books of the Bible. I was very impressed and a little intimidated because I had no previous Bible teaching. Grandmother had mostly spoken of the love of God. She was the only Christian I had ever known personally. I wanted to ask questions, but I didn't want everybody looking at me as though I was dumb. The Sunday School teacher went over memorizing the books in the Bible, the spiritual fathers, and parables. She gave us prizes for participation. I wanted to learn, just as all the other kids had. I spoke to the bible teacher after class to ask her how the kids knew so much about the bible. She smiled and told me that most of her students grew up in the church and have had teachings since they were babies.

She went on to say, "You can catch up, but it'll take some time studying your lessons. I give homework weekly to give you kids a focus point. If you start coming to church more regularly and do the studies assigned, then it's possible you can catch up." I didn't want to tell her that it was out of my control whether or not I could get to church every Sunday. I made up my mind; I would do my part, and that was to complete all of the assignments she gave me.

I was missing every other Sunday, but Aunt Rachel loved to help me with the assignments that came home from church. I would be excited every time I got to go back. The bible teacher would go through a "Bible drill" which consisted of many questions from previous assignments and lessons. It almost seemed like she would be looking my way for me to raise my hand. If I didn't know the answer, I wouldn't raise my hand and guess like the other kids. I thought if I were quiet, I would look smarter. I thought that if I didn't, I might say something considered "dumb", and I didn't want to be that kid. However, our Bible teacher firmly believed in our participation. I would be the one kid she would be sure to call on at least once every class. Before I left that church, I was grounded with Jesus' mission and who he was. I had learned some of the order of the bible from the Old Testament. I also remember a few Bible stories and parables. There was so much more to learn, and I couldn't get enough. We went to church for a year regularly until my Aunt Rachel started getting sick.

Aunt Rachel sickness started off gradually. She would feel bad every now and then, having her good days and bad days. In time, she started having worse than good days. We were very sporadically able to go to church. When Aunt Rachel got worse, we stopped attending all together. Church wasn't the only thing that changed in our schedules. Aunt Rachel started off just taking naps during the day and going to bed earlier. As time went on, she seemed to be tired all the time and would be in the bed for more than half the day. She would only be out of the bed long enough to cook and then would immediately get back in. I was always asking her if she was okay. She would always respond, "I'm a little tired but I'll be alright."

I was eventually told that she had rheumatoid arthritis. I didn't quite understand what Aunt's sickness was. Though, from what I did notice was that everything she enjoyed doing with her hands and feet was compromised. Aunt stopped sewing or making things with her hands at all. It became very difficult for her to cook, or to do Sarah and I's hair. All of us kids took on more cleaning responsibilities because she just couldn't do it. I started noticing my Uncle grilling more often, so Aunt Rachel wouldn't have to cook or get out the bed. When Aunt Rachel had her good days, she always wanted to do something fun with us to make up for those not so good days.

There was one time when Uncle Taylor and Aunt Rachel went to the skating rink with us, even though Aunt Rachel's energy level wasn't the best. She told Uncle Taylor that her pain level was down, and she missed spending time as a family. Uncle Taylor was against the idea, but he would not argue with aunt after she had told him it would make her feel better. She loved to see us kids having fun. Uncle Taylor understood that you could have fun watching others have fun. This was a way to keep Aunt Rachel's mind off of what she was going through. Uncle Taylor was one to ride bikes with us and race us on foot. He loved basketball and skating, and he really was just a kid at heart. He would tell us, "Why should I allow you kids to have all the fun?" Uncle rented a pair of skates to skate with us that day at the rink. Aunt Rachel's plan was to sit back and watch. Uncle Taylor was on and off the skating rink floor. He was keeping an eye on Aunt Rachel. Rayan was the oldest out of all us kids, and also the most experienced when it came to skating. When he got on that skating rink floor no one challenged him. Rayan was like an eagle flying from a mountain top. Rayan could skate backwards, sideways, and in circles around anyone. That was except for Uncle Taylor; he was the only one who could keep up with Rayan. Rayan would let me hang on his shirt in the back: That was the only time I could catch up with the speed of the others. Skating became a tradition in the household. The skating rink was within walking distance to Aunt's house. Us kids used to go every Friday afternoon by ourselves. Sarah and Rayan had their own personal shakes, which meant they never had to rent skates like Kaleb and me. Though, I was never bothered by it: I just felt fortunate to be able to have an opportunity to go skating at all. Additionally, I thought about what a drag it would be to lug those heavy skates all the way down the street when we had to walk, which was most of the time.

On one particular occasion Rayan was pulling me like he would normally do: just a much faster speed. Normally I would let go before we would get too close to the curve. I did not this time because Rayan was going too fast, and I was afraid. I knew it would be tricky to go around the curve but not impossible for me. I was sure it was too late to let go because I had no clue how to slow myself down at the speed I was going. I had one option which was to hang on and hope Rayan slowed down on his own. At the beginning of the turning point of the curve I let go of my cousin's shirt because my skates got hulked on each other. I remember going at an uncontrollable speed and couldn't slow down. I hit the concrete wall with the right side of my body: bracing myself with my hand and wrist. Then I fell on the floor of the skating rink. Immediately after, somebody came behind me and ran over my right wrist with their skates. This caused the bone in my wrist to stick out, without breaking through the skin. I had never experienced pain in my life like this. Other skaters tripped over me trying to pass. Two of them fell on me; not being able to avoid it. I looked up and Rayan was already halfway around the rink before he noticed what had happened. Uncle Taylor had to have seen it because he was already halfway over to me.

I knew I had to go to the hospital right away. When Uncle Taylor got to me; he picked me off the rink and carried me to a lounge chair. The manager was with him trying to see if I was okay. He explained to us that in the event of any accidents he had been instructed to call an ambulance. Uncle Taylor made it clear he was going to take care of me, and that there was no need to call an ambulance. The manager told him that we would need to sign a waiver release that stated we refused the ambulance; we wouldn't be allowed back until we brought the waiver filled out. Uncle Taylor became upset and started to go off at the man. Which is when Aunt Rachel interjected and took the waiver and said, "It's going to be alright, let's just get out of here." This was the first time that I had ever seen Uncle Taylor this angry. We all filed into the car and Rayan said to me, "I didn't know you were still holding on to me. Why didn't you let go like you always do?".

"You know she doesn't have common sense," Sarah interjected. "She's dumb as a box of rocks." As I was getting ready to defend myself, Uncle Taylor cut me off and told everyone to be quiet and not say another word.

He then turned to Aunt Rachel and I could hear him say, "We're definitely not eating this bill. You need to contact their mother. There's no reason for these kids not to have insurance coverage. We'll have to ask the hospital if they can set up a payment plan…" The hospital ended up making Uncle Taylor pay for half of the bill before they would see me, and then they set up a payment arrangement for the remainder. They tried to reach mom when we were still at the hospital, but they were unsuccessful. Later on, when Aunt Rachel got ahold of Mom, she told them that she wasn't in a position to afford health insurance and right now was a bad time for her to send them any money. I had never heard Uncle Taylor use bad language before, and especially not in front of us. That was the exact moment when I became aware that mom had never sent any money to Uncle Taylor and Aunt Rachel to take care of Kaleb and me. They hadn't received anything for food, clothes, extra activities, or even emergencies. To think about the holidays we spent with them, Mom never sent Christmas or birthday money. I was quickly able to reconnect with Kaleb's feelings of abandonment. I felt like a burden to my Uncle Taylor and Aunt Rachel. They had done so much for us within those three years. I know that it was not Uncle Taylor's intention to make us feel like burdens, but he was right in his actions and even myself at 9 years old knew that to be the truth. How could you just drop your kids off with someone and expect them to incur all their expenses? Uncle and Aunt had treated us as their own. We were never made a difference from their own kids: We were always treated equally.

From what I know, Uncle Taylor or Aunt Rachel never received any reimbursement for the medical bills or any other expenses from the time that we lived there. Things changed after the incident; my uncle seemed to always have things on his mind. He became serious-minded and quiet. On top of everything else you could see he was worried about Aunt Rachel. Due to the state of Aunt Rachel's health, it got to a point where they could no longer take care of us financially or even physically. Aunt Rachel was too sick to care for herself. Rayan was in his first year of college by this point and was home for summer break. Uncle Taylor spoke to Rayan about him taking off a year from college to be there for Aunt Rachel.

Long before this point they had already informed Mom that she needed to pick us up. She once again told them it was not a good time, but Uncle Taylor told her it wasn't for them either. Mom no longer lived in South Carolina; she had moved miles away to Colorado. Aunt Rachel sat down with Kaleb and I and told us that she'd spoken to our mom. Apparently, Mom told Aunt Rachel that she would be coming to get us soon. She said that Mom did not indicate how soon she would be getting us; just that she would let us know.

Kaleb was excited but I was not: I did not want to leave Aunt Rachel. To be honest, I was still mad that mom hadn't kept in contact with us during the few years we'd been staying with Aunt Rachel. On top of that, I had several other reasons at the time why I didn't want to go back to my mother. Now looking back on that, I feel as though most of those reasons were just an excuse for me feeling like Mom had rejected and abandoned me. But was I really abandoned? The word abandoned means to be blackballed, blacklisted, shunned, shut out, and forsaken. The devil has a way of making our feelings about ourselves more than about the truth of a situation. God has a way of shining the light on the truth in the darkness of our perception. You just have to look for it.

Deuteronomy 31:8(NKJV), "And the Lord, He is the One who goes before you. He will be with you. He will not leave you nor forsake you; do not fear nor be dismayed."

Yes, Mom left us, but it was with our family. Relatives that loved us as one of their own and were able to provide for us. We were not placed in an orphanage or a foster family. In a true perspective, a lot of the suffering we were going through when we had been with Mom was stopped because she entrusted us to Aunt Rachel and Uncle Taylor. She did this to be able to get herself in position to care for us again without our dad being a part of our lives... The most beneficial thing that came out of this time spent with my family was the connection I received with God's word through Aunt Rachel and her church. I will forever be blessed and thankful for Aunt Rachel's church. Even as a child, I knew things were a lot harder after Dad left Mom, but **God kept me**. Now as I reflect from the eyes and mindset of maturity and wisdom. What God was saying about it all?

Romans 8:28 (NKJV), "And we know that all things work together for good to those who love God, to those who are the called according to His purpose.

Eph 1:9 (NKJV), "Having made known to us the mystery of His will, according to His good pleasure which He purposed in Himself."

Months passed after Aunt Rachel had spoken to us about mom coming to get us, and no one had heard anything else from mom. Aunt Rachel became sicker and had little or no strength to be out of the bed for any length of time. She only ever really left the house, and her bed, to go to her appointments. Uncle Taylor always took off from work to take her to the doctor. Rayan was off to college; meaning Sarah, Kaleb, and I were trying to manage most of the time by ourselves. Uncle Taylor started buying food that was already cooked and all we needed to do was warm it up. Sometimes Greatma would cook dishes and we would just warm them up. There were always things in the refrigerator we could make sandwiches with. No one dared to complain.

On one of the days Uncle Taylor took Aunt Rachel to the doctor, we all were in the family room playing a board game while we waited for them to come home. We mostly just wanted to hear that things were getting better with her more than anything else. I do not know about the rest of them, but I refuse to give up hope even though there were no signs of improvement. I had this strong belief that one day I would wake up and things would be back to normal. We heard the car pull up. Rayan ran and opened the door for them. When they came in, Uncle Taylor was carrying Aunt Rachel as she shivered from head to toe. She could barely stand, nor keep her balance. I'd never seen anyone be in this kind of pain before. I looked at Uncle Taylor to see his eyes if they were red and watery as though he wanted to cry but wouldn't. I ran to my room because I didn't want anyone to see me cry.

Boiling hot water was something Aunt Rachel needed to have done three times a day. I had never gone in her room to see what Uncle was using the hot water for. I know it had something to do with Aunt Rachel's medical treatment. Uncle Taylor was completely hands on when it came to taking care of Aunt Rachel. At night he would be home prepared to do whatever was needed to help care for Aunt

Rachel. Rayan came home from college to be there when Uncle Taylor couldn't be. There was a morning where Uncle Taylor was at work and Rayan had an appointment with a college counselor at a local Community Campus. There was no one to look after Aunt Rachel except for Sarah, Kaleb, and I. Sarah and Kaleb were in a hurry to go to the basketball court to play. I knew that Sarah was not good at being around Aunt Rachel because she did not like to see her in pain, no one did, but I told her I would take the boiling hot water to Aunt Rachel and sit with her if she didn't want to. I didn't expect this would make Sarah and I closer, I just wanted to be able to help Aunt at least once to show her that I loved her.

She immediately said, "Okay. Don't forget to turn the stove off after you bring the hot water to her." This was the first time Sarah had said anything nice to me since I'd started living with them. I took the boiling water into Aunt Rachel's bedroom and poured the water into a bed pan that was beside her bed. She had some white powdery substance that she mixed into the water. I asked Aunt Rachel what the powder was. She said it was her medicine, and it helped with the pain. I watched as the steam came off of the water. Aunt Rachel said she needed to let the water cool for 5 minutes before she could properly use it. I then helped her to the bathroom and left to go check to make sure I'd turned the stove off. After I came back to the room, she was already ready to go back to her bed. She'd already started shaking again since I'd come and gone. She leaned half of her weight on me, and we walked very slowly back to her bed which was only about five feet away from her bathroom. Aunt Rachel had these large plastic bags that she put over each one of her feet that went all the way up to her knees; there were ties on the ends of each of them. She had a miniature pitcher laying next to the bed pan which was filled with boiling water. Aunt Rachel stuck the pitcher in the water using it to stir. As she stirred it, it turned into liquid wax. Steam was coming out of the waxy liquid as though I had just taken it off the stove. Aunt Rachel placed one of her legs in the large bag and filled the pitcher up with the hot waxy liquid. I told Aunt Rachel, "That it looks too hot for you to pour on your skin!"

She said, "The sting from the heated liquid-wax doesn't last that long. The pain that I'm feeling now is much worse than the hot wax. Once the wax has cooled, it will help settle the pain." That's when I felt the worst for Aunt Rachel. I couldn't even begin to imagine the amount of pain she was in. As she poured the hot waxy liquid over her feet and legs, she let out a cry. It felt as though someone had just kicked me in the stomach. All of a sudden, I felt sick and overwhelmed for Aunt Rachel. As much as I wanted to get up and run out of her room, I didn't. I just could not bring myself to leave her alone while she was doing that.

As she poured that hot liquid wax on her bare skin, all I could say was, "I'm sorry Auntie, I'm so sorry, I'm so very sorry Auntie." I wish I could've said that I didn't shed a tear, but I did. We both cried together. When the whole ordeal was over, Aunt Rachel was completely wiped out. Once the wax was covering both of her legs and, it cooled very quickly; just as she said it would. It turned into a mold of her knees down. She then proceeded to do her arms one at a time, which was a lot easier because it wasn't as much to cover. Then the wax was pulled off and disposed of. She was falling asleep before I could even finish cleaning up everything. So, I let her lay down while I finished cleaning up all the used wax. Then I quickly and quietly left her room. After the encounter with the reality of Aunt Rachel's condition I was never the same. From then on, I made a point not to get into quarrels with Sarah or Kaleb. If I needed help doing anything and could not get either of them to help me; I did without it. Uncle Taylor's hands were too full to deal with us kids and our little complaints. At this point I made up my mind to go ahead and start packing for whenever Mom came, just like Kaleb had done. He had been packed for the 2 months since Aunt Rachel first spoke to us about her return. Approximately 2weeks after I did, mom showed up without notifying anyone. We received a phone call from her telling us that she was in town and would be there to pick us up the next morning. Mom showed up that morning and told us to bring all our stuff to the back door. She didn't spend time visiting or making small talk with Uncle Taylor or Aunt Rachel; I didn't even hear any gratitude expressed for what they'd done. As soon as we brought our bags to the back door, Mom loaded them up. She told us to say goodbye and get in the car. To me it was a flashback of what had happened when mom first brought us and left us with Aunt Rachel and Uncle Taylor. I felt it was too quick and impersonal. I must admit though that my views as a nine-year-old girl may have been a little narrow minded in thinking a social visit should have taken place of some sort. I wasn't aware of the original agreement that had been made between mom and Aunt Rachel; nor did I know the contents of the months of conversation that took place between the two of them. It was obvious that Mom had a little animosity both times. There was only one thing I could be sure of: Mom wasn't able to take care of my brother and I after her separation from Dad. Uncle Taylor and Aunt Rachel accepted the challenge to care for us until mom could get on her feet. Now that Aunt Rachel was sick; I needed to accept that it was time for me to go back with mom. As children, we want to be able to hold people accountable for our sadness or for things not going the way we think they should; and that's where I was mentally at the time. Right or wrong, Mom didn't have to give us an ounce of an explanation as to what was going on. Sure, if mom had given us an explanation it could've made our transition a lot easier in coming and going. Though maybe she didn't know how. I know back in the days; kids were treated the same as luggage. We were talked at and not to. Whatever your parents told you to do, you were expected to do it without any questions asked. There was no doubt in that fact that Mom was still dealing with how we would make it. I was hoping that she was financially better off than how she had been before she'd left us. We were always told she never had money to help out with us. Looking back on that statement, I feel as though if Mom did have the money to send then she wouldn't have needed us to stay with Uncle Taylor and Aunt Rachel. I can honestly say that I never knew Mom to be selfish before all of this had taken place. That was not mom's character, and I knew she loved us. Now that I am older, I understand people make choices based on what they've experienced, or their lack of experience. Our immaturity in the knowledge of God hinders us from trusting God. The Bible is our guide to righteousness and to the blessings from Father God. It helps us from repeating the cycle of sin that keeps us unfruitful and nonproductive in life. The word of God helps us make Godly decisions and keeps us on an obedient path, which keeps us from unwanted consequences. God is clear that we have the choice to love Him and follow Him, or to not. Sometimes people use God as a scapegoat for the bad things that happen in their life. Mom was raised in the church and in the word of God; but something had happened in her life that caused her to turn away from God. It could've been one thing or the culmination of many things that only she and God know. These things will now forever have an impact on Kaleb and me because she made a choice to move us out of state and raise us away from all our family. Mom's choices were based on the pain that was afflicted on her and on my grandmother, who died before her time. Mom chose not to forgive certain individuals in our family and all together just block them all out of our life. The other decision Mom made was a judgment against God by saying God allowed it to happen because "He's all powerful and could've stopped it." This response, which is unfortunate, happens all too often in the church. We as people judge God wrongly and forget who He really is. God is love before He's anything else. God created man out of love for Himself, and God has given salvation for free out of love through His only begotten son Jesus. The bloodshed of Jesus was given out of love for our righteousness, and the restoring of God's church was out of love through the resurrection of Christ. And now because of Christ's love for His church we have the ability to be more like Christ through God's spirit, who equips us daily until the second coming of Christ. That means everything God did, and is still doing, comes from a place of love and he cannot go back on his word by intervening in man's free will.

Num 23:19(NKJV), "God is not a man, that He should lie, nor a son of man, that He should repent. Has He said and will He not do? Or has He spoken, and will He not do? Or has He spoken, and will He not make it good?"

Isaiah 43:18(NKJV), "Do not remember the former things, nor consider the things of old. Behold I will do a new thing now it shall spring forth; shall you not know it?" God is telling all of us to lay down the past: What should've and could've happened but didn't. God is saying if we continue to focus on the failure and offence of man; we'll miss out on the new things the Father wants to do for us and within us. I've learned that it's hard when we let those things consume us. We become hard-hearted and bitter. We leave no room for the love God wants to give us to replace the pain and to bring healing in our lives because we're too busy faulting God for man's choice.

Colo 3:6 (NKJV), "Because of these things the wrath of God is coming upon the sons of disobedience."

James 4:10 (NKJV), "Humble yourselves in the sight of the Lord, and He will lift you up."

James 4:12 (NKJV), "There is one Lawgiver who is able to save and to destroy. Who are you to judge another?"

Mom had a friend named "Israel" that helped her drive from Colorado to get us. We didn't know him; he was someone who Mom had met since we'd been away. After Mom had picked us up; she stopped by Kaleb and my school to get our school records. We then e left South Carolina and drove straight to Colorado. On our drive, we barely heard from her other than when she asked if we were hungry or if we needed to stop to use the restroom. There was zero conversation concerning how we had been or what we'd been up to. We rode for two and half days in the car before we arrived; it was a long drive. Mom and Israel took turns driving.

Chapter 3
Reality Sets In.

WHEN WE ARRIVED IN COLORADO, MOM HAD A HOUSE THAT she was renting from the owner. My younger sister Tina had been with a friend of my mother's. Mom went to pick her up once we arrived in Colorado. She explained to us that she was enrolling us into the neighborhood school in the morning, and that she was going to start right away looking for childcare for after-school. That way she could take evening classes since she wanted to get her GED in the next couple of weeks. The next morning, we woke early to get ready and go to school. Mom enrolled us in school and signed us up for a free breakfast and lunch program. She also spoke to the school about their after-school program. She wasn't able to sign us up for it because it was too expensive. Mom didn't have a regular paying job; she worked as a maid when work became available. One good thing that Mom had going for her was she had a good work reference. All of the people whom she'd

ever worked for said she was very dependable, trustworthy and thorough when it came to her job. Most of Mom's jobs came from word of mouth: People needed maids that they could depend on. She would schedule her shifts around our school hours; but after her night school started, she would need to have a sitter, or some other childcare arranged. For now, if mom didn't get finished with work before we got out of school we were instructed to walk home, make no stops on the way, and lock ourselves in the house once we made it there. We knew to get our homework done before watching T.V. She tried to never leave us by ourselves longer than an hour or two. Mom spent all her off days putting in applications for other jobs, but because she didn't have a high school diploma or any other work experience no one would take a chance in hiring her. Mom's rent was 2 months behind, and our food was becoming more and more scarce. We had a sympathetic landlord that worked with Mom as long as she kept him informed on her plans to pay and was giving him at least some money. I never knew how much a blessing the school lunch program was until we came to live with Mom. When we didn't have food at home, at least we had breakfast and lunch at school. One thing about holidays with mom meant that we may not get gifts, but we always had a full-course meal on Christmas Day and during birthdays. If it was our birthday, we got to choose the meal that mom was going to cook. My favorite meal was potato salad, fried okra and fried pork chops. We couldn't always count on a cake but anything sweet was a plus. Outside of that, our regular meals were pot pies, cold cut sandwiches, T.V. dinners, and those little party pizzas. The change in our lives was quite noticeable compared to how it was at Uncle Taylor and Aunt Rachel's house. I never forgot Mom did everything on her own without Dad's financial support.

There was one day when the landlord stopped by to pick up rent from mom; he was finally able to meet Kaleb and I. Mom asked him if he knew anyone who did in-home sitting because she needed childcare for us. He told her that there was a retired couple that lived three houses down and that they've lived there as long as he's been in his house. He told mom that they were a really nice and friendly couple. One day after school, Mom took us by there to talk to the couple and they invited us in. Mom started by telling them who suggested that we stop in and speak to them. She further explained that she was a single parent with no family that lived nearby to help her out. She continued with how she's been having a hard time getting a job, so she wants to go back to school to get her G.E.D. but doesn't have anyone to watch us kids. The neighbors, who introduced themselves as Mr. and Mrs. Oakley, said that they had two kids whose ages were around the age of our mom and only one of them had kids. They went on to say that all of them are living outside of Colorado, so they do not get to see them very often.

Mr. Oakley said, "We would love to adopt your kids as our grandkids."

Mrs. Oakley said, "It wouldn't be a problem for us to watch them here until you get out of class. Plus, I need someone else to cook for because Mr. Oakley doesn't eat much anymore. Every day, you can get out of school and walk straight over to our house."

"How much would you charge me?" Mom asked.

"You can pay me when you can, and however much you believe is fair and that you can afford," Mrs. Oakley said.

After we left their house, Mom had a peaceful smile on her face for the first time since we had been back with her. I was excited to start spending time with them. They seemed to be a loving and caring couple. The rest of the evening was quiet, and everyone spent time in their own room preparing for the next day. Tina and I always shared rooms: We each slept in twin size beds. My relationship with her was nothing compared to the one I had with my cousin Sarah. Tina was 8 now, and I was 9, only a year older. Since she was the baby of the family, Mom babies her most of the time. She could do no wrong and if she ever did do something, Mom would hold me accountable for it because I was the oldest. I was always given the responsibility to watch over her, and Tina took advantage of that. Whenever mom was not home, she would refuse to listen to me; even if it were something Mom had specifically instructed us to do or not do. She seemed to always act like a renegade, never following rules and was just causing problems unnecessarily. I believe it was because she knew mom would let her get away with anything. There were only two things that really bothered me about Tina at that time; one being that Mom would literarily whip me for things she did wrong, and she could not care less. Then two, she was never given any responsibilities. Tina was automatically exempt from daily chores. I would find myself being the only one of Mom's kids who was forced to be in the kitchen and to clean the bathroom. Anytime Mom cooked, I had to be in there to help. Learning to cook and clean up daily was expected out of me. Kaleb, who was 12 years old, was exempt from most cleaning exhibits because he was a boy. Mom seemed to always be the hardest on me and said how she was tired of me comparing her to Aunt Rachel. It was obvious that we were each treated differently, which was unfair; during my time spent with my aunt, she never exempts anyone from anything. We were given age-appropriate chores and duties and were responsible to follow through on all that was given. No one was held accountable for anyone else. I could see what mom meant when she said I was always comparing her to Aunt Rachel. I really did not mean to but, I felt encouraged whenever I thought injustice was taking place; not that it ever made a difference. So why did I? Mom made me aware that she knew, but she didn't care. It was always going to be her way or the highway. Unfortunately, it continued to get worse as I got older. I felt like a stepchild that was a burden to my Mom. Due to this, Tina and I never became close or played together.

Tina has always been bigger than I am, and throughout our life people who saw us together would assume her to be the oldest. When Mom and Dad were still together, Mom would always dress us up as if we were twins. I was told that my personality favored Dad's and Tina's favored Mom's but even to this day I highly disagree with that. I was always called dramatic because I was sensitive. I was told I played too much and could be a bit silly when in a peaceful environment. Tina on the other hand never really cared about the things that I cared about. Her interests stemmed off of other people's, and they were rarely off of her own curiosity. She wasn't a dreamer like me: she was much more of a follower. Now that I'm older, I can see that I pushed Tina away because of jealousy over the favoritism Mom gave her. She always made friends easier than I did because she never held a standard over people. If you didn't agree with me on what I wanted to play and how I wanted to play it, then I would play alone and feel zero remorse. I did not realize that the spirit of rejection and abandonment was fueling my emotions, which was caused from being left at Aunt Rachel's for those years. Most of the friends I connected with liked me and what I was interested in. The time I spent with Aunt Rachel and sharing a room with my cousin Sarah led me to grow up quite a bit.

My cousin Sarah's bullying caused me to constantly live with my guard up, which enforced me in my ways of being a "loner". To this day, I believe that I treated Tina the way my cousin Sarah treated me. I have no real relationship with Tina because of the standards and expectations I placed on her throughout our life. I have come to the truth in time and had to rather recently apologize for the childlike behavior that I've carried into my adult life. It is what has brought division between the two of us. I can confidently say that some of the things that Mom did wasn't fair to me, but Tina had no hand in them and shouldn't have been held accountable for someone else's behavior. Mom had a hidden past that I didn't know anything about at the time. She displayed her feelings against me just the same as I did with Tina. I didn't cause them and didn't deserve the repercussions of it. Hers were caused by Aunt Rachel and their childhood. Mom struggled with forgiveness over the abuse that took place when she was younger. Who would have known that the Aunt Rachel I loved so much had this history of offence with mom; especially now that her daughter Sarah brought that same type of offense towards me? It has been nothing but jealousy and envy between Aunt Rachel and Mom, which is paralleled through Sarah and me. Though, without forgiving previous offences, we can further the spread of it down through generations. We call life normal and acceptable to see ourselves with fruitless and, often lifeless relationships that Satan uses to hinder our walk with God and each other. If only I knew then what I know now: God's word is resurrecting and life giving to all who will apply it.

Daniel 9:9(NKJV), "To the Lord our God belong mercy and forgiveness, though we have rebelled against Him."

Colossians 1:13-14 (NKJV), "He has delivered us from the power of darkness and conveyed us into the Kingdom of the Son of His love, in whom we have redemption through His blood, the forgiveness."

Matthew 6:15(NKJV), "But if you do not forgive men their trespasses, neither will your Father forgive your trespasses."

Proverbs 17:9(NKJV), "He who covers a transgression seeks love, but he who repeats a matter separates friends."

Proverbs 10:12(NKJV), "Hatred stirs up strife, But love covers all sins."

Kaleb was by himself most of the time, locked up in his room and watching television. He used his free time now catching up on the television shows. There wasn't any sort of restriction on what shows he could watch, and how much time he could spend watching it. He did not have anyone to hound him anymore about reading nor practicing any schoolwork.

That next day after meeting with our neighbors, we got dressed quickly and walked to school early to make sure we didn't miss out on breakfast. This was going to be the first day we were able to get out of school and walk to The Oakley's house. The school day went by fast: after which Kaleb met Tina and I in the front of the school so we could walk home together; just as he always did. Mom wanted us to walk home together regardless of who got out first. Once we arrived at the Oakley's house, Mrs. Oakley had a hot meal sitting there waiting for us. It appeared as though she had been waiting on us all day. She had cooked a pot roast and vegetables and cornbread. It had been a while since I remember eating like that. Mr. Oakley greeted us while we were eating, and he asked us about our day. He shared with us that he spends most of his time in his garage which he converted into a workshop. I wasn't sure what that meant, but I wasn't going to be the one to ask and look dumb because I should've known. He also told us that he was retired from the Marines and had served in World War 2 as an officer. He said his favorite thing in coming home was Mrs. Oakley's cooking.

"Let them finish up eating so they can get all their homework done before it gets to be late" Mrs. Oakley said.

"Okay, okay fine but do you guys know how to play cards? If not, I'll teach you after your homework is all done." Mrs. Oakley then had us sit down and work on homework and for those of us who didn't have any assignments, she had us read a book. Mrs. Oakley had a dayroom that was filled with books. That room resembled a small library. It had books on any subject you could think that were fit for all ages. She had told us she was a retired schoolteacher and she volunteered at the library whenever they needed help. You could really tell she had been a teacher because she was very patient with us, and knowledgeable on any subject you brought up to her. Once we were finished with everything Mrs. Oakley asked us to do, she allowed us to watch television. However, Mr. Oakley was standing there wanting to know if we were ready to play cards. As we sat down to play, Mom rang the doorbell. Time had gone by so fast; I forgot that she was coming early to pick us up. As Mom stepped into the house Mrs. Oakley was urging her to sit down to eat: This gave us a little more time to spend with Mr. Oakley. Our relationship with the Oakley's was incredibly impactful. As I look back on that season of my life with Mr. and Mrs. Oakley it brings to mind:

Isaiah 46:10 (NKJV), "Declaring the end from the beginning, and from ancient times things that are not yet done, saying, 'My counsel shall stand, and I will do all my pleasure.'" This passage of scripture speaks to me saying that no matter what issues you have which hinders your faith in God, you and your loved ones are not unreachable by God. God can and will restore you to His will and good purpose.

Hebrews 1:14 (NKJV), "Are they not all ministering spirits sent forth to minister for those who will inherit salvation." The Oakley's were used by God to minister to our family, showing the love of God in kindness, generosity, and compassion. Who has God sent to you to be the hands, feet, and mouth of Jesus while expecting nothing in return?

Hebrews 13:2 (NKJV), "Do not forget to entertain strangers, for by so doing some have unwittingly entertained angels." *"God eagerly awaits on the manifestation of his son and daughter to awaken and take their place in the body" (Rom 8:19).*

The weather in Colorado was much different than what we were used to; but like everything else it was just an adjustment that needed to be made. During most summer days it would never get over 80 degrees... During the fall and into the winter, the temperature really cooled down fast. Most of those days we were in sweaters, jackets, and clothing that was layered. There was one particular day that those layers would not be enough. We got dressed to go to school just like any other morning: but as we tried to go outside, the front door would not budge. It appeared to have been bolted from the opposite side. Mom further investigated by looking outside, and as far as the eyes could see there was nothing but white snow. Mom had to climb out of one of our windows to get outside. Before the front door would open, she had to shovel tons of snow away from the front door. Mom climbed back in through the window twice to warm herself before she was able to clear enough snow to open the front door. Seeing how deep the snow was on the ground was both amazing and scary at the same time. The snow came up to mom's waist when she stood on the sidewalk after a path was dug. It was too much snow to dig with a regular shovel; it would've taken mom all day to clear a small path on the porch and stairs. Lucky for mom: the neighbors had a plow. After one of our male neighbors helped mom; we had the front door and a half of sidewalk that led to the front yard clear. When I stood on the sidewalk that had been cleared, the surrounding snow came up to my neck. Walking through the snow was not an option for any of us: it was way too deep. As I stood outside for a few minutes, the saliva on my lips froze. The cold air cut straight through my winter clothes and cut through my bones. It felt as if I had just taken a bath and was still wet: It was the same coldness that hits you before you dry off. It was too cold for me to be outside. Mom had to catch a ride to the store because our car was blocked in by the snow: A week later mom had to get someone with a larger plow to clear a path around the car to the street. School ended up being closed for a month. We had to forfeit our Spring Break to make up for all of the days we missed. Many kids and teachers were upset about it, but we did not care one way or another. Mom did not have enough money anyway to do anything special for us if we did have Spring Break, so it would not have really changed anything for us.

Throughout the time we lived in Colorado, Mom never really made any close friends outside of the Oakley's. However, there was this one lady named Maria which mom called her friend. She was a Spanish psychic that had her own business doing palm readings and reading of cards. She had a small little shop that sold all types of stuff that was supposed to bring people good luck. Mom spent any money she had to spare buying candles for every area of her life she needed improvement in. These candles were supposed to last three weeks on a continuous burn and bring luck in the area that was listed outside of the candle. Mom had a candle for love, money, happiness, peace and protection. Sometimes there were other candles she would buy however these were the go-to when money was tight. Mom kept them burning around the house constantly. At that time, I thought it was just a silly intuition. She also allowed Maria to read her future. When we would go there, I stayed outside in the front of her store waiting for mom to visit and leave. It was something about her store that creeped me out: including Maria herself. Mom never gave me a hard time about going in. On one occasion, Maria told Mom to have me come inside because she didn't like the idea of me being outside alone while strangers were passing by. Mom made me come in; and I was not happy about it. I refused to go all the way into the store: I stood by the entrance of the front door. Maria walked up to me and asked me to let her read my hand. I immediately balled my hands up and put them behind my back and looked down to the floor. Every time I was around her it reminded me of an unknown darkness. Then she would say, "Let me read your cards," and giggled, "you don't have anything to be scared of." Mom and Tina both with zero hesitation would put their hands out to receive a reading by Maria. She would read Mom's cards too. I didn't know much about psychics, but I had an uneasy feeling about Maria. I would get a sick feeling in my stomach from being in her shop. It was like seeing scary movies on television and being nervous because you don't know what's going to happen next. There were other things Mom did that was clearly superstitious. She would yell at us if we walked on the wrong side of any telephone pole, and she would also say there was a right and wrong side to pass people which would bring bad luck if we made the wrong choice. If mom saw a black cat, she got paranoid and did not let it cross in front of us; it didn't matter if she had to go out of her way to avoid the cat. She also said an umbrella would bring bad luck if it was opened up indoors. Every morning Mom would read her horoscope to predict her day. There were other things like 7 years of bad luck for breaking a mirror. She would regularly quote our Zodiac sign and hers by the month we were born. According to Mom, the zodiac signs couldn't lie; they were our true character and personality. I personally thought it was a pain to try to remember all of that stuff. It definitely kept mom so unpeaceful and gave Mom an excuse for her bad attitude and moods. She also had become paranoid over so many little things. It scared me that she used to get as mad as she did about them. I personally didn't feel that any of them held any truth. Yes, there were some coincidences, and many happen by chance. But for me it was easier to believe that God loved me enough to keep me safe from all of that crazy stuff. I didn't know God's word like I do now. Though, I can still say this scripture lines up with him being in the midst of me, even though my small amount of faith at the time.

45

Roman 8:31 (NKJV), "What then shall we then say to these things? If God be for us, who can be against us?"

Deuteronomy 31:8(NIV), "The Lord Himself goes before you and will be with you; He will never leave you nor forsake you. Do not be afraid; do not be discouraged."

Now that I am older, I realize that no matter how small of a door people open to the unseen rhyme; the devil will get in and cause a spiritual attack that manifests itself in the natural through fear (night terrors & demonic visitations), sickness, poverty, bad relationships and death. As a child I didn't realize mom had opened a spiritual portal through witchcraft in all these things that she was doing. Mom thought she was bringing herself good luck through all these mediums. The truth was she had invited the demonic and satanic spirits into our home and life. The reason that there was an ongoing battle of good and evil in the life of my siblings and I and mom's life was because of these open doors. In the back of this book, you will find prayers to shut those doors and put you back on the right path of freedom and prosperity. My first night in the house mom was renting out; I started having tormenting dreams and dominic visitation unlike the dreams I had at my aunt Rachel's house. No longer did I see my garden angel at night. I started feeling like a dark present of a man or monster would come into my room and get in my bed with me, trying to choke me or lay on top of me and touch my body. I was full of fear each time it happened to the point that I would be paralyzed and not be able to move or get out of my bed to go get help. Every time I tried to scream no words would come out. The only thing I did that would help me every time would be to close my eyes tight and start calling out the name of Jesus. No sound would come out because of the fear that I was gripped with. I kept saying it anyway over and over and over until I fell asleep or until the scarry present would leave me. I didn't know that the night tarras was tied to all this crazy stuff mom was doing until much later in life. I never did share with mom about the night tarras; fearing she would force me to talk with Maria the psychic. There was a door that had been open through my mom in the supernatural rhyme of darkness. During the time period I was with my Aunt having the repeated dreams of the King Cobra Snake Kingdom; I was able to see my gardening angel. Now I no longer could see my angel; after I left my aunt's house. I thought she had left me. Now that I'm older I understand the spirit rhyme and how it works. Angels are assigned by God to keep us in all our ways and make sure God's word goes forth as it is written. However, demons can torment and bring fear when sin is present in your life. This is what I was experiencing. I had gotten older and my new environment with mom suppressed my ability to see the angel. Plus, I had gotten older and no-longer had an innocent spirit but a heart that had me operating out of judgment and offence towards others which is sin. This will limit your ability to see your angels. Not only that I was in mom's custody now and she was the responsible party for keeping us covered and protected. Mom herself was operating in sin and had unforgiveness with family and God. Known or unknown this opened a portal to the demonic rhyme that was attacking me nightly in our house. The seeking of supernatural powers other than God has been around since the beginning of times. Satan has used witchcraft to prevent people from finding holy spirituality in God alone. Satan uses mediums, horoscopes to entice people away from God and toward a power that gives self-enlightenment.

Lev 19:31 (NIV), "Do not turn to mediums or seek out spiritists, for you will be defiled by them. I am the Lord your God." God tells us through his word not to walk in the way of the world nor wisdom of man or self for this is disobedient.

1 Sam 15:23 (NIV),"For rebellion is like the sin of divination, and arrogance like the evil of idolatry. Because you have rejected the word of the Lord." Thank God for his word that kept me alive.

Psalm 34:7, "The angel of the Lord encamps around those who fear Him, and He delivers them."

Exodus 23:20, "See, I am sending an angel ahead of you to guard you along the way and to bring you to the place I have prepared." Even as a little kid I knew God and his angels were still watching over me.

Deu 31:6 (NKJV), "Be Strong and of Good Courage, do not Fear or be Afraid of them; for the Lord your God, He is the One who goes with you. He will not leave you nor forsake you."

Winter had come and gone. Spring went quickly and we were now transitioning out of Summer into Fall. My siblings and I were truly thankful for the

Oakley's because of their love for our family. Even when school was out, we were over their house daily enjoying their kindness. Because of Mrs. Oakley we never missed a hot meal when the school was closed for summer break. Not much had changed mom was still taking night class to get her G.E.D and still looking for work. She picked up jobs here and there doing self-contracted work in cleaning homes for people. The Oakley's jumped in anytime they saw an open door to be a blessing to mom and us kids if mom would allow it. During the fall, around early part of November, Mom had gotten so behind on the rent that she sat us kids down in the living room in a circle on the floor. She said that she needed to talk to us about what she was dealing with. She said that she had gotten so behind on the rent that it wasn't possible to catch up unless she got another job this week. She went on to say that the landlord had been here every week asking for money. He told Mom that he can no longer allow us to stay if we're not going to pay our rent. She was not mad at him, because he had given out a grace period for months at a time since we've lived there... She said how it was not an option to drop out of night school because she was halfway through it; plus, most jobs required you to have a minimum of a high school diploma or a GED. We were also told that we would be lucky to have a place to stay by the time that Thanksgiving and Christmas rolled around. Mom asked me to get up and get the Bible off the mantle on top of the fireplace. I was happy that she was finally turning to God: However, I was concerned that we may be living on the street soon. When I saw the bible laying there, it was covered in dust and was totally white. I lifted it up and dust filled the room. I started coughing and choking as soon as I removed it from the ledge. Mom turned towards me and said, "Girl, hurry up and bring that Bible and sit back down." I did as I was told. She put one of her hands on the bible and the other hand she grabbed Tina's hand. Mom told us to all hold hands. Then mom began to pray. Her prayer to God was that he had a right to leave us in the situation we were in because of the life she was living. Mom asked God if He would have mercy on her because of us kids. Then she said she would change her ways and do better if He'd bless her with another job during this week to help pay bills. Mom continued to tell God that she would do anything to save us from being homeless. It was a heartfelt prayer, and I had faith that God would help us. Not only that, but I also believed that Mom was going to turn her life around. I felt there would be no more trust in psychics and other superstitious beliefs. The next day, Mom asked Mrs. Oakley if she could keep us overnight because she was looking for work. She made sure to say that she would come by early in the morning to make sure we got to school on time. Mrs. Oakley had been trying to get mom to let us spend the night ever since we had started coming over there. She appeared to be more excited than we were. The following day when mom picked us up from Mrs. Oakleys, she was smiling and in a good mood. Mrs. Oakley asked her to share some good news. Mom said she had found another job: I was extremely happy. For one thing, God didn't let us down. I was also hoping that it would be a new beginning for our family, and that we would start going to church and praying more often. Though, Mom did not change her way with the Lord, even after He came through on His agreement; above and beyond what she had even asked for. Mom had not only found a job, but her maid job had given her a pay advance on a job that they contracted her to do at a later time. It was just enough to pay one month's rent and to get us some groceries. Not only were we going to keep having a place to live, but a nice Thanksgiving dinner too. Mom never did acknowledge God though even after all of his blessings upon our family. My heart was broken, and my spirit was grieved. I felt that mom had used God. I have learned throughout my lifetime that God's mercy and grace has been given to all his children and has no limits; even in situations such as these.

Lamentations 3:22-23 (NKJV), "Through the Lord's mercies we are not consumed, because His compassion never fails. They are new every morning; Great is your faithfulness." There is a flip side to the unlimited mercy of God. I previously spoke about how one of the greatest gifts God has given man outside of salvation is free will. That is the ability to make the decision to live your life for God, or to not.

Deuteronomy 30:19(NKJV), "I call Heaven and Earth as witnesses today against you, that I have set before you life and death, blessing and cursing: Therefore, choose life, that both you and your descendants may live." The plan God has for man is for good not evil, to prosper you not to harm you, it is a plan filled with hope and a future. If we choose a path outside of God's will, then it is not God's will that anyone should perish; but that all men should come to Him and receive eternal life and more than just that man would live abundant life here on earth.

2 Peter 3:9 (NKJV), "The Lord is not slack concerning His promise, as some count slackness, but is longsuffering toward us not willing that any should perish but that all should come to repentance." God was working on mom's heart by showing her His unconditional love and faithfulness as the Father. The story of the Prodigal Son, also known as the parable of the "Lost Son", follows immediately after the parables of the "Lost Sheep" and the "Lost Coin" in Luke 15 in the Bible. In these three parables, Jesus demonstrated what it means to be lost, how heaven celebrates with joy when the lost are found, and how the loving Father longs to save people.

We started to spend more time over at the Oakley's house because mom had to work. We all were happy to spend more time with them, especially Kaleb. I had never seen Kaleb take a liking to anyone like he did with Mr. Oakley. He looked forward to hearing his military stories and to playing checkers or cards with him. Kaleb would start yelling for everyone to be quiet any time Mr. Oakley told a story, even if he'd heard it before. Tina and I on the other hand loved to sit and listen to Mrs. Oakley read to us out loud. She had the most interesting books. They treated us like we were family. Whenever mom would give Mrs. Oakley money for watching us. She would always tell her not to worry about it and that they already had everything they needed; but Mom would not have any of it. So, Mrs. Oakley would always take the money and go buy us the things we needed for school or other personal items like shoes and clothing. Mrs. Oakley told us kids that she admired our Mom: She said she was a go-getter. As I look back on it now, what she meant was that Mom would never take handouts or charity. She was a very hard-working person. Mom finally graduated and got her GED after months of work. Mom had also been speaking to her lady friend from Eastern Texas who had been asking her to come live up there with her family. She was a single parent like mom and had three kids. We had never met them nor been anywhere close to Texas. Mom suddenly told us that we were moving up there. Two days later we had everything packed and Mom had rented a U-Haul. Mom's friend helped by driving our personal car while Mom drove the U-Haul. All of us hated the thought of leaving the Oakley's; but mom promised things would get better once we moved. She explained to us how in East Texas she'd have someone that could help pay half of the bills since we'd be sharing the house with another family. Plus, she said that they would help her get a decent job with them meaning she would no longer have to work two jobs. Mom was excited and that helped us feel encouraged about accepting the move.

Chapter 4
When the Fun Takes a Turn

WE NOW LIVED IN LONGVIEW, TEXAS IN A NICE FOUR-BED-room house with another single family. The three other girls stayed in one of the bedrooms, while Kaleb, Tina, and I stayed in another. Then their mother Linda had her own bedroom and so did our Mom. This house had a big backyard and plenty of room for parking. It was much nicer than our house in Colorado. Right away, Mom was able to get a job working with Ms. Linda. Ms. Linda had grown up and always lived in Longview; so, there were not many people that they didn't know in town. Every Saturday, Mrs. Linda

and Mom had a party at the house. Which meant on Fridays they had all of us kids clean the house from front to back. One thing that I noticed was how Ms. Linda made no difference in her kids. Her two youngest girls had just as many chores as everyone else, they were just slightly different. For the first time in her life, Tina was held accountable for chores and her behavior. Mom and Mrs. Linda would stock up on alcohol and food on Saturday morning for their party. By 5pm, Ms. Linda and Mom expected us to have eaten and taken baths and to be in our bedroom for the night. When their company came by, we would be yelled at, grounded, and sometimes we'd be whipped if we came out of the bedroom during the party. We enjoyed playing together so we used that time to ask if we could all slumber party in the same room. Most of the time, we were allowed. A couple of times police came out to tell them they were disturbing the neighbors. The music would be turned down for 30 minutes, or at least until cops left, and then it would be turned back up. On one occasion, there was a fight that broke out that Mom and Ms. Linda had no control over. These people were rowdy and drunk and wanted to fight each other for fun. The police were called, and someone was taken away, but the party went on. Us kids were nosy so we would go to the master bathroom and while we were in the hallway, we would look to see how many people Mom and Ms. Linda was entertaining. People were all over the place, standing against every wall in the living room, dining room, and kitchen areas. The nightmare for us came the following morning. All day on Sundays, us kids were responsible for cleaning up after the party. We had 3 sometimes 4 large black garbage bags of empty alcohol containers, beer bottles, and cigarette buds. The kitchen and dining room looked terrible. There wasn't a clean dish in the house and the carpet and floors always had spills. The guest bathroom looked like a gas station bathroom. Pee and sometimes throw-up would be on the floor or in the bathtub. It usually took most of the day for us to clean up. We would get grounded or whipped if we did not clean everything up. We were told we could not watch T.V. or do anything else until the house was totally clean. Ms. Linda would sleep most of the day, and Mom would leave most Sunday and "sneak out" to see Dad. From what we were told, our dad lived less than 10 minutes down the street from our house. We were never allowed to go with mom, nor did dad make any effort to see us. It amazed me then, and still does now, how God can be everything you need in an earthly and spiritual Father if you allow Him. When you have no father in your life, God has a way of showing you love through his sons and daughters within the church as well as others that are placed in your path. God has an answer for those who have broken families, and for those who have endured abuse all throughout their lives; He gives light through His word.

Psalm 147:3(NKJV), "He heals the brokenhearted and binds up their wounds."
The first step to healing is through forgiveness. We all have to come to a place of realization in knowing that the offender is in no type of pain in most cases; because if he or she were, they would have come asking for forgiveness after their offence. Part of giving our pain to the Father is releasing the offender of their offence. And that does not mean that they just get away with what they've done: Justice is the Lord!

Hebrews 10:30(NKJV), "For we know Him who said, ʻVengeance is mine, I will repay,ʼ says the Lord and again, ʻThe Lord will judge His people.ʼ" God then takes his position in your life and by being the good father that He is, He brings forth healing to your soul.

Psalm 107:20(NKJV), "He sent His word and healed them, and delivered them from their destruction." No matter which category you fall into, remember you're not alone and God will help you through or bring you out of it. Do not turn down the many ways that God can connect with you and bless you.

Ms. Linda was not connected to any church, but she had friends that did go. During the summer, she talked mom into letting us go to a summer Bible camp for kids. Her intention was to eliminate some of the free time we had while school was out. The church would feed kids for free and provide snacks in between lunch. We would also be presented with the opportunity to connect with other kids our age through doing constructive activities that were related to the Bible throughout the entire day. It would only be for one week out of the entire summer. It really wasn't a long time, but one week for our moms to not have to worry about what we were doing while they were at work was a nice break for them; plus, they also wouldn't have to feed us. I was excited, and did not know what to expect, but anything was better than sitting at home all day every day while bored out of my mind from playing the same games. The church we attended for the Bible camp was in a little neighborhood church; it was a little bigger than my grand-ma's church. There were so many kids that signed up to go, that they didn't have enough volunteer adults to oversee all of us. The leaders tried to break everyone up into the smallest groups that they could: Which meant that there were 35 kids per teacher, and with there being 7 groups it made a total of 250 kids, give or take a few. In my group, every time the teacher tried to teach us a Bible lesson, she would have to deal with a handful of troublemakers. When she was correcting them, the other kids would become distracted and act out. We never got through a lesson that wasn't interrupted multiple times. After the second day, the teachers decided it would be better to just have games set up to keep the kids active because it was taking too much effort to try and teach the Bible lessons. Most kids were hindered from learning in any way because of all that was going on. The games were held outside, which was way too hot for me and some of the others. After 15 minutes, we were sweating as though someone had thrown water on us. There wasn't a shady tree around, and the air was muggy with no breeze to be felt. The last couple of days, I didn't want to go because of the chaos and because we had to stay outside the entire time. However, Mom made us go every day except for the last day because she was getting off early for a doctor's appointment that she had previously scheduled. That week I learned one thing: a child reflects the standard the parents teach them.

Proverbs 22:6 (NKJV), "Train up a child in the way he or she should go, and when they are older, they will not depart from it."

Proverbs 20:11 (NKJV), "Even a child makes himself known by his acts, by whether his conduct is pure and upright." I never consider myself an angel and am far from it. I know I wasn't brought up in the word of God by my mom; but I had a sense of respect for God's church and his people, so His reverence was in me. Some kids naturally have that fear of God, and others don't. As you learn more about myself and my story, you'll see that I faced many struggles that could've been avoided, but rather God used it to raise something good out of me. Amen! After raising my own children in the word of God, I understand that a child's behavior can't be placed entirely upon the parents; we also cannot expect the church and our schools to raise our kids for us. A child's rearing is a twofold principle and still we have to be in continual prayer as parents for them to keep them covered and focused. Even after all of that, they may still be led astray; but God will bring them back. This is His promise. God will turn everything around that the devil meant to be evil and renew it in the good of God's Kingdom. First, they have to be taught God's standard by demonstration: In which, they see parents setting an example for them in their relationship with Christ. Then, we have to teach them the word of God daily at home. This is so that the children will have a foundation to come back to, if they do happen to stray away from God's teaching as adults, which happens more often than most people realize. There is no perfect parent, and there will never be but through the teachings of our Lord Jesus Christ, He will make up for where we mess up. He's our safety blanket, and He will not let us walk through this alone.

Mom and Ms. Linda then decided that they wanted to give us kids something to do during the hot days, which there were many of in Texas, so that we wouldn't mind going outside. The days were so hot here that It made it undesirable to go outside. It was like a smothering heat with very little breeze. It was the opposite of extreme from Colorado cold and snow. We had a big backyard, so Ms. Linda talked Mom into going half in on an above ground pool. I couldn't swim, but I was still excited about it because I knew it would be the perfect thing to help cool off some of those hot scorching days in Texas. I was 11 years old, and Tina was 10, Ms. Linda's oldest daughter, Sabrina, was 13, her middle daughter, Erica, was 6 years old, and her baby girl, Eleanor, was 5. My brother Kaleb was the oldest of all of us; he was 14. During the summer when Mom and Ms. Linda were at work, we were completely by ourselves. We would play school and find all kinds of games to play inside. We weren't allowed to go outside if a grownup wasn't home. We would sing, dance, make drawings and art activities, and play school or house. Kaleb rarely played with us girls. He stayed locked up in his room reading comics, drawing, or watching television. Food was not a problem when we stayed with Ms. Linda. Mom and Ms. Linda kept groceries in the house always. I would say that having another person to help Mom off set her bills allowed her a little more freedom. She had made more friends from work and in the neighborhood than she ever did in Colorado; mainly because Longview was considered a small country town: The population was 62,762 at the time. Everyone from Longview always says how everybody knows everybody else, by name or by face. Ms. Linda and her family and ex-husband all grew up there.

When school started back up, Tina and I went to the same school and Kaleb attended another school. Ms. Linda's girls were in private schools. Our school was dominantly white kids, which really did not bother me. However, racism was very noticeable in most public schools, which is one of the reasons why Ms. Linda had her girls go to private schools. Mom on the other hand, did not have financial support from our Dad like Ms. Linda had for her girls; so, we could not afford to go. I had problems with a select few of my teachers treating me differently because of my skin color. There were times I would raise my hand and I would blatantly be ignored by the teachers. These teachers never hid their true feelings about the color of my skin. There were many times that I needed a teacher to assist with my classwork and I would be verbally disrespected in front of the entire classroom. I was told that I should already know the answer, and still not given any help. Most days, I was treated as though I had no rights to be a part of a classroom discussion and was asked to be quieted by the teacher if I tried to participate like the other kids. I was told, "No one is talking to you," if I responded to a question that the teacher posed to the class. This opened the door for some kids to pick on Tina and me. There were many times when I would see Tina at recess while her class was still finishing up. One time, I saw two white boys saying something to her, so I put my lunch tray down and ran outside to see if she was being harassed. As I approached her; a teacher saw me and then decided to intervene. This teacher had to have seen what had happened because she was on recess duty supposedly watching all of the kids. Yet, until she saw me run in that direction, she made no attempt to see what was going on. I got there before the teacher did and Tina told me they had pushed her off the swing and took it from her.

I immediately grabbed the swing from one of the boys and the teacher said, "What's going on?"

The boys said, "She fell out of the swing."

I said, "Y'all pushed my sister out of the swing, and I saw you through the cafeteria window!

The teacher then told the boys to go play and leave Tina alone. I knew if I hadn't made it there before the teacher did, then it would've been an entirely different story. Unlike me, Tina didn't want to make a big deal about the things that went on. But I was all about enforcing what was right and what was wrong.

We faced the worst of the discrimination on our school bus. Tina and I were told where we could and could not sit and the bus driver allowed it. We were the only black kids on the bus, and for the most part the only black kids in our classes. When we would get on the bus, the kids would spread out and take up all the seats leaving nowhere for us to sit down. Tina always ignored them, but I would end up getting into verbal altercations with them all. There were even times when Tina and I were both left standing up just because the bullying from the kids on the bus refused to allow us to sit down with any of them nor would they share sets with each other because it would open up a set for us. It became so tiresome because this was happening daily to and from school. The bus driver would smile as though he was in agreement with the kids on the bus and never to intervene on our behalf. There was times Tina, and I would stand instead of making an issue out of it. There was this one time however when we were leaving school on the bus ride home. Kids started cutting in front of us in line and began to save sets. On this day Tina and I had to stand up once again the entire trip home: The next day, I got out of my last class quickly to rush and stand in line for the bus in order to reserve a seat for Tina and me. The more and more kids broke in line in front of me, the more I had less of a chance to sit down. Once we were on the bus, just as I predicted, the kids had blocked all the seats once again. It still didn't stop me from asking everyone if Tina and I could share seats with them so we could sit down. There was one little boy who felt sorry for us and allowed Tina to sit with him; but nobody would allow me. There was this one girl that was sitting by herself and she wouldn't allow me to sit. She started calling me "Dirty nigger," "Trashy nigger, you don't deserve to sit." Without thinking, I slapped her face and she pushed me back. I then grabbed her hair to hold her head still and started punching her in the face. Two white boys came behind me, one hit me in my back and the other one was blocked by Tina. I felt like my sister and I were fighting back-to-back with half the bus because everyone else had gotten up to try and take their swing at us. The bus driver turned the bus around, back to the school, and dragged Tina and I off by our arms.

He looked at me and said, "That's why you people need to stay with your own kind." We sat in the principal's office until Mom got off work and picked us up. The principal set up a meeting with Mom for the next morning. She was angry at us because she had to leave work early to come get us and go in late the next day because of the meeting. The next morning, we sat waiting on the principal for an hour. Once he brought us in the office, he gave us a one-week suspension.

"What about the other kids?" my Mom questioned.

"Well, everyone on the bus, including the driver, said that your girls started the fight," he said.

"Well, you haven't heard their side of things. You have to hear them out before you put all the blame on them."

"It won't change anything. I've already made up my mind, but if I must: I'll hear their story," he said. After we told our side, he said it didn't change anything. Then he went on to say even if what u girls said was true, you should've been in this office long before it got out of control. He told mom that he was giving us an out of school suspension for a week. Mom was terribly angry that we had been treated miss fairy.

Mankind has to ask the right question: When will this world be awakened to God's truth? The truth is Adam was created in the likeness of God and brought alive by His spirit with nothing missing or lacking from being a perfect creation. In fact, God said after creating both Adam and Eve that His work was very good! God said it's not good for man, or any being, to be alone. Then God put Adam asleep and took his rib and created Eve; she would act as a helpmate for Adam. At this point, man had a spirit of good and righteousness in them, otherwise known as the Holy Spirit. Sin had not entered them as of yet: It wasn't until after Eve ate and gave Adam the forbidden fruit from the tree of knowledge. The disobedience of man brought sin and corruption to mankind. The Holy Spirit is the spirit of truth; He left man when Adam and Eve sinned. Only through the death, burial, and resurrection of Jesus can man be made righteous again and restored to God's likeness (image). So, what does all this have to do with race? Racism is part of that sin that Jesus died for. It's a spirit of division. This is the same spirit that separated man from God to make man believe that they could be God or like God. All men came from Adam and Eve, so there is no separation of races in God's sight. We are sons and daughters of God or by choice we are the sons and daughters of Satan.

1 John 2:9-11 (NKJV), "He who says he is in the light, and hates his brother, is in darkness. He who loves his brother abides in the light, and there is no cause for stumbling in him. But he who hates his brother is in darkness and walks in darkness, and does not know where he is going, because the darkness has blinded his eyes."

Unfortunately, racism will always be part of the earth until God silences the devil and all his followers for good, through confining them into the pit of eternal damnation. As a son or daughter of God, we have to take our place at the feet of Jesus in heaven. We can't feed on the ignorance of mankind. In **Hosea 4:6,** Jesus says, "My people are destroyed because they lack knowledge. It's time to rise above all traps of the devil. God is our defender!" **Rev 12:11** tells us that we overcome him by the blood of the lamb, by the words of our testimony, and we love not our own lives to death. Now that I'm older I understand what all this means. **Proverbs 4:23** is fundamental for us to] keep a non-offendable conscience. It tells us to guard our heart with all diligence because out of the heart springs the issues of life. During this time period of offence, Mom did well in protecting us from Satan's fiery arrows. A fiery arrow is a lie, false judgment or accusation, and anything or anyone that tells you that you are less than what God and His word say that you are. Keeping focus is key in persevering past the roadblocks of the devil. At that time, we had no power in the world nor over the people in it because we were out of fellowship with God; but we had a choice on how we would respond to their offence against our skin color. Mom taught us well: She told Tina and I that she was going to use some of her vacation time and take off from work to take us to the Six Flags in Dallas and stay for a couple of days. We had the most wonderful time. I believe this was the only time we ever got to go on a vacation with Mom in our entire life. Ms. Linda was able to take time off from work and pull her kids out of school and bring them along with us. Mom and Ms. Linda usually acted like sisters, but during this trip it was noticeable that mom had an offence with Ms. Linda. Their dialogue was filled with "joking attacks in a tasteless manner, which had both of them responding to each other in a defensive tone. I noticed once we returned back to Longview that the smallest things would offend Mom when it came to Ms. Linda and her innocent jokes. Ms. Linda became agitated with that because it was obviously that mom was being too serious and negative. Their relationship had always been transparent, and they were honest with each other. On top of that, it used to be a preconceived as a love- hate relationship where neither would normally take anything personal. Now things have changed.

Mom had to be thinking about moving to Dallas for some time now, and we were not aware of it. That was until a month after our vacation when Mom picked up and moved us there. She rented a U-Haul and paid someone to help move us down there. Once we arrived, there was an apartment already rented and ready for us to move into. Unknown to us Mom had everything lined up. I was excited about there being no more weekend parties. Moving to the big city would be a little scary for a couple of reasons though. First of all, we had never lived in the city before. We're back to being in a place where we're surrounded by nothing but strangers. Secondly, back when mom had no one helping with bills it was a lot harder on all of us. Though, Mom did tell us that she had made a trip to Dallas before we got here and had put in several applications for different jobs. She said that the one job she had her mind set on more than any others was driving the city bus, working for public transit (known as DART). She explained that this job would pay well and have good benefits. Mom had already interviewed with them and passed their test. She was waiting to hear back from them the week we moved to Dallas. We kept to ourselves when we got to Dallas: Mom would rarely allow us to go outside until she enrolled us in school. She would drive us to school and pick us up even though there was a school bus assigned to our area. I was relieved about that after the last school bus incident. Within the first month of moving to Dallas, Mom was officially hired and in training for her new job at DART. My skepticism had been for nothing. Mom had done it and we were very proud of her accomplishments in such a short period of time. She had done very well in providing for us as a single parent who had no support from our father. Though, she did still struggle with many hidden areas in her life that would bring a deep sadness over her on most days. She also dealt with other symptoms of mood disorder. There was one time that we were sitting and watching the television as a family and talking among each other about the movie. Mom got up, left the room to go to the bathroom and came back yelling that we could be doing something productive like cleaning out our closets or restacking the pots under the cabinet. I was totally puzzled. Just before she went into the bathroom, she was smiling and laughing at the movie and having normal discussions with the rest of us. This happened frequently; and it didn't necessarily have to happen while looking at the television. There were times when we were having a conversation about school or something that happened in the apartments. Mom would be smiling and joking and then she would get quiet for a moment as though she lost her train of thought. Then she would interject with a topic from a foreign subject which confirmed to us she was totally disconnected from everyone in the room, as well as the subject that was just being discussed; in an instant her personality changed. All I can tell you at that point was Mom's mood went from one extreme to another with nothing reasonable to set her off. When Mom became drunk this compounded her delusion: She would become violent and destructive. Mom would never remember her alcoholic outbursts after she became sober the next day. That was almost scarier than when Mom would go on binge drinking a couple times a month. The older we got; the more Mom would binge drink. When she had been binge drinking, she wouldn't go to work. She would be at home closed up in her room drinking day and night; for days at a time and not eating. Mom had binged drinked up to 14days at one period. A lot of time Mom had no choice but to go back to work, because on many occasions she had spent all of her money on drinking and our bills were falling behind. This is when we started moving from apartment to apartment every 3 to 4 months; before our 6-month lease would end we would be going through eviction for lack of rent payment. Mom would get a doctor's note and go back to work trying to work double shifts, sometimes triple shifts, to make up for the money she drank up. From the ages of 12 to 16, I had never been in the same school district for longer than a semester. This affected my grades, as well as me being able to learn like a normal kid. Struggling to catch up was the only thing I did for five years straight in middle school and high school. Every school district we moved to have a different curriculum than the school I was coming from. Most of the time, the district I was leaving was a semester or two behind the one I was going to. Mom wasn't hard on us when it came to our grades. Tina averaged D's and F's and I averaged C's and D's. Kaleb started skipping school at age 15, and by the time he turned 16 he had dropped out altogether. Kaleb was given a lot of grace from Mom, so much so when he decided to drop out of school, she allowed it. She also allowed him to drink her beer and smoke her weed when she was home and had enough to share. I was truly too embarrassed to invite any of my school friends over because of my dysfunctional family. Every now and then I would hear Mom say negative things about our family. Anytime I brought up the name of one of her relatives, or more specifically my Aunt Rachel or her mother, she would go off on me and become very angry for long periods of time. Mom's drinking was on a scale larger than ever before since we'd moved to the city. Because I know this, I did my best not to bring them up or any subject that was connected to our family. As a young person even, I could see that the root of mom's pain and sickness was only going to be healed by God.

Most of the men mom worked with drank, and ninety percent of her coworkers were men. They would go straight to the liquor store after getting their paychecks every Friday. There had been a few times when Mom was off on payday and we would go with her to pick up her check. There was a liquor store almost walking distance from her job and all of the bus drivers would meet up in the parking lot. They all would stay in the parking lot for a couple of hours drinking and talking. The few times I went with mom it had to be around 75 to 100 men standing around this liquor store parking lot hanging out. Mom would bring home a case of "Schlitz Malt Liquor Bull" beer and "Smirnoff 100 Pf" vodka on payday. For many years those were Moms' exclusive selection of alcohol. You could guarantee our refrigerator would never be without them.

All I could do was hold on to God's promise in his word. Daily I cried out to God like an Israelite in the Old Testament who were in captivity for 400 years. They were enslaved by the Egyptians before God was moved by their continuous prayer for freedom. Then God orchestrated a release through His faithful servant Moses. I knew one day mom would be saved, delivered, and set free by God. Prayer and the word of God is the only weapon we have to help a loved one who's trapped with an addiction of any kind. We cannot give up on them. It's impossible for God to turn away from His word. **It's impossible to pray and have nothing**

happen. I was too young to pray for Mom's mother before she died, but I refused to let the devil have my mom! It was up to me to keep the faith. Mom would not be leaving this earth before her time. Mom stayed on the top of my prayer list no matter what else was going on in my life or between us. I can happily say that **God's been keeping mom.** She's been completely sober since 2008, that's 12 years sober and recommitted to God and His plan for her life.

She will tell you sometimes are harder than others depending on the part of the years that she's dealing with loss in her life. The struggle is always there, but it's worth it every day that we can pick up the phone and say, "I love you" and have a drama free conversation. Mom is alive to see her great grandkids and is a living testimony of God's goodness.

I'd like to take a moment and share the Heavenly Fathers point of view. Everyone's story is different and even if it's similar it's not going to be handled the same. Outside of what I've already shared be **Philippians 4:6 (NKJV) Be anxious for nothing, but in everything by prayer and supplication with thanksgiving let your requests be made known to God.** Philippians is saying before you get advice or counsel we are to pray and after we get advice and counsel we are to pray.

1 Thessalonians 5:17 (NKJV), "Pray without ceasing."

Luke 7:47 (NKJV), "Therefore I say to you, her sins, which are many, are forgiven, for she loved much. But to whom little is forgiven, the same loves little." Father is telling the offended and the offender that forgiveness is the only way to enter into your healing journey. When offence is embedded in your heart, it will hinder the healing process from going forth. Forgiveness is freely given to us through the blood shed of Jesus on the cross. Why do we want to hold back what Christ gives free to those who we ordained as not worthy? We will never experience the full magnitude of God's love if we don't release judgement to God. You cannot love anyone when you do not love yourself first by forgiving yourself and releasing yourself from the past.

1 John 2:16 (NKJV), "For all that is in the world-the lust of the flesh, the lust of the eyes, and the pride of life, is not of the Father but is of the world." Everything in the world can be a hindrance to us walking in relationship to God. To acquire the abundance God has promised His children, we have to put him first in all things. Be aware that anything that is put before God is an idol and will block the blessing and favor of God in your life. God is a jealous God.

At the end of this book, I created prayers for forgiveness, deliverance, and healing. Feel free to write them down and pray with them daily until you see God change your situation.

Chapter 5
It's Not Always How It Seems

I WAS 12 NOW, AND I HAD JUST STARTED TO GO THROUGH puberty. Alongside my cycle, I started having debilitating monthly cramps, and at the same time I began to have severe headaches which Mom called "migraines".

Many times, if I were dealing with either one of them, I became totally unable to function; so, I would miss school in most cases. Mom said she had struggled with both of them at one point in her life and still did every now and then. She never gave me a hard time when I was dealing with either and had to miss school. Mom would say, "Unless you've experienced it; you wouldn't be able to relate." A heating pad, extra- strength Excedrin, and laying down just wasn't enough. I would be balled up in a knot crying. Mom started giving me over the counter pain pills. Within six months or

less, my body became immune to whatever medicine she gave me. I would be back at square one in struggling with the pain: Which led to Mom sharing her prescription pain pills with me. She would give me half of what her recommended dosage was. Mom told me that for years she and Grandmother both had suffered from chronic migraines. She said that it was part of life, and I just have to learn to deal with it. When I was sick was the only time that Mom and I would get along or see eye to eye. Outside of that, I was getting cursed out and called out of my name all day long, every single day. I wasn't the only one that was ever called out. Mom had a vocabulary of her own and none of it came from the "Webster Dictionary". The only other place I had heard a mouth as foul as Mom's was on television in a sitcom about drunken sailors. Being around questionable vocabulary wasn't a big deal to mom. She said it's in the world, it's part of the world, so we better get used to it. I strongly disagree, I was very offended by it every time I'd hear her speak in that manner. I was the only one of Mom's kids that couldn't get used to it or was bold enough to complain. I taught myself to have selective hearing; maybe a little too well. At that time, I didn't realize that it couldn't be turned on and off so easily. I taught myself to zone out completely from any loud, harsh, and offensive noises. Mom's natural tone was yelling and hollering. Profanity was the chosen vocabulary mom used regardless of if she was upset or not. I got to the point where I was able to stand right next to mom, while she was yelling and cursing, and I wouldn't hear anything that was said. If you've ever watched Charlie Brown's cartoon you would see that none of the adults talk in an actual language, rather they speak in "Wah Wah" which is voiced through a trombone: Looking back, that is exactly what Mom sounded like to me, once I drowned her out. As I got older, I started to notice that I was drowning most things out without being aware of it, not just Mom. People I met through school or just saw in general would need to repeat themselves several times. A lot of the time if I didn't make eye contact with whoever was speaking to me, I would automatically have a deaf ear to them. My last year in high school, I started to notice it became very hard to listen. I would repeat what was being said to me, to make sure I was the one being spoken to. Also, this would help me be able to be corrected by the person speaking, which would help me to format what was being said. My mind would wander off just because my body felt trapped in chaos. I began to daydream a lot. That was the only way I could experience peace around my family. It helped me feel less attacked and oppressed when being around Mom. One day, I asked her why she had to use vulgar language all the time. She slapped me in the face and told me if I ever questioned her about anything she did or said ever again she would take my (mo-fo-ass) out of this world; just like she brought me into this (mo-fo-ass) world. Yes, the slap hurt, but not as much as her verbal threat. Mom had a way of imparting the fear of death in you. Since we moved to Dallas, I had become terrified of Mom causing bodily harm to me. Her whipping was on another level and it began to threaten my life. There were no limits in what she would use to whip us or how far she would go. Since my children's rearing, whipping has been outlawed in society. I do believe that we shouldn't tolerate child abuse, but on the flip side children do need to be properly taught the boundaries of right and wrong.

Proverbs 13:24 (NKJV), "He who spares his rod hates his son: But he who loves him disciplines him promptly." This was written by the wisest man in the Bible, King Solomon. This verse tells us that discipline is not only needed but required in every child's life. Though, what this verse doesn't share is that there is a balance which is required in all things to makes a person either be righteous or unrighteous. In my personal opinion whipping may be appropriate when a child is: In an extremely unsafe situation, deliberately defiant and disobedient, or severely disrespectful. Whipping is NOT appropriate when a child is: simply being childish, impulsive, or having an accident. When I raised my children, communication was the key for both them and me. Whipping can be an important moment of connection when it's done with calmness, explanation, and immediate reconnection. My son's personality as a child was one of getting a mutual understanding which would avoid whipping. If I didn't make a rule concerning something, he'd ask and never assume otherwise. We had an honor code between us. He could talk to me about anything and not feel threatened or judged. My daughter's personality responded more to the act of "being grounded" as a punishment rather than whipping. The honor code was not there, even when I intentionally tried to connect with her so we would be on the same page. Most rules she respected but others she would try to get around. At one time or another both kids pushed past the boundaries I set and received whippings in response. I learned to pick and choose my battles, and some just weren't worth the fight. I worked hard on being a friend to my children, which is a mistake. Kids will use this type of a relationship as a weakness. There was one time when my son told me that there were people in the world that whenever they see a sucker — they'll lick it. He was trying to tell me not to always see the best in people, because they could take advantage of me for the worst. My response to him was we as Christians have to be more concerned over what Jesus would say than what man will do, because Jesus has our back. Balance is the key. God's word brings balance and gives knowledge, wisdom, and understanding in all cases.

2 Timothy 3:16,17 (NKJV), "All scripture is breathed out by God and profitable for teaching, for reproof, for correction, and for training in righteousness, that the man of God may be complete, equipped for every good work."

On the other hand, causing fear in a child's life is never okay. A child has to understand that you love them and want to protect them. As a parent, I always referred to the Bible before implementing a punishment; even if it's something that I thought they knew already. I could always find a related story in the Bible that would help my child think "What would Jesus say?" and "What would Jesus do?"

Proverbs 22:6 (NKJV), "Train up a child in the way he should go, and when he is old, he will not depart from it."

If your child doesn't understand why he or she is being punished, or they do understand but don't agree then there is a possibility of having a repeat incident. In these cases, sharing your heart and listening to their point of view is the best strategy. You show your children honor and love by humbling yourself to listen to their heart. After this is done, there should always be clarity of what you expect from them. There shouldn't be any guessing of your decision and what the consequences will be if violated. There should always be a mutual honor and love between a child and their parents.

I understand that many parents fall into a web from their past, just like my Mom. Many are raised in abusive or neglected environments and have no example of a healthy parent relationship. I can't hold Mom responsible for things she didn't know or things she did out of pain. Though, I also can't sit here and make excuse after excuse for her behavior to justify why I had to go through what I went through. It will never make it right or okay that it happened that way. I had to release her to God and forgive her for every offense. One thing we have to always remember is: We're not deserving or worthy of salvation. When we were still sinners, Jesus died for us. What Jesus gave out of love and obedience to the Father for our forgiveness was His life. So, I cannot charge someone for something that I got free. Forgiveness is not an option; it is a requirement to obtain your inheritance from the Kingdom of God.

In school, I didn't think I fit in anywhere. I didn't care for the popular kids because of their "uppity" personalities. I didn't care for the nerdy kids because I felt I had enough strange people in my life that I already couldn't connect with. I was good at being a loner. Peace and focus were the benefit of being a loner. I needed more of that than anything. Knowing I wasn't going to be in a school for a long period of time meant that spending a lot of time making friends wasn't really a wise decision. After I entered high school, the kid ratio changed. It wasn't intentional, but for whatever reason I always had 3 or 4 kids that would be around me all the time. I would try to avoid them without hurting their feelings, and ask them if they had anything else, they needed to do besides follow me. They'd always respond the same, "Yes, but we like to hang out with you." I never understood that. I was quiet, didn't put up with gossip or bullying, and if they started to act that way, I wouldn't put up with it. I never tried to make a conversation, nor did I get into anyone's business; even when they freely shared it. I would listen, but never had any opinion to share. I figured if any of them really knew what my home environment was like, I would be the center of their discussions every day. My focus was on school. Mom may not have cared about my grades, but it bothered me to make C's and below. Math and English were very challenging for me because I never had a good teacher. Half of my teachers were just focused on getting a paycheck and going home at the end of the day. The other half were too busy complaining about their working conditions and the impossible standards the principal and school district put on them. Teachers would spend more time preparing for the "Star testing" than on the regular curriculum: Purely because if your school scored higher than other schools then the teachers, staff, and principal would all get bonuses and special funding in certain areas of the school. Math and English required additional focus and practice for me. I still found myself not doing great, but I reached out to my teachers for tutoring. The best I would be offered was a makeup assignment which would replace a lower grade. Most of the time it had nothing to do with what I needed help on. I worked hard to stay on top of my assignments, even when it became about just passing and not learning. I had finally thought that I was caught up, and then Mom came and told us we had to be out of our apartment by the weekend, so she'd be pulling us from school once again.

Mom had me do a larger part of the cleaning than my siblings in our home. Each of us was responsible for our own room. Mom had us all on a rotation of cleaning the kitchen and the main bathroom and vacuuming and dusting the living room was a daily activity. Mom's room and bathroom was my responsibility. She was a perfectionist when it came to having a clean apartment. Anything that was asked of you was to be done in a timely and perfect manner. That meant before she got home from work every day, it better had been done. Mom was faithful in inspecting all delegated chores for quality work daily. No one would be allowed to go anywhere if their chores weren't finished. And to only do half of the chores was just as bad as not doing it at all. You'd usually end up getting whipped and grounded at the same time. Cooking on the other hand was something Mom had been having me do since I got back from Aunt Rachel's house. Neither of my siblings ever asked to help with the cooking. I was either being the assistant cook, and making meals when Mom didn't or couldn't, or I'd be in the kitchen helping her. Most of the time I didn't have a problem with any of it. When her favoritism for Tina became obvious, I knew better than to say anything. Mom would consider that as being disrespectful. Every now and then when I caught myself getting an attitude, I would take it out on Tina by not talking to her or playing with her. It was the same as what my cousin Sarah did to me, and my Aunt Rachel did to mom. Now that I am older, I understand the errors in my ways. The Lord revealed to me that it was my fault that Tina and I had never been close as sisters should be. For many years I never saw it that way. I was always so quick to fault her for something that she had nothing to do with. Not only that, but I intentionally inflicted pain on her. For over forty years, my sister has lived less than 15 minutes away and yet we only see each other once or twice a year. We never talk to each other unless we need to connect on behalf of our kids or Mom. Holidays have generally been spent avoiding each other, unless Mom was in town; but even then, we would fight about whose house we were going to meet at. Last year, I formally apologized to Tina. I told her that she wasn't responsible for what our mother did and that I shouldn't have treated her as though she was. I asked her to forgive me for my years of distancing myself and the negativity I further perpetuated into her life. She said that she forgave me, but our relationship hasn't changed to this day. I realize it's something I have to continue to pray about and give to God. All you can do as an offender is apologize. As much as you want to take back the offence, it can't be erased on either side. However, we are obligated to pray for the person that we hurt or that hurt us. Prayer brings closure and healing quicker than we can ever imagine. God is the only one who can change a man's heart.

Ezekiel 36:26-27 (NKJV), "And I will give you a new heart, and a new spirit I will put within you. And I will remove the heart of stone from your flesh and give you a heart of flesh. I will put My Spirit within you and **cause you to walk in My statutes, and you will keep My judgments and do them."**

Unfortunately, my Aunt Rachel and her daughter, Sarah, died early in life. Mom and I didn't get the opportunity to settle the offence between them before their passing. That doesn't change the power and promise that God has given us to heal the broken hearted and bind up our wounds. I released my cousin Sarah years ago and forgave her. Mom is still struggling with issues of the heart from Aunt Rachel as well as other family members. I pray for Mom daily and have been able to forgive her of all offenses both known and unknown. As nice as it would be to hear her apologize for something, I no longer need that. Mom has forgotten many things that happened during my childhood when she was struggling heavily with alcoholism. I still pray **Ezekiel 36:26,27** for mom so that she will one day be able to let go of her past and be healed of the pain she harbors which caused her to drink in the first place. When she found out I was writing this book she became angry and told me that I need not to bring up the past, and that she did not want to help me with any of it. I respected that she didn't want to know about this book or have anything to do with it. She suffers with many health issues and I believe if she let go of the past then the devil cannot continue to afflict her body. I also believe that time doesn't heal any wound: Wounds are only healed from us facing the truth about the offence. What is the truth? Yes, it happened, yes it should not have happened, and I cannot change that; but I can change how I allow it to make me feel. I chose to give the offence to God. God's word has promised me justice on behalf of His position in my life as my Heavenly Father.

Romans 12:19 (NKJV), "Beloved, never avenge yourselves, but leave it to the wrath of God, for it is written, Vengeance is mine, I will repay, says the Lord."

I was able to forgive all of the people that were involved. Blocking it out and acting like it never occurred will never bring forth closure nor healing. Harboring unforgiveness, hinders our body from being able to heal itself. Forgiveness must be released in order to allow healing to take place.

Luke 6:37 (NKJV), "Judge not, and you will not be judged; condemn not, and you will not be condemned; forgive, and you will be forgiven." Old wounds can be the deadliest wound and eventually take us to our grave if we allow it.

"Hebrews 12:15 (NKJV), "Looking carefully lest anyone fall short of the grace of God; lest any root of bitterness spring up cause trouble, and by this many become defiled." Then ask God to heal you. God is faithful and just to perform.

Numbers 23:19 (NKJV), "God is not man, that he should lie, or a son of man, that he should change His mind. Has he said, and will he not fulfill it?"

When we first moved to Dallas, I felt compelled to find a church to connect to. I remembered how much peace I felt from being around God and his people when I would attend church with my grandmother. From ages of 12 to 13, I looked for people in whom I could go to church with. I didn't have to look far; surprisingly every apartment we lived in had churches that would bus children from their apartment complex to the actual church. Every Sunday I would get up urgently, get dressed, and go catch that church bus. At first Tina and Kaleb marked me for going. However, Mom would ask me to pray for her each time I went. She was very neutral when it came to me wanting to go to church; it didn't matter to her either way. When I did go, she didn't seem curious about what I was being taught. The churches that I would end up in were typically Baptists': not that I knew the difference at that time. I thank God that I didn't have to unlearn any orthodox teachings from other religious beliefs. These Baptist churches were dominantly filled with white members, except for us kids that came from the apartment complex bus. I never was treated differently because of my race when I went to church. The children's pastor at the church would always give out treats and prizes for those who attended and those who participated during the teaching segment of church. Every time I went to church, I would forget about my problems at home. I felt uplifted when I returned home. It was during those times I felt I would be able to make it. Every time I went back home, Tina and Kaleb would regret that they tested me and didn't come. As long as they were nice, I would share what I brought back. Finally, my brother said, "Karen's having all the fun and getting all the candy and prizes; we need to go with her." The following Sunday they got up and accompanied me to church. The pastors were excited to have both of them come. They loaded them up with all kinds of goodies. They started attending regularly with me for a while, at least until my brother started getting in trouble.

I heard one of the pastors tell him," We love having you, but it's important that you don't fight with the other kids. We have rules in place for your safety; so, it's important you follow them to stay safe." I knew from that moment that Kaleb had been acting up. He always needed someone to pay special attention to him: He would do stuff intentionally to get attention. Most of the time it was something that he knew better than to do. I never understood it, but Mom treated him like the man of the house and let him have his way most of the time. After that conversation that Kaleb had with the pastor, he never returned. Tina on the other hand had a problem getting out of the bed early Sunday mornings.

If she felt like getting up, she would but a lot of times she would say, "That's alright you go head by yourself." I was alright; It didn't really bother me either way if they came or not. I was taught many of the old testament stories, but it was nothing like Aunt Rachel's church where they would challenge us to memorize certain things in the Bible. One of the differences I liked about the Baptist churches was the songs that were created alongside the storyline of the Bible. The songs would help you to remember the important things in the Bible. Since I wasn't challenged with Sunday school homework, it helped me have more time to memorize these songs. It wasn't hard for me to connect to this congregation even though in my past I was discriminated against by white people. I knew all white people were not alike just like all black people weren't alike, so I never built up a wall around them.

I would watch a program series that came on every year called "Root's". Many black Americans got angry when watching this program because of the harshness of oppression and brutality that black slaves were faced with. It was hurtful for me to see the torment that was brought against the black community in my forefathers' time, but I was inspired to see how far the world had come. Not only that, but there was a charter called "Toby" who blessed me with the power of seeing just how strong and brave he was in every episode. He endured hell on earth and still persevered against the odds. His character was one who would never give up. Toby would rather die than to accept things the way they were. That encouraged me to think outside the box which people often placed me in. I don't have to be subject to man's opinion of myself or by the life they want me to live. As long as I have life, I can improve my situation one day at a time just by changing my mindset. Change is inevitable; nothing stays the same except for our Heavenly Father and his word. I didn't like seeing our ancestors being beaten and killed, but it made me appreciate and value my life so much more. It made me feel my problems were not as bad as they could've been helping to put things further into perspective. I never missed a single episode. I realize that many people did not share my opinion about "Roots". This program was taken off television in time because many African Americans would get caught up in the movement of slavery and their hatred against white Americans. Blacks fault the white community for what their ancestors went through. I had been told by African American's that I was brainwashed by the white community. That didn't make me angry because I know that wasn't true. I have firsthand experienced racism; but unlike many, I have been liberated from the world's view to God's view. The older I got, the more I noticed the Lord showing me that he loved the sinners and hated the sin in the world. The devil has been defeated through the death, burial, and resurrection of Jesus. Man has a choice between doing good or doing evil. This is where we as Christians have to have a forgiving heart and a praying spirit for our lost brothers and sisters. I know this world still has a significant amount of racism that's breeding. The following two scriptures tell us how we're going to stay focused and live a blessed life that Jesus offers us in the midst of a fallen world.

Proverbs 4:23 (NKJV), "Keep your heart with all diligence, for out of it spring the issues of life."

John 16:33 (NKJV), "These things I have spoken unto you, that in me ye might have peace. In the world ye shall have tribulation: but be of good cheer; I have overcome the world." I believe your life is what you make it to be. No one can hold or keep you back other than yourself when you have God on your side.

Isaiah 41:10 (NKJV), "Fear not, I am with you; Be not dismayed, for I am your God. I will strengthen you, Yes, I will help you, I will uphold you with My righteous right hand."

We may not be where we want to be right now, but we are better off than our ancestors were. The United States has come a long way and we have to continue to persevere, even if people are still dying at the hands of racism and injustice. God's people have been awoken to the authority we have through Jesus Christ. Let us all arise into the maturity of faith in Jesus and His word.

Exodus 14:14 (NKJV), "The Lord will fight for you, and you shall hold your peace."

Gen 12:3 (NKJV), "I will bless those who bless you, And I will curse him who curses you. And in you all the families of the earth will be blessed."

Isaiah 54:17 (NKJV), "No weapon formed against You shall prosper. And every tongue which rises against you in judgment You shall condemn. This is the heritage of the servants Lord, and their righteousness is from me. Says the Lord." God's word is unchanged and forever true for His sons and daughters. This is why it's important to position yourself in Christ as a son or daughter and to stand firm in His word, because it will keep you in all your ways.

For many years mom kept strangers out of our house as much as possible. We had this one apartment property we lived in that had a lady named Sally who was a little younger than Mom. Sally looked frail and acted paranoid every time you saw her. She had no kids; only a husband who was fresh out of prison. When we first met Sally; she told us her husband worked handyman jobs and other small construction jobs. She only came over when her husband, Harold, was working or not at home. We assumed he was at work most days, because she was at our house every day during the week. Sally would say regularly that she needed to get home before Harold got there. From the first day Mom met her; she was overly friendly. Daily we started seeing her come over to our apartment, even if she was never invited in the first place. Mom would say every day as she was walking in from work, "I sure hope Sally keeps her ass home today." Within 15 to 20min Sally would be walking into our apartment soon after Mom got home. She talked a lot and very fast; Mom never had a chance to interject. If you ever met someone who talked like this, you would ask yourself if they were breathing while they spoke. I know I did. In most sentences Sally would even answer her own question or remarks. Mom used to call her "Birdbrain" because she always acted so strange. Mom always looked at her as harmless and never saw her as a threat to our family. I would say most times she would get on Mom's nerves, and I never understood why mom would not just tell Sally how she felt. She would tell everyone else how she felt with zero regard to their feelings, but not Sally. She was known as the gossip queen in the apartment complex. How she knew everyone's business; I'll never know because she was over at our house the majority of the time except for when she was at home. Mom never shared anything personal with her: not that she would've been able to get a word in anyway. I always thought Sally was nosy because she walked around our house looking at our stuff; asking where we got certain things. It was impossible to bring home anything new without Sally spotting it and asking where we got it and how much it cost. Sally never told us what her husband served prison time for. She would just say he did a little of everything that was illegal.

"You name it, he did it." At one point he was employed by the property management for the apartments we were living in. We did not know anything concerning it; she never talked about him. I was sure that's where Sally got all her gossip from. One day we finally met Harold. He stopped by our apartment to get her one afternoon. He acted as though he didn't want to come in. He stood outside our front door yelling and hollering at Sally into the living room. He called her all kinds of names in front of us. He was saying she was lazy and good for nothing. He even called her the "B-word". Then once she exited out our house, he hit her in the head and face three times. Mom told Harold that they needed to take that commotion away from our front door. Harold left and continued acting hostile and loud in the courtyard of the apartment building. I was embarrassed for Sally because of the scene that Harold made in front of everyone. Sally never once raised her voice to defend herself during this altercation, nor did she try to hit him back. I don't know if he was still employed by the apartments are not after that incident: I just know that we didn't want him anywhere near our apartment unit. You never know what's going on behind the doors of people's homes; I was glad that mom had never ran her off. Sally needed friends that showed love and mom sensed that. At the time, we lived upstairs next to an empty apartment. We haven't had any next-door neighbors since we moved into that apartment. A week after Sally and Harold's altercation, we didn't see her for a week. I became concerned and I asked Mom if she thought she was okay. Mom said we got business; we don't need to be in anyone else's business. Two days after that Sally showed up. She looked around like she usually does, got a beer from Mom; drank it and left. That was the quickest visit I'd ever seen Sally make. Then we didn't see her for three more days and were faced with yet another short encounter. The next day following Sally's second short visit; we noticed when we got home from school that anything that had value was gone. Mom was still at work when we found out. Someone had come in through the bathroom wall that was connected to the vacant apartment. They had taken 2VCRs, 2 televisions, all of Mom's jewelry, her turntable and sound system with speakers, and a few other things that she had collected over the years. We did not have any insurance, so the only thing Mom could do was file a police report and replace the things herself as she became able to.

The following Monday, Sally came by and Mom asked her with boldness, "Does Harold still work for this apartment?"

Sally said, "No, he was fired."

"What is he doing now?"

"He's in between jobs right now, why do you ask?"

Mom told Sally about the burglary in our apartment that took place Friday.

"Even if Harold were still robbing people, he'd never mess with my friends. Maybe if you do not trust me then you shouldn't have me around," Sally said, clearly offended.

"Maybe you shouldn't," Mom firmly said, and Sally left. A week later, Sally returned and asked Mom if she had any money that she could borrow. After Mom asked Sally what the money was for, she said that Harold had been arrested again.

"I need the money to bail him out."

Mom said, "For what? So, he can bet your head in again. Let that (Mother Fucker) stay in there, that's the best place he could be." Sally quietly left and never returned to our apartment. A week later, Mom was contacted by the detective that was investigating our break-in. He had received a few items from a burglary that they needed her to look at, to see if she could identify any of our missing items. Mom met the detective and had serial numbers that matched our Televisions and DVDs. Mom told the detective about Harold and Sally and how he was recently arrested for burglary. The detective said that Harold had been locked up and connected to a series of robberies and that Sally will now be considered an accomplice because of the time she spent in our apartment. Mom didn't want her to go to jail, but there was nothing she could do about it. The evidence pointed out very clearly that she was helping her husband. Without Sally, Harold wouldn't have known what time to break in and if we had anything worth breaking in for. Mom became more cautious in allowing strangers from our neighborhood to come spend time at our house. The Bible teaches us to be open to entertaining strangers because we don't want to get ourselves in a position to reject an angel of the Lord (**Heb 13:2**). But with all things we have to use wisdom and we acknowledge the fruits a person displays from their words and action and lifestyle. The Bible teaches us that if we resist the devil, he'll flee from us. Sally had many red flags that God had highlighted to us, but we felt sorry for her and overlooked them and allowed her into our home.

Exodus 23:1-3 (NIV), "Do not spread false reports. Do not help a guilty person by being a malicious witness. Do not follow the crowd in doing wrong. When you give testimony in a lawsuit, do not pervert justice by siding with the crowd, and do not show favoritism to a poor person in a lawsuit."

These three scriptures in Exodus have given God people a standard of living to go by when we deal with strangers. The fact that Sally was secretive about her husband's previous conviction was a sign that she would cover for him in any crime past or current. We knew something was wrong with a person who was spreading continuous gossip about others yet was concealing their own personal life. Sally's mental state was questionable and should not have been taken lightly.

Psalm 101:5 (NIV), "Whoever slanders their neighbor in secret, I will put to silence; whoever has haughty eyes and a proud heart, I will not tolerate." If mom had been applying God's word; I strongly believe that we wouldn't have allowed the devil to take from us. Satan has taken from many good people. Just being a good person is not good enough unless you've been made right through Christ Jesus righteousness. Jesus' righteousness gave man enough authority to be reconnected to God. By No Means am I saying Christian are perfect and they don't get robbed, No! Christian realizes their imperfection and weakness, so they do not rely on themselves. They rely on God when dealing with all matters. What I am saying is we can prevent most things if we are operating in the wisdom of God which is His word and by His spirit. God's blueprint for our lives is the Bible. If we do end up in a predicament of foul play; then God has a way of working, it out for our good and His glory.

A month later mom packed us up and moved to another apartment complex. You would've thought that we would become used to moving every 4 to 6months. But it didn't matter how long we had been in an apartment nor if it was us breaking the lease or if it was from an eviction. Mom had us clean every aspect of that apartment. She made sure that the apartment looked as good as it did when we first moved in it. Mom didn't believe in having no one clean some else's filth. Most times the apartment looked better than what it did when we first moved in. She never prolonged the unpacking either. She wanted our house in order, and right away. Mom had us label every box before moving; for the room it was to go in. Once everything was moved in, we would set aside one day to unpack everything and put it in its correct place. Every move I prayed and asked God to bless me to be able to raise my kids in a stable environment, where we wouldn't have to be moving all around. Years later, He answered that prayer.

Chapter 6
No way out!

I WAS 13 NOW, SO TINA WAS 12, AND WHEN IT CAME TO BOYS approaching us, we would get scared and start looking around to see if Mom were nearby. She would tell us that if we messed with a boy, we would get preg-nant and be homeless and live on the street for the rest of our lives. Mom would tell us boys were never interested in girls for any-thing other than sex and once they got it, they'd be gone. I didn't understand why she would go on and on about boys every time we got ready to go outside. Tina and I had no interest in boys at the time. Mom would say that it doesn't matter if you're not inter-ested because boys know how to wrap you around their finger. I never heard mom talk to Kaleb about getting girls pregnant. Mom always had Tina and I stayed within yelling distance or visual distance from the apart-

ment if we were to go outside to play. When mom called you and you didn't come; she'd come get you. You could count on being embarrassed once she got to where you were at. We were outside playing hopscotch with some other girls in our apartments one time, and Mom had been calling me, but I didn't know it. On this particular day, all of the other kids seemed to be out playing. One group was playing football, another group was playing dodgeball, and some other kids were playing double Dutch jump rope with Tina; I was hopscotching with some others. Mom came down the stairs yelling and cursing. Everyone that was outside stopped what they were doing and started staring. I didn't hear or see her until one of the girls I was playing with said, "Isn't that your mother?" As I turned around, Mom was already halfway to me. My heart started racing and I was scared of what she was going to do. I turned around and dropped everything and ran at her. She had called me the "Bitch" and "Wench".

I said, "I'm sorry for not coming Mom, I didn't hear you." She started slapping my head and face and proceeded to grab my ear and drag me into the house.

I heard all the kids saying, "Wow their Mom doesn't play." Apparently, Mom had been calling me into the house to help her cook. After that incident, I never did go back outside at that complex as long as we lived there. I was too embarrassed to ever face those kids. I had to refocus. My thing now was to keep up my grades and do the very best I could. At times it felt redundant to do so knowing in a matter of time Mom would pull us out of school and all my hard work wouldn't count because of the incomplete I would get for the rest of the semester after being withdrawn. Maybe that's why Kaleb and Tina throw their hands up and not make school their priority.

I always thought about my future and what difference I could make in the world. Going into the right field of work was important. Yes, graduating was a priority for me, and I had to stay focused on the things that could give me an opportunity for a better life. I wasn't sure what direction I would go in after graduating, but it would likely be the military or a community college. Going to a University was not a viable option just because I had struggled in school for most of my life and some of my weakest areas were the basic subjects. If I chose to go into the military directly after graduating, I would still enroll in Community college after I returned home from active duty. It would give me an opportunity to improve my GPA and catch up in the areas that I struggled with in school. I knew that God had a great plan for me, even if I didn't know what it was as of yet. How could He not have a plan? I was always self-driven and determined when it came to most things. I also felt God had been calling me since I was five years old. I always had a hunger for God's word and to be connected to God's people. One thing for sure was I needed to stay alive to be able to find out what God's plan was. I feared mom in such a way that if I continued to stay with her; the possibility of me ever finding my purpose in this world was very slim.

Christmas holiday break was near and I had term paper and a book report to get in before the holiday break started. I felt rushed because the end of the semester was in a few weeks. I never was a person that loved reading, it seemed like a chore to me. I had to push myself to focus and work hard to get this book read. Once I had done that, it was time for me to write the report. The term paper was a whole 'nother story. I had researched exactly what I needed to do before I even started on it. I knew I had to score high on both of these assignments because I didn't have a passing grade at the time. I was new to the school district and had many incompletes because I hadn't been enrolled at the beginning of the school year like the rest of the kids. It was impossible for me to go back and try to complete all of those assignments. Though, if I could score a B, which was 80 percent, or higher on both assignments that would give me a passing grade for the semester with a 70 percent. If I didn't pass, I would've had to do dozens of make-up assignments which would be much harder. My plan was to do the report that night so that I could turn it in. That would give me the rest of the week to finish the other assignment and get it in by Friday. If they both weren't turned in this week that would take points off of my final grade. I came straight home like always and got my chores out of the way and went straight to work on my report. Mom had come home on her lunch break that day and cooked so that dinner would be there for us when we got home. I went straight to my room to work on my report. I knew that it was my turn to clean the kitchen after everyone ate dinner. Meaning that I had until Mom got off of work, since she was the last one to get home and eat. As soon as she got home, she started yelling for me to come clean the kitchen. I started feeling stressed because I had barely got started and had a long way to go until I finished the report. I came into the kitchen where Mom was and asked her if I could clean the kitchen before, I went to bed. I thought that would give me more time to get most of my thoughts into an outline to be able to start writing my report out. Right away, I could tell mom had been heavily drinking by her red eyes and loud sluggish speech. To my surprise, she didn't fuss with me on the issue when I asked. She just told me not to fall asleep before I got the kitchen clean. At that time, it was already 6 in the evening. I went straight into my bedroom and applied myself to the best of my abilities. Before I knew it, time had quickly passed by. It was now 11 p.m. Mom was yelling for me to get my ass into the kitchen. Once I got in there, Mom was cursing me out for not having yet washed the dishes. She was speaking as if she'd completely forgotten that she gave me permission to clean the dishes before I went to bed. I knew it had gotten late, but I hadn't fallen asleep, I was just waiting until I got to a good stopping point. Mom refused to let me speak or say anything concerning what we discussed. Mom picked up a large drinking glass up off the counter, turned to one of the upper cabinet doors, and hit the glass against it; to sharpen the rim of it. Mom pressed the sharp part of the glass against my throat. She muttered, "I'll take you out of this world, just like I brought you into it. If you think you're going to live in my house and do whatever the hell you want to do you have another mother fucking thing coming." For 30 minutes she held that glass to my neck, telling me that I better not blink or breathe; she threw in insulting and vulgar language with every sentence she spoke. I had never been so scared of Mom like I was that night. I dared not to speak. I slowed my breathing down the best way I could to keep from breaking down... She was too drunk to communicate with, I dare not try to reason with her it would've been the death of me. Mom had cut her hand and blood was everywhere. Because of how sharp the glass was, and it being pressed against my neck it automatically cut me. It wasn't deep, just a flesh wound. With all the blood between the both of us, you would've thought something would have clicked in mom's head to bring her out of that comatose state of hostility; though it was almost as if she didn't feel or see anything. There had been other times either Mom had whipped me with an extension cord or used her hands to slap me in my face and head continually with force. I felt that the extreme force and focus mom used had a lot of hate in it. I see now that's what Satan wanted me to believe. The truth is it never had anything to do with the issue at hand. Mom had this thing she did often where she would zone out; it was as though her body would be there, but her mind was in another time zone. After that night I didn't see any way that I would be able to stay with Mom until after I had graduated. There are other times she was sober and went off into a zone: Mom would never remember a thing. The fear that Satan was planting in me was rooted and real. I feared one day she would kill me and wake up the next day and not remember how it happened. Mom raised a severe threat to Tina and Kaleb also, but never oppressed anyone like she did me. Every now and then, Mom would snap and go off on them in a crazy way, but with me it was a daily verbal and physical abuse. Now that I'm older, God has opened my eyes to the revelation of the truth that is only revealed through God's Spirit and not man's natural eye or wisdom. This may or may not be a familiar scripture to you. God says in His word in **Hosea 4:1** that; His people are destroyed daily because they lack knowledge.

Ephesians 6:12(KJV) For we wrestle not against flesh and blood, but against principalities, against powers, against the rulers of this world, against spiritual wickedness in high places.

It is particularly important that you understand what **Eph 6:12** is saying. This scripture is telling us no matter who or what the offense is coming from, don't take it personal. It has nothing to do with you, or them, as a whole. Sin and unforgiveness open up the door for Satan to enter. Earlier in this book in chapter 2 we talked about open doors from the kingdom of darkness because of witchcraft and other medium participation that mom had opened up. It's important you know that these doors don't close by themselves. You have to renounce and cut all connections of the occulted realm. Satan's mission is to come against those who God has chosen. It aims to stop God's plan for their life. At the time, my belief was that Mom hated me and was eventually going to kill me. But the truth is; if mom wanted to kill me, she could have and would have. The truth is Satan is the one that wanted to kill me not my mom. If Satan can get his way, he will have us both dead. Mom was brought up in the church and in a house of nothing but believers of Jesus. What took place in their home that turned mom against God it has never been disclosed: However, I know it was enough to draw her away from family members and give her an offence against God. Now ask yourself is that God's will or Satan's? If you are ever unsure if something is the will of God, then ask yourself this one question. Will that thing if it's done increase the kingdom of God or increase the kingdom of Satan? Then you will have your answer.

Eph 4:20-24 (NIV), "That, however, is not the way of life you learned when you heard about Christ and were taught in him in accordance with the truth that is in Jesus. You were taught, with regard to your former way of life, to put off your old self, which is being corrupted by its deceitful desires; to be made new in the attitude of your minds; and to put on the new self, created to be like God in true righteousness and holiness." This scripture points out that many know Jesus and His teachings (Satan knows God's word), However they are still walking around as if we do not know Him. That would've made them hearers of the word and not doers. The Bible teaches and warns against that. Satan can use the smallest things to make Christianity look to be unappealing and to give Jesus a bad rap. All men have their own perspective when the word and the spirit of God is not rooted in them.

Jeremiah 17:9 (Amplified), "The heart is deceitful above all things, and it is exceedingly perverse, corrupt and severely mortally sick! Who can know it (perceive, understand, or be acquainted) with his own heart and mind?" I love the breakdown of this verse. It pretty much speaks for itself. What I hear the Lord saying through it is; because man has been corrupted through people and things in the world that it's not possible to trust our true feelings about anything. *Proverbs 4:23* says we are to guard our heart above all else; because the issues of life flow from it. This Proverbs tells us if we are taking anything personal; then we are being deceived (**know that it's Satan that temp's man into sin not God, then Satan enters as a hidden offender through man's sin**), and we are not guarding our heart with all diligence like the word of God tells us to do in Proverbs. Man's heart belongs to Father God, the creator of Heaven and earth. Satan's trap is to bring offense against man, so man will turn against man, and then against God. Next, Satan plants lies and judgment against God by saying it's God's fault for not stopping the offenses or threats. Once sin has entered man, this separates God's presence from man, and he begins functioning out of flesh (sin) and outside of

God's will and plan. Another question that Satan plants in people's heads is, "Why does God allow evil to rain if he's God the All Powerful One?" God doesn't allow evil to rain or rule, man does through his disobedience to God. Man gives evil ruling power through choices made outside of God's will. This empowers Satan to bring havoc into people's lives.

Romans 1:21 (Amp), "Because when they knew and recognized Him as the God, they did not honor and glorify Him as God, or give Him thanks, but instead they became futile and godless in their thinking with vain imaginings, foolish reasoning and stupid speculations and their senseless minds were darkened." This verse also says that man is walking in the deception of Satan when he or she lives in sin. God calls darkness of the mind of man is deception or a lie. Satan is the father of darkness and lies. He saturates people's minds who are not abiding by God's word.

Acts 26:18 (NKJV), "To open their eyes in order to turn them from darkness to light, and from the power of Satan to the power of God, that they may receive forgiveness of sins and an inheritance among those who are sanctified by faith in me." God is telling his sons and daughters in *Acts 26:18* and in *John 12:46* that they do not have to remain in darkness because He has come into the world as the light, so that everyone who believes in Him, does not have to remain in darkness.

Mom had an old saying that she believed and spoke into existence, "If it's not one thing it's another." What that meant was something bad would always dominate our life and keep us from succeeding or getting ahead. Now that I am older, I know that this is a lie from hell, and I will never want to adopt that saying in my life nor speak it over my house. It's intended to keep you in a defeated spirit and curse you from the blessing of God. Now that I look back over my life, I had to believe it because it was like a record playing every day when anything negative happened to us that is what we heard mom saying. I believe if you expect something good then good is going to happen and if you're always expecting something bad to happen, then bad is what would be highlighted in your life. Our words bring power into our situation. **Proverbs 18:21** Tells us that the tongue has the power of life and death.

The first time I ran away was to a family friend I knew through Mom her name was Mrs. Evelyn. She was an older lady and acted more like a mother figure to Mom due to her age: She had two grown kids that were Mom's age. Her daughter was the oldest and she had two boys who were 12 and 15 years old. Her son had a daughter who was 8years old. Most weekends Mrs. Evelyn would keep her grandkids at her house to give her children a break. Mom started taking us over there on some Saturdays so she could get a break or go out of town. It was a blessing for Mrs. Evelyn because she was a widow and very lonely most days. Kaleb and Tina loved going to play with Mrs. Evelyn grandkids, but I enjoyed sitting and listening to Mrs. Evelyn tells stories about her past. If Mom were around, she would make me go outside with the other kids and play while she and Mrs. Evelyn were talking. We would usually spend a day there, but It was rare that we got to spend the night unless mom would be out of town. On this particular occasion Mom was helping a friend throw a party and didn't have time to worry if we were staying out of trouble or not. At first mom dropped us off for just a few hours on Friday evening, but then Mrs. Evelyn convinced mom to allow us to stay because we're all having so much fun. That's when it became an overnight stay until the next morning. We all camped out on Mrs. Evelyn's living room floor and watched movies and ate popcorn all night long. I used that opportunity to share my heart with Mrs. Evelyn. I told her that I loved Mom, but I didn't want to live at home anymore because I felt like she was out to kill me. She tried to be sympathetic and comforting. She told me that the only reason mothers discipline the children is because they love them and care. Mrs. Evelyn said I am not trying to take your mom's side, but I want you to look at it from another perspective. As I listened to her, I was sure she wasn't going to be persuaded to be on my side. After Mrs. Evelyn told me all of the reasons why I shouldn't feel the way I felt. Then she went on to say, "If I talk to your mom and she allows you to stay; you're more than welcome."

"Does your mom know how you're feeling?"

"I don't know…I'm too afraid to share with her because of how violent she gets with me," I said

"You know, you really need to talk to her." I felt like the world was ending when she said that. I knew that would be an impossible task.

"Do you want me to help you try and talk to her about it?" she said. I knew that wasn't a good Idea unless she was totally on my side. Mom would be upset that I told her our business to an outsider no matter who it was. That night when Mom called to check on us Mrs. Evelyn shared with her that I had expressed feelings to come live with her. Right away Mom became defensive and said that she wasn't surprised one bit because I was so dramatic about everything.

Mom said, "Karen isn't going anywhere, so she needs to pull herself together and be ready to come home tomorrow." That night I thought about running away so Mom couldn't come back and get me; but Mrs. Evelyn wouldn't let me out of her sight. The next morning when Mom came and got us, she looked at me and said, "I will deal with your ass when we get home." When we arrived home, I was surprised to not have received a whipping, but Mom had me clean the house until it was time for me to go to bed. She never ran out of things for me to clean. It was my punishment for bringing drama into someone else's house. Mom went on making my life miserable as if to say, "I dare you ever cross me again." All I could think about was hurrying up to graduate so that I could move after. I was only 13 and in the eighth grade and still had four and half years before I could graduate and was still way too young to work. The more I endured the verbal attacks the more I came to realize I would not last in the same house with Mom for another year yet alone four. I knew I had to figure something out

Chapter 7

Don't Give Up (Help is on the way)

For the first time since Dad left, I was thinking about him. When you're feeling desperate, you don't think about the things that drove a wedge between relationships. You're looking for a way out of what seems to be a life-or-death situation. Now my thoughts were, "Where is he?" "Would he take me in?" "Is he in position to care for me?" "Had he gotten married again?" To entertain these thoughts meant something inside of me was saying, "I'll do whatever I have to do to live again and to stay alive I need to do it soon." My other parent seemed to be the only option at the time. I decided to wait until Mom calmed down to ask her where my father was now; had he still been in Longview? I waited until  the next week to bring up the subject. When I did ask Mom, she went from being zero threat to rearing up to a 100 percent threat in terms of being out of control.

I wasn't shocked: I stopped being shocked at Mom's response to anything long before. The important thing now was to see if this was a viable exit for me.

After Mom spent 30 minutes telling me how terrible and awful that Dad was, and how he didn't care about me or anyone other than himself, she immediately said it would be fine with her if I went to stay with him. "I'll do you one better than that," she said. "I'll give you his phone number and address and help you pack."

That day Mom contacted Dad and told him that I wanted to come and live with him. Dad had remarried again: The lady he was married to was named "Sherry". She had two boys, one was 5 years old named Zaiden, and the other 8 whose name was June. At this time, I had recently turned 13 and was in the eighth grade. Mom had me pack and I was on my way within 24 hours of contacting Dad. She drove me to their house which only was 20 minutes away from where we lived. Dad's wife, Sherry, was a science and art teacher for one of the North Dallas high schools. You could tell she had reservations about me coming to stay with them and was not in a hurry to make me feel at home or allow me to be a part of their family. Sherry made it clear that I didn't have a right to touch anything in her house that didn't belong to me. Sherry handed me a pillow and a couple of blankets and placed them on the couch saying, "These are mine also, but I will loan them to you for now." I believe her point was to let me know that this is her house and everything in it: Nothing belongs to dad. Sherry owned a 3-bedroom house in the southern part of Dallas before she married my father. Right at the beginning of my stay, I was being brushed off onto Sherry by my dad. Dad was spending most of his time at work or in bed asleep. I refused to look at it in a negative way, even though Sherry did: It was still better than the alternative. She told Dad right in front of me on more than one occasion that I was his responsibility: not hers. Sherry spent more time making sure I wasn't stealing anything or bothering her or the boys. What she didn't realize was that keeping to myself was something I did well. I had no desire to be a busybody in her house. As tired as I grew of not being trusted, I appreciated that more than being verbally and physically abused. Sherry didn't drink, or curse, or hit anyone with her hands, so I was able to respect her shortcomings in wanting to put up with me living there. After being with them for a month my mom dropped Tina off. Now Sherry had two squatters living in her house. After talking to Tina, she said it was her choice to come and get a break from Mom's abuse. Tina didn't have a chance to ask me of my opinion of Dad's wife: but she sure did form her own opinion right off the bat. Sherry gave her the "low-down "just like she did with me concerning everything that belonged to her and her boys. We were not allowed to touch anything in the house.

Tina asked Sherry, "Well, what if we asked first?"

Sherry said, "Even if you asked; so, don't ask." I looked at Tina and did a half smile and shrugged my shoulders. I believe it bothered Tina much more than me because it gave off a clear statement: "I don't want you here!" I looked at it as a place to lay my head and not have to worry about facing physical harm or worse. To me, it brought peace to my heart to no longer hear cursing and name calling. Living under that type of abuse will motivate you to move even when you don't have anywhere to go. Tina and I never talked about it; we just knew that was the unspoken life we lived behind closed doors. We were finally being given a bed to sleep in. Sherry put Tina and I in her oldest son's room June and we shared his bunk beds. Sherry moved June to his little brother's room where there was a queen size bed: June and Zaiden shared the queen size bed. June was very much like his mother. He was selfish and always acted inconvenienced. He never looked at us as family but rather as intruders. The younger brother Zaiden was nothing like his mother or his older brother. He was excited about me moving in from day one and was always trying to get me to go play with him in his room. From that day on, I became his protector; from 8-year-old June and anyone else that wanted to give little 5-year-old Zaiden a hard time. He loved me and my sister Tina. Whenever we went in public, he'd be right there holding my hand. Sherry started noticing how good we were with Zaiden, and over time felt that she could trust Tina and me. She started to do little things for us like hot combing and styling our hair nicely and bought Borax to keep it looking cute. Sherry wasn't as organized or clean as Mom was. We didn't have a daily chore list at her house: All she asked of us was to keep things straightened up if we used them, such as making our beds or putting dirty clothes away properly. Sherry used her dishwasher, so we didn't have to even worry about doing dishes, other than rinsing our dirty utensils before placing them in the washer. She never asked me to cook either. There were a few times she had us go rake leaves or sweep the sidewalk.

We were adjusting to a stepmom that looked at us as a thorn in her side. It was very obvious that Sherry's time and money meant more to her than becoming a family. Her and Dad began to have regular fights about that. I sided more with Sherry during those arguments: She was using all her personal money to meet our needs and every time she would ask Dad for money for us, he would never have it. Most times it was something we had to have like shoes or clothes or school supplies. Dad told Sherry to keep all her receipts for the money she spent on Tonya and me. She did for a while, and he was paying her back too, but in time Dad got back to where he wasn't keeping his reimbursement agreement. Sherry was getting sick and tired of fighting with Dad all the time. Five days a week she was dealing with other people's kids at work, and then she came home and had to deal with us too. Dad never tried to give Sherry a break by taking all of us off her hands so she could have some time for herself.

Sherry and dad fought about other issues they had with keeping the house together too. I knew he worked a lot, so even as a 13-year-old I was curious about my dad's money. He was very stingy with it unless we were in an emergency situation. He would give Sherry a little money and expect her to cover the rest no matter what it was; or she could just do without it. I understood Sherry's side and why it was an ongoing and almost daily argument. Dad had no compassion for anyone or anything. His way of providing was helping with a major bill or two, and not by meeting our personal needs or the needs of the household. He didn't want to spend money on groceries nor any other necessities. Sherry didn't have a problem talking about it in front of us. She wanted us to know how much she really contributed when it came to managing her house. Even when Sherry was speaking with Dad, she would use the words "mine" or "my" a lot in order to show ownership of things; not knowing it also showed the disconnect and division in their marriage. I don't know if that bothered Dad or not. Surely it didn't make things any better. I've learned now since I've grown up that marriage has to be a commitment, not a contract. You do things out of love not obligations. If one is forced or made to feel obligated to contribute it brings a sense of control or domination in a marriage or relationship. I am definitely not saying Sherry was the culprit in their marriage problems. I will say two wrongs don't make a right. Sherry's oldest boy, June, was just like her. He didn't want anyone touching anything of his stuff. That was hard not to do since we were staying in his room. He would always be spying on us. June wasn't the easiest person to get along with, plus being 6 years older than him made it so he couldn't bully me. But he seemed to be always angry and a big tattletale like my cousin Sarah. We stayed with them for one school year and within that time I don't recall him being sociable or trying to connect once. I ask myself now, "Was I sociable?" I surely thought I was trying to be however he wouldn't receive it; so, it only became pointless over time. Zaiden on the other hand was excited that June could no longer bully him because I refused to allow it. It really made June angry when Zaiden would invite Tina and I to play in his room. June shared Zaiden's room but he didn't have control over it. Little Zaiden was a talented kid and very prestigious, and in a unique way cute. Sherry was very sure he would be an actor and, or a model. She started Zaiden out early running him all over Dallas for competition, pageant and acting interviews. He might have done a few kids clothing contracts but nothing permanent or long lasting. I believe that was a lot of June's jealousy stem from. Zaiden had high yellow skin and natural curly hair; he could pass for a mixed ethics background. June had a different father who left him with a very dark brown skin color, darker than even Tina and me. I thought June had this intelligent (professor) look about himself and could come off acting and looking older than he was. With June being the oldest I understood how it might have felt having a little sibling that was favorite. Now that I wasn't in that situation, I believe for the first and only time my sister connected. In this season of my life not to compete with both of my siblings for mom's love was a much-needed rest I enjoyed.

We attended the neighborhood school, which was only a little way down the street from Sherry's house. I met a friend named "Tammy" who was around my age that went to school with me: She lived on the same street as we did. Her parents would drive her and her brother to school most days, but they would walk home with us after school. Any time I was allowed to go outside to play, I would run to her house. School seemed normal for the first time ever. Sherry helped us with our homework and encouraged us to be more involved in outside activities that were connected to the school. One of the extracurriculars I ended up taking part in was a science fair, and I did an excellent job all thanks to Sherry. During the month of October, the school had a costume contest and I placed 3rd out of the entire school because Sherry helped me create a custom. Before the end of the school year, we had built a trusting and loving relationship.

One weekend, Sherry decided to teach Tina and I proper etiquette. I thought it was fun, until we had to walk with books on our heads for hours to learn how to balance properly. Tina on the other hand thought it was stupid; she always had been a tomboy. Sherry's teaching included: Eating properly with the right utensils, no elbows on the table, how-to properly set the table, and walking and sitting like a young lady should be. She told us that she didn't want us to look like a hatching if we had a formal engagement to go to: This made us feel more a part of the family. Dad was gone so much it kind of felt that we just lived with Sherry and her boys. Tina and I had lots of fun playing the games we had learned from Ms. Linda's girls in Longview, anytime we were left home, never a dull moment. Sherry's mom and dad had a house down the street. Her parents were a precious Christian couple with nothing but love for all people. They were very friendly and outgoing, especially her mother which we called Granny. Both of Sherry's parents treated us as their own grandkids. Any time they had a fellowship of any kind we were invited. We went to a couple of barbecues over there on the weekend. I had never heard of a block party, but Sherry was good at helping put together and host any type of party. What I understood was Sherry's family getting the community together for a potluck dinner on the purpose to meet and greet new residents. Granny thought it highly important to build healthy relationships and support in their community. Granny had it on her entire street. This is why it was called a block party. All the people on the street were invited to bring a dish and card tables and lawn chairs and any board games or card game. Sherry had a live DJ who played a variety of music. I never saw such a friendly fellowship of community coming together. We were always introduced as family. Sherry's parents were very active in the community and knew just about everyone and their children's children.

Dad acted like a boarder in Sherry's house and that he only lives there to have a place to eat and sleep, which is how it was when he was with Mom. Though, there was one thing that caught Dad's eye and that was little Zaiden. Dad loved him as though he was his only child. I was okay with Dad never looking at us like that. I had remembered what my Grandma Ethel Lou had once said about Dad, how he was not really mad at us or how he did love us. She said that dad struggled with connecting with people and showing love. However, he did love us all. Dad was the only father figure Zaiden had ever known. Zaiden was the last thing in his arms when he left for work and the first thing he picked up when he came home. No one else got hugs or that kind of attention given to them except for Little Zaiden. Zaiden had so much love to give back to everyone that you couldn't be jealous of him. He was so innocent, plus I looked at him as though he were my little brother because he looked at me as his big sister. He would even embrace my mom as if she was his second mom and not think about it even for a second. June kept resentment in his heart concerning all of us, including Dad.

Sherry tried hard to plan things for the family to do together, but Dad's response was always, "I'm tired" or "I have to go to work." We also never attended church while living with Dad. However, there was a time or two when we went to the lake and Dad took us out on his canoe. I was weary about going on the canoe because I didn't know how to swim. I let Dad and Tina convince me to ride in the canoe one time. Of course, the one time I went out with Dad, his canoe rolled into the deep waters and only a few inches of it stayed above the water. I called out to God saying, if you get me back on dry land, I promise I will never get into another canoe as long as I live." Sherry was the wiser one; she refused to get into Dad's canoe in the first place. She would go to the lake, but she wasn't going to get into Dad's canoe. As far as I'm concerned, God kept His agreement with me; and I made it safely back onto land. Tina and Dad convinced me once again to get back into the canoe, which was just as horrifying as the first time. Though, by doing this I started thinking: If I was going to die, at least it would be while having fun, and not by the hands of someone with. This helped me wash away my fears.

Sherry had a close lady friend named "Grace" that lived in North Dallas and we would go over to her house to swim and play with her children; we used to have barbecues over there. Every time we went over Mrs. Grace's house, I was amazed with her pet parrots and cockatoos. They were tamed birds that Grace had raised and trained to speak and do an assortment of tricks. These birds were beautiful and intelligent. Grace had two kids, a son who was three years older than I and a five-year-old daughter. Sam, her son, was more of a quiet spirit, his talents were in creating music. He didn't care too much for company or for engaging with us or whatever we wanted to do when we would come over. That never stopped Mrs. Grace from inviting us over to swim or hangout because she and Sherry were closer than most sisters. Also, his little sister, Cindy, was much more friendly and outgoing with us than Sam was. Zaiden and Cindy were also both in the modeling and acting industries; something we'd never really given much thought to before meeting Sherry. Grace homeschooled her kids and worked part-time at a college. Grace's husband, John, seemed to be quiet and inverted, just like his son, but he was very smart. He was into building computers and worked for IBM as a computer analyst... I thought it was weird, them being a white family and all. I had never seen a connection like Sherry and Grace had before. Mrs. Grace was sweet, funny, and outgoing: just the same as her daughter Cindy. Dad may have visited with us on a holiday once or twice, but he would never accompany us over to their house most of the time. Dad never had a conversation that lasted longer than a greeting with John. During the times Dad did come, he would be sitting staring off into space or daydreaming: He had always been a professional mechanic and worked with his hands, never really a people person.

When the school year came to a close, Dad reached out to Mom and told her to come pick us up because he and Sherry would be separating. I was thirteen now; Tina was twelve. I loved Mom, but I sure was going to miss all the encouragement Sherry gave us to be successful in all we do. She had shared with us how she came from a low-income family and vowed to do something with her life no matter what. She said at one point she was a taxi driver and a single parent paying for her own college tuition while raising her child by herself. I had never had that type of encouragement or support before. Going back to Mom was not as devastating purely due to my newfound hope. Everyone has their own life challenges but maximizing your environment to the best of your abilities is essential for survival.

You need to know there's a silver lining in every dark cloud; Sherry taught us that. Throughout my life, God has placed people like Sherry in it to impart simple truths. Don't make a permanent decision on a temporary condition, because it too will pass. These may not be Biblical principles; but it is wisdom given from God Himself. Outside of learning many things from Sherry the thing she imparted into my life that changed me greatly to be a better me was not to give up too soon and always have faith in your ability to do anything that God has placed in your heart. Even though Sherry taught me that since I have grown up, I have learned that this principle aligns with the teachings of God's word.

2 Corinthians 4:18 (NKJV), "Therefore we do not lose heart. Even though our outward man is perishing, yet the inward man is being renewed day by day. For our light affliction, which is but for a moment, is working for us a far more exceeding and eternal weight of glory, while we do not look at the things which are seen, but at the things which are not seen. For the things which are seen are temporary, but the things which are not seen are eternal."

2 Corinthians 4:18 teaches us where our focus should be during troubling times, and that they are only temporary. We should not dwell on what we are going through; rather we should focus on He will guide us through it.

James 1:2-3 (NKJV), "My brethren count it all joy when you fall into various trials, knowing that the testing of your faith produces patience." **James 1:2,3** is telling us Christians that God allows struggles in our life; not to harm us, but to make us stronger in our walk with Him in both faith and patience.

Romans 8:6-8 (NKJV), "For to be carnally minded is death, but to be spiritually minded is life and peace. Because the carnal mind is enmity against God; for it is not subject to the law of God, nor indeed can be. So then, those who are in the flesh cannot please God." If we, the children of God, think and do as the world around us does, then we will die as the world will die: In agony and defeated in both the flesh and in the spirit. As Christians we should operate out of the mindset of Christ Jesus which is the mind led by the Spirit of God; and in doing so we will have victory in every situation and always be in peace.

I can clearly remember the fear I constantly lived under while growing up. Though now I live above fear, in a place of peace and I am not oppressed by it. It takes time to get an understanding of the relationship we have with Christ Jesus. Things we go through and people that we are connected to somehow can give you a twisted view of our heavenly father's true love and protection. In God's word there is relational truth that brings healing to one's soul. Aman's soul is composed of emotions, feelings, his mindset, his will and heart. Through the healing power of God's word, it can bring you liberation.

Psalm 107:20 (NKJV), "He sent forth His word and healed them, and delivered them from their destruction." I can't help to think how much better off I would've been if I could've gotten rooted in God's word much earlier in my life. As a teen, I was still lost from the truth. The father never left me or gave up on me. I was learning through trial and error as I grew up. After leaving Sherry's house, I came up with a plan before I moved back in with Mom which was to stay focused on a goal to be successful in life no matter what career I chose. I also made a commitment to myself that no matter what happened to Sherry's marriage with my Dad; I would never lose total contact with her and little Zaiden. Zaiden made me promise to always be his big sister and I did.

Chapter 8
Your Life is What You Make It.

WHEN I RETURNED TO MOM'S PLACE, SHE HAD NOT CHANGED but I was different. I was more focused and more driven to succeed. I knew my priority was school and finishing at all costs. I also realized that as long as I was in school, I needed someone to take care of me and I couldn't, as of yet, be on

my own. I had to force myself to stop being depressed and feeling so traumatized by Mom. It was time for me to deal with my emotions better than I had been before, whether I liked it or not. No matter how mom treated me, she was still the person that God put into my life to provide for me. I am 14 years old now, and a ninth grader in high school. My thoughts were surrounded around my future and wanting to succeed at something. The military entered my mind a few times: The thought of being able to join right after high school, would be great. The military also offered excellent benefits and would give me an opportunity to continue my education at a later date; paid in full. When I enrolled back in the school near my Mom's, there was an elective called "Jr-ROTC". This program was a branch that was created for students who were interested in preparing for a future career within the military. They taught you everything you needed to know about military life, including the dress and the chain of command. I would see students dress in their ROTC uniforms weekly. I noticed that the majority of kids made fun of them in their uniforms, but the ROTC students still wore their uniforms with pride. Personally, I didn't think the uniforms were too attractive. However, what drew me was the appearance of unity and order that came from wearing them. The teachers respected the ROTC students more than their other students. The ROTC taught an honor code and they meant business: I felt that fit with my personality perfectly. I stood out from all the other students but in a good way. I was a student of bold character and a focused mentality. I made that green ROTC uniform look good by wearing it with excellence. I never cared about being in clicks and I sure wasn't a follower of foolishness. I stood with the elite the purpose to succeed above all else and all others who would stand with purpose and pride. So, I joined, and I loved every minute of it. I began to excel and grow with confidence. This was the first time I had been a part of something and did well. I grew in rank and position speedily. The Jr-ROTC ward system encouraged and rewarded students of outstanding behavior in both participation and academic excellence on all levels. They believed in promoting those who put forth their best effort as well as those who excelled among their peers. One example was to wear your uniform in a manner that it was clean and ironed, your badges and ribbons were to be placed properly on the uniform and shoes must be properly shined. Another area of reward was in demonstrating good leadership skills and traits. Attendance and charter both played a key role in the Jr-ROTC program. I now had something to focus on, other than just hurrying to graduate. My first year in Jr-ROTC, they had a shooting competition called "The turkey shoot". The turkey shoot was a target shooting competition between the female teachers versus female students and the male teachers versus male students. The prize would be an actual turkey for the top two shooters. I didn't expect to win, but no other female came even close to my score. I proudly took home a turkey for my family that Thanksgiving.

My life back home with Mom, after being with Dad and Sherry for a year improved enough for me not to contemplate running away from home all the time. I enjoyed school and looked forward to going every day. I was encouraged by what the future had in store for me. I spoke to mom about getting a job after school; but it was a short conversation. I was told as long as I was in her house and in school, that it wasn't going to happen. I knew better than to ask why.

Kaleb on the other hand had a pampered life with Mom. He got away with many things us girls couldn't. Mom always seemed to be taking his responsibilities off of him. It was as if she thought his life had been hard enough already. He had never been given a curfew like Tina and I had. His chores were lighter than mine, and any time he did something that he knew was wrong Mom would sit down and have a conversation with him; or just ground him for a few days. On the other hand, us girls lived a completely restricted life. He was an athlete, he loved just about every sport that involved running and playing with a ball. When we were kids, I never did see anyone who ran faster than Kaleb: he was always down for a challenge in sports. I could look outside, and no one would be out there, the next minute Kaleb would come outside with any type of ball and all of the kids in our complex would come out to play with him. There were three siblings, two brothers and a sister, that were close to our age and continually reached out to connect with our family. The oldest brother was Richard, and he was sixteen, the same age as Kaleb, their sister was named Sophia and she was 13, which was my age. The youngest sibling was Jeremiah, and he was quite a bit younger than Tina. Jeremiah was 10 years old. They didn't live in our apartment complex on a daily basis, but their father lived in our building and they'd visit him on the weekends... Every time they visited; the brothers would come knock on our door to get Kaleb to play ball. Their sister, Sophia, enjoyed playing with Tina. However, Sophia and I didn't care for each other too much. Sophia had an extroverted personality and only connected with those who would agree to whatever she felt like playing and doing. She made the rules and led whatever was to be played; this was a perfect match for Tina. Though, there were still times where Sophia and Tina were doing something that interested me, and I would humble myself and play with them; At least until Sophia started being a cheater or a controller over the game. Then the unpreventable would happen: We would end up in confrontation. During one of the weekends Sophia and her brothers were visiting, we met their Father as he passed by us kids playing in the courtyard. He was friendly and seemed to be soft spoken in the way he greeted everyone. He told us his name was Mr. Lee, and from then on if we saw him, he would always wave at us. One time we were with Mom and just getting home from the grocery store. Mr. Lee was passing, and he waved at us kids; he had a big, warm smile on his face. Mom said, "Wow y'all know *him?*" We explained to Mom that the kids that came over to play every weekend were his. Kaleb started joking that mom had a crush on Mr. Lee right off the back, and each time he did she would tell Kaleb to shut up and be quiet. However, I started noticing every time Mom would leave the apartment, she would try to look her best. I also noticed she was always looking around to see if he was outside. Finally, Kaleb told Mom that he was going to set her up on a date with Mr. Lee.

Mom said, "You better not." The next weekend, Mr. Lee's kids came over; Kaleb shared with his kids that our mom liked their dad. They thought it was funny: They told us if our mom waited until he noticed her, she would never get asked out because he was too shy and quiet. They said he's not really forward like a lady's man is. Mr. Lee's oldest son, Richard, suggested that their first date be with all us kids. He said he could convince his father to take us all out for pizza. Richard ended up following through, and Mom acted like she was a nervous schoolgirl the entire time. She also must have remembered what his kids said about him not being forward, because before the night was over, she suggested Mr. Lee come to our house for dinner the following Sunday. He was quick to accept Mom's offer with a counteroffer. Mr. Lee shared that he was an expert cook, so Mom would have to go over to his place so he could cook one of his delicacies for her... It became a regular thing for mom and Mr. Lee to take turns cooking dinner for each other: each just wanted to outdo the other. Though, that never happened; they were both excellent cooks. They enjoyed spending time together and got along well. Mom had finally found a best friend.

Mr. Lee didn't drink hard liquor like Mom, but he did drink beer regularly and smoked his weed every now and then. Never around us kids though. He would excuse himself to the restroom and go smoke. The entire restroom would be filled with the aroma of weed. Then when Mom joined in with him, they would go smoke in her bedroom; always with the door closed. But we could smell that stuff and we weren't stupid kids; we knew what they were doing. Mom never had a hobby, so she took up Mr. Lee's hobby of going to the Casino in East Texas on the weekends and they'd also gamble at horse races at Lone Star Park in Irving. Before you knew it, Mr. Lee was spending the night at our apartment regularly. After a while, Mr. Lee and Mom decided that it was more feasible for them to become roommates and save money. So, we moved into another apartment complex which had larger rooms. They put some of Mr. Lee's furniture in storage. The only one of us kids, including Mr. Lee's, that didn't like the idea of their relationship was Sophia. She wanted Mr. Lee to get back together with her mother and she didn't care for our mom too much. The rest of us kids thought they were a great couple. Mom and Mr. Lee were both short and around the same age; plus, they had us kids in common. It was like the Brady Bunch whenever Mr. Lee's kids spent the night. They finally came to live with us full-time shortly after we moved, including Sophia. We never got the whole story of why that came to be. All we knew from the boys was that their mother was high strung like Mom and could be very dramatic and abusive. Richard was the oldest and he was a character. He had all kinds of jokes that would come out of his mouth. Mom was very fond of him because he was the lively one in the house, even when we were facing hardship. Richard would always find a way to turn things into a joke. Him and Kaleb got along well. Richard also had this natural gifting of cooking which paired well with Kaleb's natural gift of eating; so, they hit it off. Kaleb became Richard's guinea pig when it came to experimental cooking. Richard was a natural when it came to thinking outside the box when cooking. Richard would recreate any leftover meal and substitute any ingredients for another if we were out of something. If you've ever met a creative cook like Richard it wasn't too many things that he'd not tried. One day when I got home from school, I noticed there were firemen at our apartment. I couldn't even begin to imagine what had taken place. All I knew was that Mom and Mr. Lee were at work and Kaleb and Richard were home. The firemen were wrapping everything up and getting ready to leave when Tina and I walked into the apartment. When I entered the front door, the living room and kitchen was soaked with water. Mom's living and dining room furniture had been destroyed by the water and smoke. The entire kitchen was scorched with black smog which covered the walls, and smoke still lingered in the dining room. Tina and I knew Mom was going to hit the ceiling when she got home. I ask Richard what he was doing to create a mess like this. He said he had been frying pancakes and chicken. When Mom and Mr. Lee got home, just as I predicted, Mom began cursing up a storm. She told Richard that he and Kaleb were going to get a job and help pay for all the damages. She said that they should be working to help with some of the bills anyway, especially since they weren't in school. Mr. Lee said, "Man y'all really did it this time," and then he went into their bedroom and closed the door. Kaleb took a job at 7-Eleven and Richard got a job at a restaurant, and they did just as Mom told them to do. It took three months until all of the repairs had been finalized. Mom went and got new furniture on credit and paid it off gradually. Richard decided he was going to be a professional cook and go to culinary school. Sophia only lasted a few days living with us: She moved back home with her mother. I was glad, dealing with her was almost as bad as dealing with my cousin Sarah. After the boys got jobs Mom started to respect them a lot more. She would allow them to drive her car and drink her beer and eventually they started smoking their pot. The only exception was Mom would make them give her money to help replace what they used.

I liked Mr. Lee because he didn't care a lot for commotion in the house. He knew how to calm mom down when she started to be dramatic. As long as Mr. Lee was around, he wouldn't let mom go on a rampage for long periods of time. He had always treated us kids with respect and appreciation. Mr. Lee said he had a good eye for a sure thing. What he had was a bad gambling problem. It wasn't a sport that he would've placed a beat on if the offer presented itself. Let us not leave out the lottery and quick beats at the covenant stores, I've never seen him pass one up… He was so addicted to gambling; that his paycheck would be gone sometime before payday got around. Mom was mad a lot of time at Mr. Lee because this would leave all the bills on her if he lost.

One day when I got home from school, Mom was home from work. She told me that my Aunt Rachel had passed away. All I could think about was going back to South Carolina, but mom had made up her mind on the subject: I was not going anywhere. She was still angry at Aunt Rachel and hated me for loving her. I had heard bits and pieces of how badly Aunt Rachel treated mom when they were growing up, but nevertheless Mom had made Kaleb and I to stay with her for 3 years. I only knew the side of her that was loving and caring. I knew I could have gotten my Uncle to send me a plane ticket to come to the funeral, but Mom said that I was not allowed to go, and I could not call them; and that was final. She made it clear that she did not want to hear any more about it. I had never lost anyone before, and I had so much anger in my heart towards Mom. I disconnected from the entire house. I knew running away wasn't an answer anymore because of my age and because I needed to finish high school. Now that I am older, I realize that no one can understand your pain like you do. I didn't understand Mom's pain and she had no understanding of mine. Another thing to consider is that many hurt people will hurt people in response. People that are experiencing pain don't know that they are causing destruction to the people's lives around them. Wounded people tend to have tunnel vision, where there is no room for logic. That's why unforgiveness causes disconnection, division, and finally destruction of relationships. What is the Father saying about all of this can be seen in **Psalms 107:20, 147:3?**

Psalms 107:20 (NKJV), "He sent His word and healed them, And delivered them from their destructions."

Psalms 147:3 (NKJV), "He heals the brokenhearted And binds up their wounds." Both of these Psalms show that our Father God has a plan for those who are wounded in their heart. **2 Peter 3:9** It is not His will that any one of us should perish but that we all come to the maturity of faith in His word and repent

Chapter 9
Exit Strategy

I REACHED OUT TO MY FATHER AGAIN TO SEE IF I COULD COME and live with him. By this time, he had finalized his divorce from Sherry and had not been remarried. Dad lived in a 3-bedroom duplex in Oak Cliff. He allowed me to come and stay with him on one condition: I would get a job and take care of myself. I was extremely happy about that because that was something that Mom had never allowed me to do; get a job. I moved in as soon as Dad gave me the green light. Mom didn't have much to say to me other than, "Go wherever you think will give you peace." When I moved with Dad this time, I had my own room. He was never home so it felt like I had the place to myself. Dad never believed in buying  groceries. The handful of things he would bring home would be cereal, milk, bread, and sandwich meat; and nothing more. Dad stayed true to his word about me getting a job and brought me down to "Captain D's"; a restaurant down the street that he and his co-workers went for lunch every day. The minimum age limit to legally work in the state of Texas was 15 years old, and I was only 14 at the time. The entire staff liked Dad and they were willing to overlook my age. They hired me and started me off as a counter girl; greeting customers as they entered the restaurant and cleaning tables. Dad registered me at the high school down the street from his duplex. There was a neighborhood school bus that picked me up and dropped me off for school. The high school was an adjustment because I had never been to a primarily African American School. The atmosphere was different. The kids would interject more often and were generally louder. I wouldn't be lying if I used the word "hostile" to describe it too. There were more than a dozen fights everyday: If I looked at someone wrong, it could start a fight. This school also had cliques on a leave that I couldn't understand. I made zero friends and I had to focus hard on not making any enemies. In black this schools, it was a lot harder to keep to yourself because the kids will drag you down for not wanting to be a part of a clique. All of my teachers seemed to be stressed and overworked, so finding a teacher to help me get caught up on their curriculum was not going to happen. I connected with my manager, Tara, at Captain D's. She happened to be a college student herself, so I got Tara to help me with some of my school assignments. She would also take me home if I had to work late and the city buses stopped running. I truly loved my job. All of the employees were like a little family who had nothing but appreciation and love for each other. The other girls that worked with me treated me like their little sister and took me under their wings. I could talk to them about anything. Tara and the other girls would come and pick me up when we were all off. We would go to Tara's house and hangout and do our hair, nails, and do nothing but talk about girl stuff. This was the first time that I felt included and wanted in anyone's circle; it was the first time that I enjoyed having friends. Dad trusted me to go to school and work and then come back home on my own terms. Most of the time he was gone and didn't know what I was doing. He could be gone for two weeks at a time; then all of a sudden, he would stop by the duplex shower and change clothes and be gone again. Dad's place was right on the city bus line which was perfect for me to be able to go to work. After I started working school wasn't a problem anymore because Tara and the other girls, I worked with helped me get caught up and stay ahead. As much as I enjoyed ROTC this school didn't have that program. I either had money to buy food or I ate at the dinner like most of the employees. All of a sudden, Dad started going to church, and then he started being at home more often. Eventually Tina, Kaleb, and Richard came to live with us. It seemed like Mom's drinking had run just about everyone else off. I was excited and surprised that Richard came with Kaleb and Tina. Mr. Lee and Jeremiah were still there in the apartment with mom. My dad said they all were welcome to stay as long as everyone took care of themselves. Dad said he wanted Richard and Kaleb to get jobs. Richard started working with me as a cook immediately. However, that only lasted for two weeks: He had gotten into it with the head cook. I was the only one bringing home food and helping my other siblings with groceries or other household things through my paycheck. Every night I worked I would bring all of the extra fish home instead of letting my manager throw it away. Kaleb and Richard ate it up. Dad mandated that all of us were to go to church with him. He also said we needed to join the choir if we were to continue staying with him: We all did because there really wasn't much that Dad had asked from us. This church was different than any I'd been to before; they were just starting off and were looking to break ground on a new building soon. They had been holding service in a hotel. It appeared that Dad was getting closer to the Pastor there. I never asked him what happened to encourage him to go to church. I was just happy that one of my parents was in church. I watched him intently; and I noticed that everything the church needed Dad was expected to provide, do, or make happen... It seemed to put him under a lot of stress. After a month of Dad being at that church, he went and bought the church a bus and repaired. The next thing I knew dad became the regular bus driver... I was very different finally seeing dad do unself acts of love for anyone. That Pastor took advantage of that. He still wasn't dating anyone, but it looked to me that the pastor of the church became his close friend. Dad ran around doing all kinds of honey dos for him to the point where I didn't recognize him around any of the church folks. We kids never learned anything because they didn't have a youth or kids service. It all seemed quite boring to me. Plus, I didn't care too much for being in the choir; the songs were very outdated and had no life in them. Richard decided after a couple of months that enough was enough and he went back to Mom's and he easily convinced Kaleb to come with him. Tina said she didn't want to be home by herself when I was working so she left also. For about 6 months Dad supported that church, but then something happened. He just stopped going all together. It seemed to be more of a place for a weekly social gathering than for discipling Christian. If I were honest, I would say that I was relieved when dad stopped being used by that church. I wanted more than anything for him to live a saved life and grow in the word, but he didn't have to be totally consumed in the process. Now that I'm grown, I can still say that church wasn't healthy for my dad.

Galatians 6:9 (NKJV), "And let us not grow weary while doing good, for in due season we shall reap if we do not lose heart." God's work should not be tiresome or become a burden. This scripture helps one to analyze their position in the church to make sure they're working for God and not for man. Throughout the time I lived with dad, I had one girlfriend that used to come over to our house when I didn't have to work. Cammie went to my high school and rode the school bus with me daily, but we didn't have any classes together. Usually, I only saw her on the bus, aside from the days that she came over. At one point, Cammie started to tell me about a party she and her brother, Carol, were throwing. Cammie wanted me to go but I told her that I couldn't go because my father didn't like me outside of the house when he wasn't at home and especially at night by myself. That didn't stop Cammie from bugging me about coming for a month straight. Finally, one week before her party, she stopped me with this sad look on her face and told me some other things about the party that had me second guessing my decision for our friendship. The first thing she told me was that her parents were going to be out of town, and it was her older brother who was throwing the party and most of the people there she didn't know because they were his college friends. She said she really needed someone to come over to keep her company; she didn't want to be all alone. She also said that I wouldn't have to stay too long just an hour or so. Then she said she would always be indebted to me. Everything inside of me was pointing towards not going but when that night came all I could do was to think about Cammie's sad face. I told myself that I would show my face and quickly leave. Then Dad would never know I left home and went to a party. I had never been over her house, but she had pointed it out to me several times: It was walking distance from where I lived. I had seen her brother Carol one or two times when he dropped her off and picked her up at my house on various occasions. That evening, cars were parked up and down Cammie's street. You could hear the music from miles away I'm sure. I rang the doorbell after getting there and a person I didn't recognize let me in. There were so many people in Cammie's house that I barely had enough room to move around to look for her. Everyone was shoulder to shoulder. I walked towards the living room and kitchen, which both were downstairs, and she was nowhere to be found. There were college students drinking and smoking and the music was so loud you couldn't hear yourself think. I went back to the entry and stood near the front door. From there you could see the stairwells where I assume the bedrooms would be. I looked at the top of the stairs and Carol was standing and waving for me to come up. At first, I shook my head "No." He yelled Cammie's name out to me and pointed to one of the rooms upstairs with a closed door. I proceeded up the stairs to where Carol gestured, she was. He waited for me until I got to the top of the stairs and said that she was in there. I lifted my arm to knock on her door, but he reached his arm around me and turned the doorknob assuring me she was in there. Once I was in the room, he shut the door behind the two of us and locked it.

"What are you doing? Where's Cammie?" I yelled. He grinned and proceeded to pull my clothes off. The music was so loud that no one could hear me yell or fight with him. He forced himself onto me and bent me down and raped me. When he finished, I couldn't stop crying. I put my clothes back on and ran down the stairs out the front door and back home. When I got home, I balled up in a ball in my room.

The only voice I kept hearing was "You slut" in the form of my mother's voice. She had called us that many times out of just being mean and hateful, but in that moment, I felt she was right. Once the pain in between my legs subsided, I was able to go and take a hot bath. At that time, I knew I couldn't let anyone know what had happened because I shouldn't have been out at night, especially not at a party. Even after the long hot bath my entire body was hurting all over. I feared if anyone found out about it; it would be the end of my life as I knew it. That weekend I called in sick from work and stayed locked in the house and locked in my room. I didn't even come out to eat. My Dad didn't come home the entire weekend which wasn't unusual: I know it sounds bad, but I thank God for that. It kept me from having to explain why I wasn't at work or why I stayed locked in my room. Plus, I was still very scared. I felt like a loose end to someone's crime and like I needed to be dealt with. To me it felt like Carol would approach me again and try something much worse. The next Monday when I saw Cammie on the school bus, she looked at me as though she was mad. I thought oh well; I don't have to worry about saying anything to her. I'll just let her think I didn't show up; in that way, I don't have to talk. I could only guess why Cammie was mad. I felt it was because she thought I didn't show up and I wasn't going to tell her otherwise. If Cammie even though I came then there might be a possibility I slip up and tell her what had happened thinking she was a friend, I could trust. Anyone who got mad at you for staying at home and doing the right thing wasn't a real friend anyways. We never spoke again. Whenever I saw her, I would look the other way or play like I was busy doing something that involved all my attention. I was sad all the time and felt like my life was a failure. I continued to go to school and work. Though, I only worked on the weekends so during the week I would get home from school and lock myself in my room. I might have seen my dad once or twice a week for a couple of hours when he came back to shower and take and nap, then he'd leave again. I knew he had a girlfriend that he spent most of his time with outside of work; that's the only thing that would make sense. During the time I was there living with Dad Mom would call me once every other week to ask me if I was okay. I never gave her the details of how often Dad was gone in fear that she would make me come back home to live with her.

Once I turned fifteen, I was allowed to open a bank account. Outside of the time when I had been sexually assaulted, I never called in from work or was late. I took my job seriously, and I learned all my customer service skills during this time. The first four months I did nothing but greet customers as they came into the restaurant and thank them as they left. I was eventually trained to take orders and be a waitress for the dining room area of the restaurant. After I had 8 months under my belt of being faithful in those starter positions, they trained me to be a cashier. Our restaurant location won all kinds of awards for cleanliness, customer service, and food preparation.

Two months after the sexual assault, I started noticing that the skin on my feet and hands started peeling. At first, I thought maybe it was just dry skin but then I started noticing a burning sensation and discharge coming from my private area. Then other parts of my skin started getting sore for no reason. I told my dad and he called Mom. She told him that he needed to schedule an appointment for me to see the doctor and take me because I lived with him. Dad wasn't too happy about it, but he still did it. I was scared because I didn't know what to expect nor could I imagine what was going on with me. He allowed me privacy to speak with the nurse and doctor alone. The first thing they did was check to see if I was pregnant. They asked me if I was sexually active, and I told them no, but they said they had to check anyway. That's when I started getting scared. The test came negative for pregnant but positive for syphilis. I was told it was a sexually transmitted disease. My heart dropped and they went straight into a long line of questioning me about my sexual partner. All I could think of was how Mom was going to kill me. They asked all the right questions pertaining to the person who gave it to me, but I wouldn't release any information to them thinking I was protecting myself. The doctor knew I had been violated but she told me she couldn't help me if I wouldn't at least tell her who it was. To this day I believe if my mother hadn't instilled so much fear in me, I would've told them. I didn't think anyone could save me if my mom set out to kill me. They called Dad into the examination room with me and told him what I had. I felt like I was trash. The doctor said I would be given a series of six shots in my butt with an 8-inch needle over a three-month period. The doctor said that I would be getting a shot every two weeks for three months: I cried and cried.

Dad turned to me and said, "You know I have to call your mother, and it's more than likely that she'll bring you back to live with her." On the way home, the drive felt like it was never going to end. The silence that ensued was bone chilling. Dad must have called Mom that night because she was waiting for me the next day after school. Mom said, "I knew you were over here whoring around. Don't you say a word to me. Go get all your stuff I'm taking you home. I should've never let you come over here, something told me to come and get you." Not once did she give me the benefit of the doubt. Judgment and accusation and threats were all that I heard. Now that I can distinguish the enemy's voice from my heavenly father's voice, I can be confident that I am forgiven, loved, delivered from all of the devil's schemes. The devil is called many names and one of those names is the "Accuser". The Accuser wants you to feel that it was your fault that you were raped or taken advantage of or that you deserved it. This brings an enormous amount of guilt upon yourself. The next deception the Accuser brings to you is that he wants you to turn you against your Heavenly Father. You might ask, "How does that work?" Well, we know that the Creator of Heaven and earth is also called many names; one being Elohim. He is referenced to be the one and only omniscient, meaning He's all knowing in the sense that He is aware of the past, present, and future. He is also omnipotent, meaning He is all powerful and has supreme power both on and outside of earth; there are no limitations, and Elohim is omnipresent, and this means He's all present, capable of being everywhere at the same time. Indeed, these things are all true. Then why is it that God would allow such a heinous act against a precious one like you and me? The Accuser will have you believe that God is none of these things and that He is selfish, unloving, uncaring, and too busy for you. The word of God in **John 8:32** says the truth shall make you free! The Creator of Heaven and earth, Elohim, is loving and caring and selfless. He's given you a free will to choose the direction in life that you'll take and which side of good or evil you'll partner with. He will not force you to stay within His will, although it is His heart's desire. All things that man becomes subject to are because of a decision they have made outside of God's will. If you were wise not to buy into any of these deceptions, Satan still won't give up there. As the Accuser he is looking for any acquisition to entrap you by making you feel overwhelmed and confused by pain and regret.

I have shared with you in the previous chapters how serious self-deception can be. Unforgiveness can be a death trap, it'll open the door for Satan to come in like a flood. It'll block all your inheritance from the Kingdom of God starting with peace, joy, love, a sound mind, and can even bring sickness and death to your body. It is all designed to destroy relationships. I can go on and on but instead t I will just share God's word.

Deut 32:35 (NKJV), "Vengeance is Mine, and recompense; Their foot shall slip in due time; for the day of their calamity is at hand."

Matt 6:15 (NKJV), "But if you do not forgive men their trespasses, neither will your Father forgive your trespasses," said the Lord. Now that we know the truth, what do we do from here. I won't advise you myself, but I will tell you that every offense is different and no one but God can save you. He has come to save us from all things pertaining to this world. He's the same yesterday today and forever more. He's not against us but for us. *Psalm 140:12 (NKJV), "I know that the Lord will maintain The cause of the afflicted, And justice for the poor." Psalm 140* is speaking to us who have been abused and those who cannot protect or defend themselves, God is saying that He will take care of us, He will see to us, and restore us from the injustice that has been done.

Psalm 34:19 (NKJV), "Many are the afflictions of the righteous, but the Lord delivers him out of them all." Psalm 34 is also a word from the Lord for those who are and have been struggling because of sexual offenses. Elohim tells his children no matter how many offenses you are faced with, and no matter what offense you're dealing with, and no matter what the severity of it is; God is there to deliver you from them.

Chapter 10
Pushing Myself to the Limits

MOM HAD BECOME REALLY GOOD AT ENROLLING AND DISENrolling me in school. She pulled me out of school the very next day. I was

able to call my manager and tell her the abbreviated version of what happened, and she told me not to worry about my job. She said if I talked with my mother and it was okay with her, she would just have me transferred to the Captain D's near Mom's place. Mom went along with it, as long as I agreed to help her pay a bill or two. Within a week I was transferred to the Captain D's nearest to Mom's. Leaving all my friends without a goodbye was hard for me. I still felt like I was being punished for an offense that was done against me. Somehow, I looked at it as my fault for going over to that party that night, but no one would ever know. God has a way of making lemonade out of your

lemons. I was giving more blessings than I may have realized at the time. I was lucky enough that my manager could transfer me so that I could keep working. I'd also become terrified of being home alone without Dad; it wasn't that he did anything, but the whole party situation truly messed with me. I was also lucky enough to be far away from that rapist and didn't have to worry I'd somehow run into him. I didn't have a problem paying for the phone and electricity bills. I still had the rest of my paycheck to do whatever I wanted with. I also thought about not having to use my money to buy groceries anymore. Kaleb and Richard were excited about me bringing home Captain D's leftovers once again when I closed, especially if there was nothing at home to eat outside of cold cuts. However, I became sick of the smell of fish all the time. I stayed faithful when it came to doing my job but longed for a new one. Mom took me every two weeks for three months straight to get those shots to treat my case of syphilis. She saw how painful they were and started having a little bit of sympathy for me. She stopped bringing up how she thought I was the cause of it and was instead saying that we learn from our mistakes. I now had a goal to work hard and stay out of sight from Mom, especially on her bad days. Ever since I'd left mom I had missed being in the Jr-ROTC. Now I was back in a school district that I could recommitte to the program again. The military allows those students who have at least 3 years of Jr- ROTC in high school to enlist as a E-3 which is a higher grade pay then a private. I had a secret desire to join the military, so I knew I needed to be connected to a school who offered the JR-ROTC program. I craved structure, discipline, and righteous authority. I felt that would help mature me up to be all that I could be. As soon as mom transferred me back to the school district nearest to her, I was able to re-enroll in ROTC. The school that was in Dad's district didn't have ROTC, so it wasn't an option for me while I was living with him. One thing that was constant was the area we lived in. We changed schools like we changed hair styles, but mom kept us in the same part of Dallas through it all. We were always very close to the city bus barn, without staying in the same neighborhood. We mostly lived in the north east part of Dallas. Sometimes we would just be moving across the street to a different apartment property. Where we lived had 95% apartment property in this resident area. It looked like a small town with nothing but apartments as far as the eye could see. The schools were zoned in such an unusual way that made it difficult for families like mines. We could move right across the street and be a part of a totally different school district. During all of the years we lived with mom, the schools that we attended happened to be dominated by white people. Mom and Mr. Lee were still living together at this point. They had been together long enough to meet the requirement on common law marriages in the state of Texas. I knew that this wasn't God's way of envisioning relationships between men and women However, he brought the best out in Mom. Mr. Lee was the exact opposite of Mom; he helped bring balance to her most of the time. There was only one complaint anyone ever had concerning Mr. Lee: And that was his gambling addiction. No one had a problem until it started being the bill money and grocery money that he would put on the line; and would lose most of the time. Mom would become outraged. We would see her working back-to-back on a triple shift to get things covered sometimes. As much as I hated always moving, complaining would do nothing but make things worse. Once I was living back home you could guarantee that the lights would never get cut off again

Things turned around for me at the new school. I found the first teacher that ever cared about me personally and who wanted me to excel in life. She looked past all my faults to the person I could be. Her name was Mrs. Jackson, and she was my ninth grade English teacher. She was always inquisitive and never shy to make a point to have me reflect on my actions. One time she told me, "Every decision can be life changing so never be in a rush to commit to something that might change who God has created you to be." I didn't understand what she was talking about at the time. I was always trying to see if she was analyzing something I was doing or giving me advice for the future. Mrs. Jackson was very spiritual, and she could look at a person's personality and speak words of wisdom to them that would help them at a later time. She would tell me almost daily not to be in a rush to grow up or graduate. What I liked most about Mrs. Jackson was how she was always positive, even when she would catch me daydreaming in her class. She never embarrassed me in front of others. Some kids thought she was sarcastic or plain funny, but it made them act right in her presence. Mrs. Jackson would come before school or stay after to tutor me on any subject that I was having problems with. There were even two times she went out her way to pick me up for church. I really enjoyed going to her church. It was small and intimate which brought back memories of my beloved Grandma Ethel Lou church. She wasn't able to do it more than twice because it was too far for her to come driving every Sunday to pick me up and drop me off. Just the thought of her even trying in the first place was more than enough for me. I was now in the 10th grade and the school I started attending had a Jr-ROTC program which I was hoping to join once again. I was super excited about getting plugged back into the world of ROTC. After speaking with the Captain, he said he could start me off as Corporal rank because of my previous ROTC experience. This rank wasn't the ground rank, but it was a low and non-commissioned officer above a E-3 step above. I excelled during the first month and started getting all types of awards. I was encouraged to join the "Jr-ROTC Drill Team". Before the end of the first year, I had earned a rank of 1st Lieutenant and was marked as a squad leader on the JROTC Drill Team. Mom seemed to be very happy about all the awards that I brought home. I had never seen her happy about anything concerning school before. It was a breath of fresh air. The military had a summer program just for Jr-ROTC students that were serious about joining the military after high school. The students that signed up to go would leave Dallas for a week to go to Lawton, Oklahoma. We would be on an Army military base training as though we were in boot camp. I was excited to see what it would be like not only to be away from home, but to be in the military before I fully committed to signing my name for a lifetime career. I paid my $300 camp fee and bought everything I thought I'd need for the trip. I felt privileged. I was in the 10th grade at the time and the trip was only supposed to be for 11th and 12th graders; unless you were an officer, which I was... The day came where it was time to go to camp. I knew camp wasn't about being able to go there as a tourist or having free time to goof off. I expected to have a sneak preview of every area that would be made available for me to work in after boot camp or after testing during the beginning of my active military tour. Little did I know that there would be a great awakening for us all. Good or bad I committed to 7 days of completely military exposure: and that's not subtracting the 2 days for travel time. I felt it was worth it; so, I could see if this were something, I really wanted to committee my entire life to after high school. The final head count that signed up to go was 30 students: including myself. We drove all day long to get to the Fort Sill Army Base.

I knew a few of the kids but I wasn't close to any of them that went. The school had rented an air-conditioned Greyhound bus for us to travel safely and comfortably in. What I did not know was that it was going to be our last bit of comfort until we got back on this bus to return home. It didn't take long for me to figure that out. We pulled onto the army base parking lot where a group of 20 military enlisted men and women were waiting on us. After they had us get off the bus, they separated the boys from the girls right away. They had a military barber waiting on the boys. I repeatedly keep hearing, "You guys have the option to turn around now and go back home, but once the bus leaves you'll have no choice but to follow orders or receive discipline the military way. I had no idea what that meant, but 2 kids jumped back on the bus with fear. Then I saw another 3 boys get back on the bus because they refused to get their heads shaved. They made us dump our luggage out on the ground in the parking lot. They went through everyone's bags telling us what had to be left behind or trashed. During when they searched our personal items, 2 kids were not willing to have their stuff picked through; so back on the bus they went. Next, the Drill Sergeant read everyone a list of dos and don'ts that were not negotiable once you entered the military base. First on the "Do's list" was you must do whatever you're told by all your superiors with no questions asked. You must not leave your squad at any time unless you have authorization from your superior. You cannot opt out of any pre-scheduled training or events. You are to be on time for every roll call or scheduled formation. No socializing outside of your platoon was permitted during anytime, unless you had been released for downtime. There were 3 more kids getting back on the bus before they'd even finished reading off their list. Once they did come to an end, the Drill Instructor gave everyone one last chance to get back on the bus: No one else joined them and the bus departed from the parking lot. There was a total of 10 kids that were not going to attempt the military lifestyle and were on their way back home. It was made clear that you could not just wake up and be sick because you didn't want to follow orders or get out of doing the planned activities. They said sick cadets would be given light duties such as cleaning the latrines, mopping barracks, and picking up the trash on base. They told us that it's rare that anyone gets to go home just because they claim to be sick, and they don't let anyone stay in bed. None of us kids could have ever predicted this nightmare. I kept saying to myself, "I know it's the military... but this is just camp for us... I'm 15 years old and just a kid." I'm sure the rest of the students were thinking the same thing until that bus pulled off and everything we had been told was thrown into full force. Reality quickly hit us all that it was too late to turn back. We were shown to our barracks, which were our sleeping quarters. It was a room filled with 40 bunk beds stacked through the room. The latrine was connected, and it was made up of 10 commercial sinks with little mirrors over each one, and around 20 small toilet stalls, and walk-in showers with no privacy and enough space for 10 girls at a time. We were given 30 minutes to unpack our stuff and freshen up and be in formation for chow, which they called dinner. For dinner we had 20 minutes in total to stand in line, get our food, finish eating, put our food trays away, and be back in formation. Then they gave us uniforms and our schedule for the week. If you were so much as 1 minutes late for formation you would have to do push-ups in front of 4platoons; which consisted of about 100 men and women each. Even though we had 20 minutes to eat and be information, it never took me less than 15 to get through the long line of soldiers. The entire week, including breakfast, I never had more than 2minutes to eat after the lengthy process of waiting in line, getting my food, and finding a place to sit. That left me with 3 minutes to clear my remaining food from the tray and to run outside to make formation. The food served there was better than any of the restaurants that I had ever been to. The varieties of food that were offered to us during every meal setting were excellent, I would go as far to say they were 5-star meals with plenty of varieties and sides of all types of meat prepared in several different ways. It made me frustrated that I didn't have enough time to eat let alone to sit and enjoy it. I understand why people from the military eat so fast now. My second day there I was one of the ones doing pushups in front of the 4 platoons: for being late for formation after mealtime. To think that I didn't have enough time to eat after standing in the chow-line was mind blowing. On this occasion I stood in the chow-line for 25 minutes to get my food and by the time I'd received it I had to throw it out and run to get information; and I was still 2 minutes late. My Drill Sergeant made me drop and give him 20 push-ups for being late... There were 10 pushups given for each minute of being late and additional

10 pushups for each push up you did incorrectly. On that day, I ended up doing 40 pushups and having no dinner. I found myself running to formation from then on out. Daily we got our fair share of marching and hiking. We walked everywhere we went; then did our planned activity and walked back to the barracks or to the dining hall. Most of the activities were physical, and nowhere near the barracks. We would walk or hike hours to the training location. If you were out of shape you would be tired before you even got to the delegated location for training. There were no breaks given other than a couple of swigs of water and the training started with no delays. It also wouldn't be cut short, even if it's past dark and you've missed dinner; you would be gone until it was finished. When the Drill Sergeant. said we were to complete every schedule training he meant business. Training could be anywhere from 3 to 6 hours mostly physical, then it would be time to walk back to the barracks or dining hall. On average it would be an hour walk from and to our barracks. Every morning at 3 we had to be in formation with our fitness outfits on, ready for an hour of fitness every morning in the center field. After morning fitness training, you had 30 minutes to shower, change, go to the chow-haul and eat, and be back in formation completely ready. I never understood how the Drill Sergeant always managed to add an extra activity into our eating time. The only thing I could decide was that maybe eating in the military just wasn't a necessity. We also did field training exercises, weapons training, combat drills, a tear gas drill, a fitness course, and a 24-hour hike in 2different terrains, in the woods and open fields. We had only one day where we had a 2hour downtime to wash our clothes and shine our shoes. Aside from that, our schedules were completely booked. If you thought you'd be able to get souvenirs or have time to write home, then you'd be mistaken. At night, the lights were out at 9 p.m. and we would make it to our barracks usually around 8:30; only giving us 30minutes for shower and to get ready for the next day and be in bed. Every day I felt like I had been overworked and underfed. My body was far past being fatigued. I had no energy, and I was sore and ache all over. I knew I had to disconnect my thoughts of how I felt and just do whatever it took to make it through. If the Drill Sergeant heard anyone complaining you'd immediately be forced to either do push-ups, have guard duty during sleep time, or have to clean the latrines while everyone else was eating

dinner. The third day I started praying to make it through the week and with a promise to never return. I don't believe any of the drills were modified for kids. Whatever the enlisted cadets did in boot camp, that's what we did, except for the classroom teachings.

On the day we did the field fitness training, everyone was meant to face fears on a level they never had before: We had to jump out of a plane; we had to parallel down a 20-foot wall by pushing our bodies away from the wall with our feet and hanging on to a rope in a handmade body harness. The trick for me was keeping my eyes close and not looking down. We did crawling, climbing, and running exercises. There was this one drill that had a rope that looked to be 50Ft long tied to a man-made building that looked like a lookout tower. There were two men on each side of the opening of the dropout. The pit was 50 feet wide and 50 feet deep. It would be instant death if you were to fall. The rope crossed the top of the opening of the pit. The enlisted men put ropes around our legs, butt, and crotch area to create a makeshift harness for safety purposes. It was then hooked onto the rope that stretches 50 feet across, connecting to the lookout towers on each side of the pit. We had to pull ourselves across the entirety of the rope without getting stuck. The rope that was tied around me was so tight that it cut my circulation off of my legs, and it cut into my pants so every time I reached to pull myself further across, I got rope burn. I got to the middle and couldn't bear the rope burning into my crouch nor my circulation being cut off for another minute. They sent an enlisted man to pull me the rest of the way across, which was about 25 feet from the mouth of the pit. The rope had cut right through my pants and skin. It dug deep into my skin around my crotch area, but I dealt with the injury in silence because I didn't want any criticism from my Drill Sergeant or All of the other leaders, both male and female, who were placed over us seemed to be impersonal and harsh. There was no second guessing myself for a career in the military. I was totally convinced that it was not for me.

On an entirely separate day, the platoon hiked up into the mountains. It took 4 hours for us to get there. Once we arrived, there was a cabin that was empty inside of it aside from a small kitchen table in the center of it. In the middle of the table was a container filled with tear gas. Before entering the cabin, we were given gas masks. We were told to hold on to the mask until we entered the cabin and would receive further instruction on what to do next. The Drill Sergeant asked if anyone had any medical problems that they should know about. I looked around to see if anyone would raise their hand, but no one did. I felt like I should've mentioned my asthma and allergies but with all the intimidation around me, I felt reluctant. I had noticed that every time a cadet brought anything to the Drill Sergeant's attention they were marked at or insulted and sometimes even disciplined. After entering the cabin, they asked everyone to get in a circle around the table. The enlisted soldier showed us cadets how to correctly place the gas masks on our face and what to do if we're in combat and there's a gas attack. Then they had us put our own masks on. Once everyone had their mask on; one of the soldiers activated the poison gas that was sitting on the table into the air. Then they had us remove our masks and inhale deeply as each one of us leaned over the fog. There were six cadets at a time allowed in the cabin during every demonstration. When my turn came, I did as instructed and right away I had an allergic reaction. I couldn't tell if it was asthma or allergies or both. All I know is that my airway immediately closed, and my eyes swelled up; the pain was 6 times worse than it was when I would cut up a raw onion. I started going into shock from my symptoms. I had a short flashback of an experience I had at work 6 months prior. One Saturday afternoon at Captain D's it was extremely slow. I was instructed to refile all of the condiments on the tables while cleaning them off. There was only one male customer in the dining room area eating at the time. I had a complimentary piece of hard candy in my mouth, and I was sucking on it. All of a sudden, I coughed, and it became lodged in my throat. My airways were blocked, and this desperate panic came over me. The male customer saw me and came to my rescue. He tried to help me clear my throat for one minute to no avail. As I grasped my throat I was in pain, a coworker rushed behind me and plunged at my back with their fist and the candy flew out of my mouth. This vision replayed in my head as though I was reliving that incident. Then I heard someone yelling, but I couldn't make out what was being said: I had become delusional. All I knew is that I couldn't breathe, and I was choking. For a minute I was disconnected with what I was doing. A soldier pushed me out of the cabin. Even when I made it outside, I still couldn't breathe:

A soldier saw that I was still choking and hit me in the back; opening my lungs enough for me to cough and take a breath. It still took another 30 minutes for me to start breathing without coughing or gasping for air. The commander had all the cadets bused back to the barracks. My skin, eyes, and nostrils were all highly irritated and didn't go back to normal for another day or two. After all of that, returning home couldn't come fast enough. Thinking about it was comical because I had been trying to run away from home for so long, but now I was praying to go back. Mrs. Jackson was right to never be in a rush to grow up. There were many other stories I could've shared about that week; those were just the tip of the iceberg. like the day we did a 24hr hike throughout the different terraria. Once we came back my feet were swallowing, and I could barely get my military boots off and trying to put them back on the next day was like torture. I had never experienced anything close to that, not even in the country where I was born when I used to hike in the woods with my cousins and brother for fun. I can say one thing for sure about the military: It pushed me past every limitation and standard I thought I had. I slept all the way home, as did everyone else on the bus. The five hours it took to get home was nothing but dead silence. You could hear the wind against the side of the bus and the tires hitting the pavement as the driver drove. It was the first time we could get no interrupted rest without a Drill Sergeant yelling. We were far too exhausted to discuss the week with our neighboring cadets. All of our parents, including Mom, were waiting at the school excitedly when the bus arrived. Mom couldn't wait until I got in the car to start asking how my week was. My only response at the time was "I'm not committing to a career in the military!"

Mom said, "It was that bad? Maybe you need to rest and reflect back on your week." I didn't say anything else; but I knew she was disappointed. She had excitement in her voice every time I discussed ROTC or joining the military. I believe there is a lesson to learn out of everything.

Many times, we can't see through different lenses until we eject ourselves from the middle of it. We have to disconnect from our opinions, emotions, experiences and voices in the world to be able to look at something from a new perspective. This perspective is also known as hope or faith. Looking back on this particular experience, it taught me not to give up or to give in. It taught me when tough get tougher, I need to pray harder and believe that all things are possible. I am sure that I would have done great in any branch of the military I pursued, if I hadn't been shaken by fear after that week.

Now that I am older, I'm able to understand why so many nonbelievers have a hard time believing in a God that they can't see or touch. God has shown me that fear causes many to retreat or not try at all. This is where people avoid having faith. The military sets standards that a large population of people think that is impossible for them and many others. Though, there is a smaller number of people who can be convinced that they are capable. I recently met a young man in the army in that category. He said he's been challenged by the military over and over again and has been pushed to meet standards that otherwise he wouldn't have been able to. However, this same man refuses to believe in a God he can't see. God showed me that this young man has a problem with being let down by others, but more than that he also doesn't trust himself. His problem wasn't with a God he couldn't see but rather it with trusting oneself. There has to be healing that takes place in people such as this to trust on a greater scale. My prayer for this young man is not only that he gets his soul healed but also that it comes before a problem comes that's bigger than any man other than God. Where would this young man be then? I have no doubt that he'd be relying on God, like many do, during a crisis. Man has no real control over anything; everything is done through trial and error. Those who never try will stay in the unknown but those who continuously try come out of error into a faith that's been tested by recreation. There's many areas that I still struggle in when it comes to trusting man or myself, but God is on a whole 'nother level. He has given it all through His only beloved son. That is more than I can say for any of us.

John 3:16 (NKJV), "For God so loved the world that He gave His only begotten Son, that whoever believes in Him should not perish but have everlasting life."

Matt 7:11 (NKJV), "If you then, being evil, know how to give good gifts to your children, how much more will your Father who is in heaven give good things to those who ask Him!"

After my week at the Fort Sill, Oklahoma Army Base I had a new perspective on my future. What rang in my spirit was that failure was not an option. It was time to reanalyze my life and figure out where I was headed and how I was going to get there. I came home, reassessed my life, and made new goals. My first task was to start looking for a new job. I had become burned out from working at the seafood restaurant and only making minimum wage. I needed something that would pay more. Me quitting was not an option unless I found a better job to replace this one. On my off day I went to Target and put in an application for a customer service position. That same week I had an interview and was hired on the spot making an additional $3 an hour. I told the hiring manager that I didn't want to up and quit my current job and that I need to give a two-week notice. The hiring manager accepted my terms and placed me on the schedule two weeks later. I decided to open a bank account with the City Credit Union and start saving my checks. This was Mom's banking institution and she said that they had a lot of benefits for their customers. The place Dad had me bank at charged me for everything, including being a member and for every check I wrote or extra fees for ATM usage. I needed every little dime I could save. The time was coming fast when I would need money to get my own place. I also went to a furniture store located downtown because it was on the bus route and picked out furniture and placed it in a layaway. My plan was to pay 12 installments and once I paid it off; I would put the furniture in storage if I hadn't found a roommate or place to move. In addition to that, I started taking $20 to $30 dollars out of each paycheck and would go to the dollar store and buy things that I would need after I moved in for my kitchen and bathroom. Even at age 15, I was looking for God to bless me; so, Tithes wasn't an option, it was a necessity. I paid my tithes to the church that was coming to my apartment complex to take kids to church. Anytime I was off on a Sunday, I would attend. There were times I missed church for a whole month, but I made sure my tithes were mailed in. I had expected that this year was going to be a year of preparation for moving out. This coming fall I would be in the 11th grade and on my birthday, I would be turning 16 years old. The rest of the summer I worked as many hours as they would give me and did whatever it took to keep Mom from going off on me.

Chapter 11
Into Oncoming Traffic

I HAD BEEN WORKING SO DILIGENTLY THAT WHEN I FINALLY got my first Saturday morning off, I didn't know what to do with myself; but getting out of the house sounded good to me. Mr. Lee was going to "Minyards",

our neighborhood grocery store, to pick up a few things to cook with for Mom. I asked him, "Would you mind if I accompanied you?"

He said, "Sure, you can go, I'm not doing a lot of grocery shopping just picking up a few items for your mom." Once we got to Minyards, Mr. Lee parked right in front of the store which was the perfect location to see everyone who was entering or exiting the main entrance. We got out of the car and noticed an elderly white gentleman coming out of the store. He was placing his wallet in his back pocket when a young

black man ran behind him and grabbed for his pocket, but the elderly man was holding his pocket as tight as he could to keep his wallet from being taken. My first instincts were to run and help the elderly man, but Mr. Lee looked at me and shook his head as if to say, "No you better not." Mr. Lee wasn't one you wanted to test.

"Why don't you want to help the elderly man?" I said.

He responded, "It's not our business, so we need to stay out of it." Mr. Lee was not one to combat with, so I knew to let it go. That didn't stop me from saying a prayer for the old man. Mr. Lee and I stood there and watched this elderly gentleman fight off the young guy that looked to be in his early 20's and was a towering 6 feet tall. There were other customers coming in and going out of the store who saw what was happening and did nothing. In my head I thought that didn't make it okay for us to do nothing also. Here I 'am this 15year old kid and was given instruction to mind my own business. Other bystanders' only response was to grab their purses or wallets tighter while walking passed the poor old man or around them: as though the young guy was going to leave the elderly man alone and come and mess with them. At the very least I expected someone to run back into the store and notify the manager or call for help. The elderly guy couldn't have been more than 4feet from the entrance of the store; how was there not a worker or manager intervening? This incident went on for a good 20 minutes. We stood by the car waiting and watching until the struggle was over. That elderly guy held onto his wallet and let everything else go. He stayed that way until he was able to maneuver his body weight to lay on his backside and that prevented the robber from taking his wallet out of his back pocket... I couldn't believe this guy would fight with this elderly man for 20 minutes in broad daylight with so many witnesses surrounding them. Now that I'm older, I understand a couple of things a little better. In many poverty-stricken areas, you will rarely have an eyewitness come forward. Some out of fear and others out of many other reasons, thus resulting in more crimes occurring in broad daylight. Now when I look back on this heartbreaking incident, I can see more than just my own pain. This is a perfect picture of what God sees in all his Prodigal children. He is saddened when Satan kills, steals, and destroys the lives of his chosen. Satan was the cleverest out of all the creatures in the Garden of Eden. He is able to deceive men in daylight right under our noses. The thing man has to remember is that the Bible teaches in **1 John 2:15** not to love the world or things in it. It goes on to say if we love the world then the love of the Father is not in us. **1st Peter** teaches us that you may be fooling yourself but not Satan. He is on top of your open doors of sin within man's heart and will use them against you. **1st Peter** also is warning God's children that Satan doesn't give up or give in.

1 Peter 5:8 (NKJV), "Be sober, be vigilant; because your adversary the devil walks about like a roaring lion, seeking whom he may devour." I would venture out to say that this picture of the elderly white man fighting the thief is a great picture of Christians in today's church, taking their stand against the devil and letting the devil know, "Not my salvation or anything else that my Father has gifted me will be yours." Amen.

Romans 8:19 (NLT), "For all creation is waiting eagerly for that future day when God will reveal who his children really are."

Tina and I used to ride the city bus to school. We would go to downtown Dallas to transfer to a bus that would take us home. Usually when we were down there, we would stop by this popular clothing store for teens, owned by a sweet family. Every day we would go by there just to browse through the store; never once did the owners harass us about coming in and not buying anything. They were very nice people who loved to see us stop by. On this particular day, they had a rack of clothes placed in the front of their store on the outside. Tina and I got off the City Bus and proceeded to the clothing store, which was approximately 6 feet away, before reaching the front door of the store a man was running and bumped me. At first, I thought it was just someone rushing to catch another city bus. As I watched this guy pass the clothing store in front of us. He grabbed the entire rack of clothing in his arms and continued to run. Out of reaction I ran after him yelling, "Thief, thief, thief!" Not once did I think about what could've happened if he dropped those clothes and stabbed me or hit me with something. The faster he ran, the faster I ran yelling as loud as I could. I had chased him 3 blocks down the street when an officer finally spotted me from across the street and tailed after me. Within seconds there were two additional officers coming to help. The thief threw the clothes down and took off running faster across an open field. However, it was too late; the police all jumped on him while I stayed with the clothes. I had ran so far away from the store that I could no longer see the store or Tina in my view. Once the officers put him in handcuffs, I was able to catch my breath. Then I started to re-evaluate my action. What was I thinking? Obviously not of myself, but justice for the nice store owners.

The officers gave me a ride back to the store and said, "Young lady, please don't ever do that again. Your life is worth more than those clothes. You never know if a thief has any weapons on him and you could've been seriously hurt." Once I arrived back to the store the owner was hugging and thanking me. Tina on the other hand was calling me an idiot. The owner blessed me with an earring and necklace set: I didn't want or expect anything, but I sure did not turn it down. It showed me how grateful the store owner was. For months my entire family put me down for that decision with all types of jokes and other tasteless commits. I think they were trying to make me feel bad enough, so I wouldn't do it again. I have always had a heart for justice, and it pains me to see the innocent being taken for granted. Many of us are not in the position to stand up for ourselves, but there are moments when we are given opportunities. There will always be a risk in all things but if we can remember that God has got our back, the risk will be well worth it. I would like to believe that the young man's life was changed for the better after he was arrested.

Joshua 1:9 (NKJV), "Have I not commanded you? Be strong and of good courage; do not be afraid, nor be dismayed, for the Lord your God is with wherever you go."

Mom was extremely strict with Tina and I when it came to us only being allowed to get rides from her or the city bus. I always felt mom kept tabs on us wherever we went, which was in part her reasoning behind that rule. It did not bother me though, because I wasn't trying to sneak around and do anything behind moms back anyway. Tina on the other hand was always up to something. We were one grade apart and in the same school most of our lives. Tina on the other hand was a follower of the kids who were considered renegades. When Tina did show up for a class punctuality wasn't a pet P of hers. Tina would say they should be glad that I showed up at all. Also, Tina was not trying to ride the city bus even though she and I had been warned. Mom told the both of us on several occasions about not riding with students. She said we were to always leave early to make sure we didn't miss our scheduled city bus. Tina would often catch rides from male classmates against what Mom had instructed. She always begged me to go with her, but I knew Mom was harder on me than she was with her. So, I was not going to intentionally put myself in a situation like that. One day I woke up late and rushed out of the apartment to catch the bus and on my way there Tina was getting in the car with her friend. She asked me if I wanted a ride with them and like normal, I declined. As I was walking away, I saw the bus coming and started to run for it, but before I could get there it flew right on by. As I was walking back to the apartment, Tina said, "Are you sure that you want to pass up a ride to school." I know waiting for the next bus would be an hour (meaning that). I would miss my first class.

So, I thought, "*Maybe this one time.*" This guy had his music so loud I instantly knew I had made a mistake. I asked Runny, the driver, if he would turn his music down. He looked at me and only touched the volume knob, leaving the music the same. He sped out of the driveway, running two yellow lights. The next thing I knew, we were passing the city bus that had left me behind. I immediately started praying that we would get to school safely and promised God if we made it that I would never disobey Mom again. I looked up and we were approaching another red light that was yellow, but we were much further away from crossing it. All of a sudden, Runny speeds up instead of slowing down to stop at the light. I closed my eyes as we were getting ready to cross it. It felt like I had been tackled on the football field, when the two cars impacted us. Most of the damage happened on the right side, which was the side Tina, and I were both sitting on. His little Camaro spun around at least two times and then stopped. Runny jumped out of the car and started to run and Tina and I were stuck because the damage on our side of the car was total. I was in pain from head to toe but I didn't think about that: I was thinking about the butt whipping I would get when I saw Mom. A man from another car jumped out of his car and pulled Tina and I out. After the man pulled Tina out, he started helping me. As soon as I looked up and around: I noticed the city bus slowly passing by and all of the passenger's eyes were on us. I looked at Tina and said, "I should've never listened to you." The man asked us if we were alright. We both shook our heads to signal that we were. Still in shock, I said, "We have to get to school, or Mom is going to kill us."

The man said, "You almost died in that car crash, you need to go to the hospital and get checked out."

I looked at Tina and said, "If you want to go, go ahead but I'm going to school." The man was still talking to us, but I did not pay him any mind. He tried asking us about the guy who had been driving the car; the one who had jumped out and ran off after the accident. I walked away and proceeded to school on foot. I don't know what Tina told him, but within 10 minutes she was coming behind me. As we both walked to school, neither of us said a word. Throughout the rest of the day, I did not feel any peace thinking about what was going to happen if Mom found out. We rode the city bus home like we were supposed to. We cleaned up and I did all my homework as though nothing had ever happened. When Mom finally got home, she called me and Tina into the living room.

Mom's first question was, "Tell me about your day?"

I said, "Nothing really interesting happened. It was just a regular day."

She then looked at Tina and said, "Do you have anything to share?" Tina shrugged her shoulders no and then looked down towards the floor. Mom went on to say, "Then tell me... how did you two get into a car accident on the way to school?" I was speechless. This had confirmed my suspicions that Mom had those bus drivers spy on us. I knew there was nothing I could say that would keep Mom from whipping me, so I just held my tongue. Tina of course wasn't going to say anything either, she knew she had been regularly disobeying mom. Mom took off her leather uniform belt and asked us who wanted to be first to get their whipping. I never was going to be the one who wanted to be first. Somehow, I was hoping that being the last one to get whipped mom would tire out when she got to me. She never did; it was the opposite. She had just warmed up. Or maybe she was saving the best for last. I can tell you one thing: I never did that again.

Tina had a way of convincing me to either cover for her or to shadow her. I knew better but if something bad happened to her because I didn't try to protect my sister then I would've never lived it down. She came to me at school and asked me if I would ride with her to "Oak Cliff" after school. She said one of her friends lived over there and she was worried about them because they had not been to school for a week.

"If something did happen to her, then how would you be able to help?" I said.

She said, "I don't know but I have to check on her. If you don't go with me, I'm still going." I told her all the reasons why I thought it was a bad idea to go, especially alone, but Tina paid no mind to it. She assured me that if I went with her then she would just briefly check on her friend and then we could leave. I knew I wasn't able to convince her otherwise which meant I would have to go with her.

Once we got downtown to the transfer station where we would board the bus that would take us on the other side of town, I experienced culture shock for the first time. I had seen low-income type people before, but never what I experienced on this bus. Most of the women I looked at had a large part of their body exposed. The men seemed to be in three categories: homeless, gang banger, or some kind of substance abuser. To see them all together all at once seemed crazy and scary to me. Tina and I surely looked out of place on that bus. She hit me in the leg and told me to stop looking people in the face. At first that seemed backwards to me, I thought I should show no fear and that meant not to be scared to look people in the face. I started to see that Tina was right, people started acting like I was challenging them, or I was a threat to them by looking in their direction period. As we got off of the bus, the smell in the atmosphere made me nauseous. I knew better not to say anything about it, or some of the people that were to blame. Thank God this girls house wasn't too far from the bus stop. When we got to her apartments, Tina went straight to the apartment as though she had been there a dozen times before. I wouldn't be a bit surprised if she had and just didn't say anything to me. Her friend had a little brother that opened the door and let us in. He went to get his sister and she came running out of the room hugging Tina. She was very grateful and thankful for Tina and I being concerned about her whereabouts. She took Tina into the back for a minute and then we left. It was a quick visit, just like Tina had promised. I was relieved that we left quickly before it started getting dark. We were able to get home before Mom got home from work, which meant all was well for the meantime. Through this experience I learned many things: All people are different, and every person has his or her own issues; We are wrong to judge people for what they look like or where they come from; Most of all, a man's poverty level doesn't speak for his character. As a child, I responded to the people on the bus in a negative way because of the stereotypes I had been fed from the media, school, church, and the workplace. Throughout the years I've even noticed that the local news often targets low-income communities. The truth is the same crimes are committed in the black poor neighborhoods as in the rich white neighborhoods: Crime doesn't discriminate. The news is only being reported and highlighted in the black poor neighborhoods to say that these people need not to be trusted. What is God saying to us all.

Matt 7:3,4,5(NKJV), "And why do you look at the speck in your brother's eye, but do not consider the plank in your own eye? Or how can you say to your brother, "Let me remove the speck from your eye; and look, a plank is in your own eye? You Hypocrite, First remove the plank from your own eye, and then you will see clearly to remove the speck from your brother's eye."

Tina has always been very courageous; she would test or challenge anyone. She was a bit susceptible to becoming friends with the outcasts in school. They were the types of people who intentionally break rules just because they knew they could get away with it. They were dead beat students who had no interest in coming to school to learn. They were troublemakers, who came to school to skip class and harass other students. I never had a problem with them, but they would bully weaker kids. Tina never did that, but she enjoyed hanging out with them. I would be in class and see them through the classroom window hanging out on the side of the school building or in the playground and lunch areas. They would pour alcohol into a coke can and be smoking weed. I never saw Tina smoke or drink anything; she was smarter than that. I believe those outcast kids were intrigued by Tina's fearless personality and that's why they allowed her to be in their circle. I had told Tina to watch her back many times because I knew those kids couldn't be trusted.

One day at school a group of kids that had never talked to me came up to me after one of my classes and told me that something had happened to Tina. They said the ambulance just left the school with her in it. I went directly to the principal's office and inquired about the authenticity of the statement. Principal Bulark brought me into the office and started asking me questions about Tina's health.

"Has Tina ever had a seizure before?" he asked.

"No, never," I said scared.

"Has she ever done drugs before, or does she still do them?" he continued." No! She doesn't do drugs, but I don't know if she's ever tried any before."

He said, "I have one more question and then you can call your mom to come and get you. Do you know anyone who would intentionally spike her food or drink?" I really didn't know how to answer that question.

"No, I—I don't know. I don't really trust any of her friends, but that's all I can think." He told me to make a list of all of her friends for him. "But what happened to Tina?"

"I'm not too sure myself, but she was most likely exposed to a drug, either voluntarily or involuntarily, and she had a bad reaction to it."

"Where is she now then?" I asked.

"An ambulance took her to Parkland Hospital. Thank you for your time, you can call your mother now to have her come pick you up."

Mr. Lee picked me up and he said Mom was already at the hospital. Once we got to the hospital, they told mom that they were giving Tina something to counteract whatever was in her system. The doctor also told Mom that she wouldn't be leaving the hospital today because of her erratic behavior and they weren't letting anyone see her at this time.

Tina and I were together almost always when we were out of school. We shared a bedroom and so I would've known if she had been doing drugs. I'd also warned her on so many occasions about her friends, and their jealousy. I do believe that one of them likely slipped her something which caused her to have the seizure and fall into a psychotic break. Whoever gave it to her most likely lied about what it was or simply just slipped it into her food or drink. It affected her so badly that she didn't remember any details surrounding it. The hospital wouldn't let Mom see her for 3 days. They placed Tina in a padded room in a strait jacket in the psych ward. Kids weren't allowed to visit at all so I couldn't see her. Tina was kept for an entire week. Mom instructed everyone in the house to not ask any questions about the situation once Tina got home. We were told she was very fragile and confused about what had taken place. I respected that and I never brought the subject up once she came home. Tina also didn't return to school right away. Mom had me pick up her catch-up work from school. I noticed when she came home that she was a totally different person. She had a sense of sadness about herself. Mom let Tina go back to school when she felt she was able to handle the other kids. Not one of her old friends approached me to check on Tina to see how she was doing; not even the girl we traveled across town on the bus to see. That really confirmed my sister's set up to me. When Tina returned to school, she avoided all of her old friends. Anytime I had a class close to Tinas, I would walk her to class. We became much closer because this was the second time she could've died in a short period of time. I started noticing some of those same students would get arrested and sent to Juvenile Detention and two or three others started turning up dead. It was sad, but it happened. That didn't seem to affect Tina at all. She was more focused now like I was on trying to graduate and make something out of her life. Tina and I had a conversation on the bus on the way home concerning which of us would succeed first and who would have a family first. We made a bet, but I lost.

Tina has worked in law enforcement for over 30 years. I remember helping her study for the entry exams for this job; she's now eligible to retire. As an adult Tina shows no remorse when it comes to those who break the law.

Genesis 50:20 (NKJV), "But as for you, you meant evil against me; but God meant it for good, in order to bring it about as it is this day, to save many people alive."

I was still bumping heads with Mom, just not as much because I was always either at work or school. When I was off from work it seemed like she would try to make up for all the times I wasn't home cleaning up. That didn't bother me but what did was the fact that I had two siblings that weren't working; one of which had dropped out of high school. I was expected to rotate the duty of washing the dishes with them, even if I had worked and wasn't home in time for dinner. The dinner dishes would be waiting on me at 11 or 12 o'clock at night after I'd been in school all day and worked all night. Mom didn't care; I better get that kitchen clean before I went to bed. I felt like that was unfair, plus I was helping with 2 of the household bills. I didn't say a lot about the money because I know Mom's response would be, "You chose to work," and she would be right on that point. At least I was getting paid more at Target than at Captain D's. I would have to pay a cab to bring me home on the nights I worked until close. The last city bus came at around 9:45, so it was my only option. I would leave directly from school to catch the city bus to work. If I was working until close: I wouldn't get off around 10:45pm sometime 11:15pm. I tried to do most of my homework during my dinner and lunch breaks at work. Most of the time, I would have to get it finished before I went to bed at night after I had cleaned the kitchen. I was good at my job, I worked at the customer service desk with returns and exchanges. Every now and then I would be asked to cover for the receptionist on the intercom, answering the incoming phone lines and dispatch calls that would need to be connected to the right department. I was a natural when it came to dealing with people.

One day at work a customer named "Bill" came to me asking if I did any modeling and at first, I thought he just was an old guy trying to flirt but then Bill came back with a portfolio of pictures he'd taken himself. I told him that I really didn't have any interest in modeling at the time. Every time Bill came to Target, he would stop by customer service to ask me if I had changed my mind. My answer would always be the same. A month or so passed and Bill stopped by the customer service desk to see me and ask if I'd heard about the youth event that was going on at the "Gaylord" in a couple of weeks. Of course, I haven't. All I ever did was go to school and to work. Bill said he wanted me to think about going. He said that there would be a handful of young models that he wanted me to meet and some of his old clients that would share with me how rewarding modeling could be. Bill went on to say that to meet more young people my age would do me good. He said because I lack fun in my life. It sounded good and maybe Bill was right, but I wasn't willing to take off from work. Missing work and losing money to go and spending money didn't appeal to me. After Bill left, I thought about it more. I decided that if Bill asked me again and offered to pay for my ticket, without me asking him, and if my job let me come work the morning schedule so that I could be off that night I wouldn't lose anything by going. Unsurprisingly, Bill came back a week later still talking about the Gaylord event and how everyone that's anyone would be there. Before I said anything he said, "What would it take to get you to go. What if I bought your ticket?" I still didn't say yes.

I told him, "I will have to check my work schedule and figure out how I would get there."

He said right away, "What kind of man would I be, if I didn't pick you up from work and take you? There's a shower and dressing room in the hotel's workout facility." I'd never seen someone so excited about anything. It almost made me uncomfortable. Then I started to have all kinds of unsettling thoughts in my head... What was I doing? Modeling had never been a desire of mine. It hadn't been too long ago when I had almost lost my life in a car where mom had told us to not be riding with strangers. However, this guy was mom's age and had been driving before I was born. Now that I am looking back on this incident, I see how we as people will make excuses for things, we know we shouldn't do and then because of that we find ourselves praying to God for an intervention with a promise to Him to get our act together if he comes to our rescue. I never did mention anything to mom; maybe because I know she wouldn't allow it. I started planning behind her back. I went to my favorite clothing store in downtown Dallas and bought an outfit to wear. My plan was to tell Mom I was working until close that night. I planned to be home around the normal time I got off from work. After I decided to go, that Saturday came quickly. I brought my change of clothes to work that day. I got off from work at 4pm and Bill was right there to pick me up. It would be 2 hours before the event got started, which would give me time to arrive, shower, get dressed, and relax before everything began. I had everything figured out in my head. On the drive over to the Gaylord, Bill said he got a room because he wanted to stay and hangout with some of his old friends that he hadn't seen in a while. When we arrived there, it was 4:30pm and Bill said I already have my key to my room. He went on to say if it would make you more comfortable to shower in my room instead of the fitness area of the hotel you are more than welcome.

I said, "No Sir, I am not going into your room." When we arrived at the hotel, I was amazed at how big it was. It was not only big but beautiful inside and out. As we walked in, they had all kinds of events going on and people everywhere. I didn't see any advertisements for a youth event; nor did I see any young adults or teen kids hanging around. There were families and people who looked to be on business trips and vacationing. Bill showed me to the lounge and bar area. He then took me to the fitness area where the dressing rooms were and left me. He'd told me what room he was staying in, number 666, and if I needed something he would be there, or I could meet him in the lounge area at 5:30. That gave me one hour to myself. So, I went and changed clothes and walked around the hotel admiring how beautiful it was until closer to the time I thought the event would be. During that time, I spoke with guests and hotel employees and no one knew about the live concert that was supposedly being held there for youth that evening. At that point, I became nervous and uneasy. I sat on one of the couches in the lounge area waiting for Bill. I didn't want to accuse him of lying because that would open up the door for him to go off on me: Then I would be stranded and no way to get home. I convinced myself to play it cool. When Bill finally came down, he said, "So, how do you like it?"

I said, "What, the hotel? It's alright. Wasn't the concert supposed to start at 6?"

"I think so. The flyer is back in my room, you could come with me to go get it."

"I don't really want to, that's okay," I said.

"Come on, you're not doing anything else. Besides, I would like your company," he pressured. At this point I was feeling very uncomfortable. We left together to go back to his room. Once there, he opened up the door and told me to come in: His room was a mess. He told me to give him a second to find the flyer, and I stood right by the door waiting. Not surprised, he couldn't find it, but he said that was all right. Apparently, he had all the details of the event in his planner; he even showed it to me, and it said the event started at 7, not 6.

"Relax, you were worried for nothing. Just have a seat and get comfortable. If you're hungry I can have room service to bring it up."

"I would feel a lot better if we could go find out where the concert was going to be held, so that we knew where to go when the time came." Thankfully, I heard no argument from Bill. We went to the front desk and asked the customer service where the concert would be held. Bill did the talking because I really didn't have any concrete information on the event. The lady who was helping us said she didn't see anything that resembled a youth concert on her weekend events sheet, but she also said that she was going to go check with the two other employees who were working the front. At this time my heart and thoughts were racing. *"What have*

I gotten myself into and what I'm I going to do now?" After the receptionist spoke to her coworker, she came back and told Bill and I to go see the security officer in the back of the hotel. She said he has all current listings of all events, even the last-minute ones. Throughout the whole ordeal Bill was agitated and annoyed. He spoke to the employee as though they were not on top of their job or professional. I knew he was putting on this act for me. I wasn't okay with all these coincidences. I had to stop being surprised sometimes. Here I am a 15-year-old girl with this man who is my father's age or older. I had so much suspicion surrounding me; that I had to realize it wasn't anything or anybody but me. I was the fool stuck in some foolishness. On our way to the security room, we were passing a bathroom. I told Bill to wait and that I would be right back. I had to get somewhere that I could pray in peace and ask God for wisdom, guidance, and protection. I went into one of the bathroom stalls and began to pray. I'm always led to ask for forgiveness when I know that it's my own actions that have led me to a desperate prayer. Somehow the Devil always makes me feel as though I need to bargain with God to get out of a situation which was caused by a premeditated act of disobedience. I asked God if he would save me from being raped again and to please get me home safely. My comment was that I would never go behind mom's back and plan stuff without her knowing as long as I lived under her roof again. I believe that the prayer gave me the boldness to stay calm and be watchful. Before, I was too scared to even look at Bill anymore in fear of what deceitfully things he had planned for me. When I came out of the bathroom Bill said with a half grin on his face, "I thought for a moment that I needed to come in after you." I didn't respond. I tried to look as undisturbed as possible. Once we arrived at the security officers main post Bill did all the talking once again. The security officer kept staring at me for some odd reason. He also informed us that he didn't know where Bill got his information but there wasn't going to be any youth concert this weekend.

"How often do cabs run through here?" I asked.

"Quite frequently. There are a couple of cabs that are regularly waiting outside because they know we have high spending guests that are looking to sightsee or go shopping. If that's all the question you two have, I need to go make my rounds before the end of my shift." I was quiet as a mouse as we walked in the direction of his room. I knew not to make a commotion, regardless of if we were alone or in front of other people... I really felt the Lord telling me to stay watchful and keep calm.

Bill said, "I know you said you didn't want to be in my room; however, I must apologize for bringing you all the way out here. I'm just as surprised as you to hear there's not a concert. If you would give me the courtesy of a couple of hours of sleep, I'll take you home. I will not make any advances towards you." I didn't respond and kept quiet as we entered his room. I sat in one of the chairs that was there, and Bill turned on the television and flipped through all the channels asking me what I wanted to see. I told him I don't watch a lot of television, so he could put on whatever he wanted. Bill put it on a sports channel and took off his pants and shirt. He then got into bed. He said, "Will you please lay down with me? I promise I won't touch you."

I told him, "No that's alright, I'm really not sleepy."

He looked at me with this crazy look on his face and with a tone of authority he said," I'm not taking no for an answer. Get over here and lay down." So, I got up slowly and walked over to the bed and laid on the edge of it. Bill said to me, "Relax I'm not going to hurt you." He placed his arms around me, while my back was facing him. I started praying that he'd fall asleep. However, every time I moved, he grabbed me tighter. I remember what the Lord had placed in my spirit earlier. He said stay alert, be watchful and diligent, look for an opportunity to get out of there. Somehow that brought me peace and focus. It was now 9 pm and it was starting to get late. Bill had fallen asleep and woke up every time I moved. I decided to get up and use the bathroom and see if he'd fall asleep while I was in there. As I pulled away from his arms, he appeared to be asleep even though he was grabbing me. So, I removed his hands from around me and went slowly to the bathroom. I stayed in there for 15 minutes and he appeared to have turned over and was now facing where I was standing in the front of the bathroom. His eyes were closed. I slowly walked to the other side of the bed where I had been laying and grabbed my bag, which had my change of clothes in it, and tip-toed to the door. Once I was at the door, I had to take the bottom and top lock off before I could get out. After that, I was able to open the door and quietly sneak out. I went straight to where the security office was; hoping that the security guard we met earlier was still there. I was so scared and nervous I couldn't stop looking behind me. Bill's room was on the sixth floor and the security office was in the lobby floor. Exiting the elevator, I felt comfortable enough to stop looking back but I was still walking fast. Once I arrived there were two different security men. I asked both of them about the security guy I had seen earlier. They told me he'd gotten off of his shift at 9. They went on to ask if there was anything, they could help me with. I explained to them that I needed a cab, and I was in a rush to get home. The other officer told me that sometimes cabs waited outside of the hotel. The younger of the two officers said, "No problem follow me, there should be more than one waiting at this time." As I followed him back to the front of the building, he asked me if everything was alright. I told him if I could get back home before midnight, I wouldn't have to explain to anyone what happened to me tonight. We were met with 4 separate cabs once we made it out of the lobby. The security guard said, "I told you they would be out here."

This one cab driver jumps out of his cab yelling, "Madam, madam I got you!" I looked at the security officer and smiled and said thank you. I ran to get in the cab that had greeted me and waved me over. This taxi driver was very nice and talkative. I gave him my address and asked him what the expected arrival time was from where we were. He said, "11: 00p.m if there was no traffic. Is that okay?"

I was very relieved, I told him, "As long as it was before midnight all would be well." The taxi driver told me his name was Peru and that he was from Pakistan and had been in the U.S.A. for 11 years now. Peru was telling me that he just brought his mom here around a year ago. He said his mom was very elderly and can't speak English very well. He went on to say how his father passed away a few years ago and he gave his dad his word that he would take care of his mother. He said that he didn't have an immediate family left in Pakistan that would've been able to look after his mother if she stayed there without him. Meaning his only choice was to bring her to the USA.

He said, "How about you? Why were you here at this hotel at this time of night?" I told him everything that happened. He told me, "Young lady you sure are lucky to have got out of that hotel with nothing happening to you." I told him that

I thanked God for protecting me and allowing me to meet such a nice cab driver. He started laughing and said, "Oh yeah? Tell me about yourself." I told him I was a high school student that did nothing but work and go to school. He asked me how I got around, and I told him I take the city bus to and from school to work and most of the time I have to pay a taxi to take me home after work because the buses stop running by the time I get off. Peru said, "How would you like to save a little money and I'll charge you half the fare you normally pay to get home and if I have no customers you get to ride for free. The only thing I ask you is to be my friend. Sometimes it gets a little lonely to have no one to talk to."

Peru seemed genuine and nice enough that I said, "Sure, why not." He gave me his number and told me to call him. As we were pulling into my apartments, he said it was a pleasure to have met you and I'm glad God let me meet you also. I never did look at him as though he was trying to flirt or run a game on me; he seemed to be innocent. Once I got into the apartment, I was so thankful to not have had that nightmare I had envisioned because of a bad decision I made. Everyone was asleep and the dishes were clean. I texted Peru to tell him "Thanks for everything." The next day I was off from work, but I looked forward to seeing Peru on Monday after work; I had already told him that I wouldn't see him again until then. Throughout the next few weeks, he was like a big brother to me. I needed a friend also, and he fit the role perfectly. I never had anyone in my life that didn't judge me in some form or fashion. Peru would take me to lunch sometimes, or we'd sit in his cab and talk. He was always gentleman like and never said anything inappropriate or made me feel pressured into anything. He never had me waiting on him at work. Because of the culture differences I never confided in him about the problems I had at home. I was ashamed to talk about my family. That was okay though, as Peru never ran out of stuff to talk about. He would talk about his passengers and his mom most of the time; or if I asked about his culture he was honored to share. We became really good friends. He asked me how I felt about meeting his mom.

He said, "She would really like you."

I said, "How do you know that if she can't understand English?"

He said, "Well I like you. She'll like you." I knew Peru was older than me and I never looked at him in a sexual way because of his humbleness. I did end up going to meet his mom. She was all smiles and very humble like Peru. Peru had other friends from Pakistan that he introduced to me that seemed to be very kind also.

I had been doing well at school in all of my classes. I was well liked by all my coworkers, and I even had a few customers that looked forward to seeing me every time they came into Target. I never did see Bill again: I was very proud of myself. My furniture was half paid off and I had bought just about everything I needed to start myself in a new apartment whenever I was ready to move. My savings were growing and growing. I had many things to learn but I was getting wiser as I went along. One thing that I wish I had known a lot sooner was to trust the God inside of me. I've learned that man is a 3 dimensional being. We have a body, spirit, and soul. Because we have a spirit. There is a part of us that is instinctively discerning of right or wrong. Not only that, but our soul will hinder us from making sound judgments when our instincts are highlighting something that is not right, and we just ignore it. If these traits are toxic from past pain and hurt; then it will hinder sound judgment. During every experience in this chapter, some more than others, there could've been a life lost or gone too soon; but **God's word kept me**, His will drew me, and His spirit led me away to keep me from destruction. There's a question you may want to ask yourself which is, "How does God do all of this for a person who's not totally committed to serve him yet?" God's grace and mercy is sufficient.

Lam 3:22,23 (NKJV), "Through the Lord's mercies we are not consumed, because His compassions fails not. They are new every morning; Great is Your faithfulness." There's no difference between you and I. God loves you just as he loves me. But one important fact; sometimes we have to go through life experiences to bring us closer to God. If we're left without hardship, then life becomes so easy that we'll never need to call on Father God. This will hinder us from ever trusting God, nor ourselves.

Rev 12:11 (NKJV), "And they overcame him by the blood of the Lamb and by the word of their testimony, and they did not love their lives to the death."

Chapter 12
A Decision that Changed my Life Forever.

O NE DAY WHEN I GOT TO WORK, I NOTICED A VERY PRETTY little Spanish girl who was close to my age that had been hired. Every time I saw her, she was smiling. I would always try to make conversation when I passed her. She worked in the houseware department which I passed on my way to and from the break-room. She would come to the customer service department to talk to me too; one time she introduced herself to me as "Monica". We exchanged numbers and became friends almost immediately. Monica became my first true girlfriend. However, it was hard meeting up with her because she would drive up from Fort Worth which was an hour away. She had a car and would drive to see me on her

days off or come pick me up to spend the weekends with her and her family. Monica's mom was soft-spoken and humble, and she had a quiet spirit. She was barely 4 feet tall and couldn't speak any English. Anytime I came over she was right there loving on me and being an excellent host. Monica would always tell her to stop making a fuss over my company. I had never met a person as hospitable as her mother. I told Monica, "Don't treat her mean like that, and if it makes her happy to be nice let her do it. She wasn't bothering me at all." I quickly noticed that Monica wasn't the only one who would boss her mother around: It seemed to be that the whole house treated her like a maid and cook. Monica's father was the opposite personality of her mother's; he'd drink a lot like my mom. He was very loud and flirtatious with other women. He treated her mother with very little respect, which made me feel sorry for her. Every time I saw him, he had a fresh bruise somewhere on his body that would be massive. Monica said it was from him falling down when he got drunk. There was even one time where he was so drunk that he tried making a pass at me; from then on, I made a point to stay away from him. Monica had a big family and all of them were raised in America. At the time one of her brothers was in prison, but she had 3 other brothers and 4 sisters. I met them all; and they treated me like family. I was never made to feel like an outsider with any of them. Though, her older brother bought a house next door and lived there.

Monica was the first friend that I had ever felt close enough to bring to meet my mother. I believe it had a lot to do with her personality. She was very outspoken, loud, transparent, resembling some of the characteristics of my mom but more compassion. When they met, Monica connected very well with her. Mom's cursing didn't offend her one bit; she had a dirty mouth of her own. I used to encourage Monica not to use foul language, so she started speaking profanities in Spanish only. It didn't take a rocket scientist to figure out what Monica was saying, and in time I found myself understanding the Spanish as well. Monica always told me I was too sensitive and proper. That was her way of saying I needed to stop being so serious and have a little fun. She was very blunt, and I was used to that after living with my mother most of my life. She and I never competed against each other nor did we envy each other. She was the only friend that I could receive criticism from and not be offended by it.

Monica was also really hard on the men that wanted to date her. She would tell them she could do fine all by herself. She made her expectations very clear before she would give her number out. I called them roadblocks for deadbeat men. A lot of her expectations were ridiculous, but she was all about the dollar bill. Only men who were serious about her would take the challenge. She stood firmly in her belief that a man should take care of his woman, and there was nothing wrong with that. Though, I was more independent in my thinking and didn't want anything from a man unless it came from their heart. Monica also had a secret side to her that you never want to encounter. Monica was not one you would want to cross or get on her bad side. I had seen so many men be put in check by her that sometimes it broke my heart to see them encounter Monica's wrath. Different guys had their tires slashed, car windows broken, apartments destroyed, credit cards maxed out, and even had their reputations ruined. When I would see things going sideways, I would disappear until everything settled. I told Monica that I'm not going to jail for no one. She would always respond, "That 'Nager' was warned at the beginning that I don't play, so he's getting what's coming to him." She could never just leave a relationship, she had to go through and destroy everything the man had. Monica was everything a man could ever want in a woman, but he had to be prepared to put in the work.

Having a serious relationship was something that I had not desired to entertain. For one thing, I really wanted to do something with my life; and I didn't need a man to do so. So, I planned to go to community college until I could really figure out what I wanted; and I would keep saving money. Though, this was before I found myself a roommate. Monica would've been a great roommate, but her parents didn't want her on her own so early. I spoke to three of my associates at school., whom I knew were also serious about making something out of themselves and asked them what they thought about me leaving home at 16 years old. They didn't know that I had started running away from home at age 12. The fact that I was still there was only through God's grace. Two of them said it would be good if I could find someone with the same ambition as myself, and someone whom I knew was dependable in paying their portion of the bills. The other classmate said she wouldn't want to take on all those responsibilities at such a young age alone because things could become too much to manage while in school. No one knew that staying home wasn't an option for me. I had made up my mind a year ago that being on my own was the only way. Every day that passed and that I didn't have an altercation with Mom was both a blessing and a miracle. I was still afraid that she would come home drunk and beat me to death over something as small as forgetting to mop the kitchen floor. Plus, I was serious about finishing school. I had taken all my required class credits to graduate by this time, and I was only in the eleventh grade. The only thing I was working on at school were my required hours of attendance to graduate. My school had a work program, which was satisfying three-fourths of my hours. I was to go to school, check-in with the program to let them know I was leaving, and then go to work. My supervisor at Target was responsible for signing paperwork weekly that stated I was working six hours or more every school day. This program was perfect for me to get my school hours fulfilled, and to help me save up money.

I had an over-flirtatious customer that started harassing me at work one day. His name was "Andrew", and whenever he would enter the store, he'd come straight to the customer service department just to flirt with me. The biggest turn off for me, aside from him not being the least bit cute, was how arrogant he was. Andrew was full of pride and had an overly self-righteous attitude. He paid himself many compliments every time he engaged into a conversation with me. In his own words he told me, "How could you not be interested in me. I know you like my smile and swag, everyone does."

I told him, "No sir, I'm not interested in you at all."

He would say, "Yes you are, you just don't know it yet." What I was sure of, was I didn't like his push self-disposition. His attraction for me came off as being both bossy and controlling. The next day he came in wearing his work uniform: He wore it as a badge of authority that had no boundaries. He was a police officer for the county. He asked me what time I was getting off of work because we had a date. I explained to him that it wasn't very gentleman-like to be so forceful. Right away he started smiling and said, "Oh, so you're saying I'm a gentleman?"

"No!" I yelled. "You took my statement out of context. I said if you were a gentleman you wouldn't act the way that you are.". Andrew was good at twisting words in a way that would benefit him. I told him, "I have tried to keep my composure and stay professional with you; however, it's been nothing but entertainment. I don't know what else to do or say. Will you please leave me alone and stop bugging me while I'm trying to do my job?".

He responded, "That's not a problem for me, but it'll require you to do something on my behalf and I know you're not willing to."

Before he went any further, I said, "No sir! I am not trying to go anywhere with you."

Andrew said, "Girl you know you want to get to know me, don't play with me."

"You think because you're a police officer you have a right to continue to harass me, but you don't. On top of that, I'm even more sure now that going out with you would be a big mistake because you would never leave me alone!" The next day I made sure to take my lunch during the time Andrew would normally come. Just as I figured he had stopped by while I was on lunch; this time he left flowers and his business card for the third time.

On the back of his card, he wrote: "The only way I'll leave you alone is if you go on a date with me." I became sick at my stomach at the thought of it; this guy clearly was not normal. I tossed the flowers in the trash along with the business card. I told all of my fellow customer service employees that this guy was harassing me and if I saw him coming, I was going to hide, but I needed someone to cover for me. The two ladies that normally closed with me had no problem helping me avoid him. They suggested that I go to the manager and make a complaint, but I didn't think it would do any good since he was a police officer; so, I didn't bother. I started changing my lunch around every day to avoid this guy. One night he came right before closing but in his regular clothes. There wasn't anyone working with me; I was alone. He said that he knew I would be here, and he was going to wait for me to get off of work and that we were going to get ice cream. I looked at him and didn't respond to his remarks. I thought just ignoring him would be the best thing for me to do. I had told Peru about it and he was concerned: He also had advised me to speak to my manager, but I hadn't yet. Now here I was faced with a situation I could've avoided. I asked one of my coworkers to go outside and get my friend to come in. When Peru came, we were starting to lock up.

"What's the problem?" he asked. I explained to him what the guy had said, and he told me not to worry. "I am going to drive around to the back, and I'll pick you up there; that way he'll never know you left." That night I was able to get out of there without any confrontation. Monica had been gone for a week on vacation and so she didn't know what was going on. On my off day, which was the next day, Monica had returned to work. What I didn't know, or expect, was that Andrew went up to her and fast talked her into giving him my number. I couldn't believe this guy was this desperate. Monica explained, the next time I saw her at work, that Andrew had come in and said that I finally gave my number to him, but he misplaced it during work. He said it had taken an entire week for him to convince me to give it out, and now that he's lost it, he'd doubt he'd ever get it again. He also told Monica that he would be indebted to her for anything. This guy had really crossed the line, but I was scared and fed up with it. Later on, that day he popped up like clockwork at the customer service desk. I had made up my mind that I would have no dialogue with him. Unfortunately, because he's a fast talker, he doesn't need a second party to keep a conversation going. He made his regular flirtatious comments on my hair and clothes. He also said that he would finally leave me alone if I would just have coffee with him. I told him, "I don't drink coffee."

He said, "You've turned me down for dinner, how about dessert?"

I lied and said, "I'm on a diet."

Andrew responded, "Well, I guess I'll call you tonight then," and started walking away. I started weighing my options. If I reported him, he could become a stalker outside of my job. Doing nothing hasn't worked either so I couldn't continue to do that. The only thing may or may not work would be to go have a snack with him. If he's a man of his word he'd leave me alone. If he's truly not well in the head this could continue to get ugly. He called me that night like he said he would do, I told him that he has defamed the very badge he carries. I also told him I was tired of playing his little game and I needed to know if he was a man of his word. He said, "What do you mean?"

I said, "Well you told me you would leave me alone if I go out with you."

He said, "Yes I will."

"I'm not calling this a date, but anything that will get you to leave me alone will do."

He said, "Then it's a deal. How about on your off day?" I told him that was fine, and Andrew made arrangements to pick me up at my apartment and go to a pizza parlor down the street. I really felt that it was a bad idea until the evening of. He came to my apartment dressed up with flowers. He didn't have on a suit but a dress shirt and suit jacket and nice jeans and designer boots. He was driving a clean, pimped out Mercedes Benz. He opened the car door for me, as well as the door at the restaurant, and pulled out my chair; I was impressed with his manners. I couldn't believe this was the same guy that was giving me the blues. He did most of the talking, and of course it was all about himself. He said he had his own business as a private security officer and investigator on top of his job at the police department. He went on to say he had never been married or had any kids, which didn't surprise me. As he talked, I thought about my own life and what it was going to take for me to move out and away from Mom. The only thing I saw at the time were dollar signs. Someone who would be faithful in paying their portion of the bills. This man had his bachelor's degree and a career. He wasn't a looker in my eyes, but it wasn't like I was thinking about marrying him. I had lost every sense of good judgment because of a temporary need in my life. There were signs everywhere pointing to Andrew's real character and personality. However, I turned a blind eye because of my own ambitions. He had no problem in taking control and ruling over me, because I had been in that type of dictatorship all my life. Unfortunately, Peru was not a part of Andrew's equation, nor would it work the other way around. I had made a choice, and no matter how much of a blessing it was to have Peru in my life, his time was up. I didn't really realize how much it hurt him when I told him my choice. I had been so blinded that this young, innocent, sweet guy who looked at me more than just a sister. He had one day hoped that I would grow to connect to him in a more intimate way. Though, my decision had been made. My goals were grounded, and I was going to use this Andrew guy as much as possible without committing my entire life to him. For the next six months Andrew and I became friends. He never tried to get me to sleep with him because he knew my age. I had been to his apartment and he cooked dinner for me a couple of times. I respected that a lot. I wasn't sexually attracted to him, but I knew the time would come when he would want more out of our relationship; for now, I didn't have to worry though. He began to take time out of his day to teach me how to drive. I was surprised that he let me get behind the wheel of his "Mercedes-Benz CL-500".

My sixteenth birthday was coming in the next two weeks, and Andrew asked me what my plans concerning my future were. I told him I hadn't made any definite plans for anything, but I wanted to have my own place, but I couldn't afford to pay for it by myself right now. I told Andrew how I had paid off my furniture and acquired everything I needed for an apartment except for a bed. He responded, "Well, why don't you move in with me?" I got quiet and didn't respond. I wasn't ready to sleep with him and I know that if we moved in together that would be the next thing I would be faced with. Andrew asked me what's wrong, but I didn't respond. He smiled and said, "I don't bite." I told him I would think about it. Even to think about sleeping with Andrew made me wheeze in my stomach. I still had this fear I was dealing with from two years ago when Cammie's brother had violated me. The closer my birthday got the more nervous I became. I started shutting down around Andrew. He was buying me all kinds of gifts the week of my birthday, as though I had already agreed to move in with him. Andrew was buying me clothes, jewelry, flowers, and always sticking money in my hand. I knew how Andrew felt about me and my feelings weren't mutual. I felt I would possibly be going into a "shacking relationship" and this was something that I didn't desire. If there would've been an agreement of no sex in our relationship, then it would've been much easier on me. I didn't want to ask because I knew that would be a touchy subject, seeing as Andrew had already assumed, he was dating me for the last six months. After analyzing the entire situation, it ended with me choosing a man that I thought had plenty of money and would help me accomplish my goals in my life at the time. Also, I had a feeling of obligation to Andrew for the months we were friends; mainly because he had bought me a lot of materialistic gifts.

The day before my birthday I didn't answer his calls and I avoided seeing him. I needed time to think. I know this decision would change my life forever.

On my birthday, Mom made me a homemade chocolate cake and cooked my favorite meal, fried okra, fried pork chops, and macaroni & cheese. I had not mentioned to her or anyone else the choice I was faced with. It was the first time I didn't have an appetite for my favorite meal. Kaleb and Richard assured me that the food would not go to waste; I smiled for the first time in a while. The next morning, I went to school and then to work and Andrew showed up with flowers again telling me he hoped I enjoyed my birthday with my family yesterday; but today was his day with me. He said, "Have you told your mom that you're moving yet?"

I said, "No I haven't."

He said, "You might as well. I can pick you and all your stuff up this evening." I didn't respond, I just dropped my head, but he lifted it with his hands and said, "I love you." That was really scary to me. I rode the bus home and thought about what to say to Mom. Thinking about it gave me a lump in my throat. I was more scared of Andrew than I was of her now. I got home and started packing and told Tina that I was moving. She asked me why and I told her with red eyes that it was finally time for me to move on.

She gave me a hug and said, "It's going to be alright." I believe Tina thought my worries were of mom than anything else. If she really knew she wouldn't let me go. Once mom was home I stayed in my room until her and Mr. Lee got into bed. Then I knocked on the bedroom door and asked to come in to speak to them both.

I told Mom, "I'm moving out today."

She said, "Out where and with who?"

I said, "that Andrew guy that I've been spending time with. He has an apartment and I'm going to be his roommate."

Mom said, "Roommate? What you mean his sex slave?" I didn't respond.

I dropped my head and said, "Mom my stuff is packed, and he'll be here in 30 minutes to pick me up."

Mom said, "Okay, well take care of yourself."

Mr. Lee said, "Yeah be careful." That night I left thinking I had no other choice. This guy had done so much stuff for me and I felt that I was obligated. Andrew picked me and all of my stuff up and we drove straight to his place.

After he unloaded all my stuff, he said, "Do you want some wine?"

I said, "No, you know I don't drink."

He said, "I know you don't, but this will help you relax." I told him that I didn't feel good, and I just wanted to lay down. He said, "Great, I'm a little tired myself." I went into the bathroom and put my night clothes on, and he took off all of his clothes except for his under shorts. I told him I didn't feel comfortable sleeping with him yet and he said, "Where do you want to sleep? on the couch?"

I said, "Yes please." He said fine. However, he went into the living room with me and laid down beside me and started touching me all over. I kept trying to move his hand away, but he started taking my clothes off. I told him to stop but he ignored me and continued until he was putting his private area in mine with my underwear still on. The penetration was so painful I yelled, "You're hurting me!" He kept going as though he had no sense of consciousness. When he had finished, he held me and wouldn't let go. I was in pain throughout the entire night, and I was scared to talk and tell him how I really felt. The next day I was completely disconnected from him. I had shut down. I was in a situation I didn't want to be in, and I didn't know how to get out. I was confused on how I could've let things get so out of control and end up in the position I did. He took me to work, and I was consumed by thoughts of it all day. I felt that I had one chance to correct everything I did; every mistake I felt I made. I would tell Andrew to take me back home and to forget about me. I didn't know if it would work but I had to try. I knew I didn't want to live shacking up with a man that I didn't care about. That night, once we got back to his apartment, I told him the way I felt. I told him that I felt that I was rushed into something I wasn't ready for. I told him I didn't believe in men and women shacking up.

Andrew said, "I understand completely but what you don't understand is that I care about you a lot and I know we could make it if you give it a chance." I told him that I didn't want to give him a chance. "If by the end of the week you haven't yet changed your mind then I will take you home." Every night I begged him to leave me alone and every night he took advantage of me until I just gave up. At the end of the week, I told Andrew I still wanted to go back to my mom. He told me he couldn't allow that and that he knew that our relationship would grow on me. The next time I was at work I prayed to talk to Monica because she was the only person, I could trust to give me sound judgement. I hadn't seen or talked to her since before my birthday. The supervisor said she had been calling in, so they cut down on her hours.

I had become more terrified of Andrew and felt trapped. His character continued to evolve into a less and less conscious person; even when we were in the public together. Someone approached the both of us and they were speaking to me. Andrew responded in an extremely rude manner to them and did not allow me to say a word. Anything I asked Andrew for, he'd tell me I didn't need it; even something as simple as headache medicine. My family would call to see how I was doing, and he would tell them I couldn't come to the phone and ask them what they needed. I wasn't allowed to answer the phone. I missed my prom because I was afraid that the way he treated me in public would embarrass me. He told me I didn't need to go to any of those stupid high school senior events anyways. On the upside of it, I didn't want anyone I knew to meet Andrew anyways. He had a bad temper, and he would embarrass me over the smallest things.

I finally saw my girl Monica and when I did, I ran to hug her. Monica told me that her mother had been sick, and she had to stay home to take care of her. She asked me what was wrong, and I told her everything. Monica said, "I will kill that son of a bitch if he ever touches you again. You are coming with me to Fort Worth; he doesn't know where I live." I felt relieved to finally have help. Not once was I worried about the stuff that I had left behind. As far as I was concerned, that stuff could all be replaced. I told my job that I need to take an emergency leave of absence for a week. I had never called in before and I worked whatever schedule they gave to me, including the reception when they couldn't get that shift covered. Me taking off time wasn't a problem for them. After work she drove me to her parent's house. Her mother was sweet as she could be. She kept trying to cook for me and serve me. At the end of the week, I had to decide if I was going back to work or if I was going to ask for another week off.

I talked to my supervisor and explained what was wrong. She said, "You should have said something sooner." She told me to come back to work and that I could work the reception position. I never thought about how it was hidden in a little room that no one can see you except other employees. She told me to take the rest of the weekend off and to come in on Monday and work the reception. I was glad to see her, and I felt thankful and a lot more peaceful; now I figured out something with my job.

Monica and I wore the same size in clothes, so I were wearing her stuff. She said, "Andrew was up at Target looking for you and he came to ask if I had seen you. I told him no I haven't but if I did, I would give you the message." We went to Dave and Busters that night and when we got back to her place Andrew was sitting in her driveway and waiting on us in his car. I told Monica to keep driving and he recognized her car and started to follow us. We drove around until we were able to lose him. I told Monica that maybe we could get a hotel, but she said, "No the safest place would be at my house because my dad and brother can go crazy on him." I was terrified. I didn't want anyone to get hurt. I was able to convince her to at least wait for a while before we returned to her house. When we did return to her house, Andrew was gone but all her brothers were there waiting on us. I was relieved. The next day was Sunday. I was so paranoid, and Monica said, "Karen I've never seen you like this and I hate it. Are you able to go back home?" I told her, "I suppose I could, but I would hate to bring my mom into the middle of this because someone will get hurt in the end." Monica's mom started yelling something in Spanish I didn't know what she was saying, and Monica came running saying it's him again. I said, "What do you want me to do? I'll go out there. I don't want anyone to get hurt." Monica's mom told me not to go out there and something else in Spanish that I couldn't understand. Monica went out there to talk to Andrew and tried to get him to leave. Not one of her brothers was around; and he refused to leave. I started to think about what Monica had said earlier about going back home and what my reasons were for not. I brought this mess over to her family's house, rather than my own. I told Monica that I was going to go with him because I felt it wasn't right having her family drawn into something like this.

Once I went outside Andrew said, "You need to leave with me." I told him that I didn't want to be with him anymore. He said, "That's too bad because if I can't have you then no one can." At that point I knew I had no other choice than to go with him. I got in the car and left. He took me back to his apartment, I showered and changed clothes and I was totally zoned out with no expression on my face. He pulled out a bunch of DVDs containing sex movies. I got up and went into the bedroom and closed the door so that I didn't have to hear those sounds being made. It disgusted me. He called me back into the room and asked me to watch with him, but I told him no that's not something that I'm going to do. Then I went back into the bedroom and shut the door. The night came and Andrew said, "You will sleep in the bed tonight and I have bought you some new pajamas because I don't like those old maid ones you wear. He had bought me lingerie. I told him that I would get cold wearing that. He said, "You'll be alright." He ended up taking it off to have sex again. I thought about the last thing that Mom had said to me before I left. She said I was going to be someone's sex slave, and she was right. Andrew started keeping a close watch over me so that I couldn't run away again. I never found out how he figured out where Monica lived. He would have followed her home any day that week and decided to wait until the weekend to approach the house. I also started seeing signs that he had another girlfriend on the side. In this case, I was pleased because that meant he could get his sexual needs taken care of by her instead of me. I have officially graduated now, and Tina called to tell me that the school needed an address to mail my diploma to. I had the school mail it to Mom's apartment. I told Tina what I was going to do and that she needed to be on the watch for it. She also told me that Mom and Mr. Lee officially got married, finally. I was glad for her.

There was an American Express check cashing place right next to Andrew's apartment and I was looking into placing an application there to be closer to the apartment. In a couple of months, I would be starting at the community college down the street... I also went to a Ford Dealership and put in an application for a car. I didn't have any credit built up, but my work experience helped a lot. I got my first car and was able to drive it right off the lot. It was a red "Chrysler Aldi". I had barely had my license for a year. A week later I started working at the little check cashing place across the street from Andrew apartments. I left Target all together. That first week I started having all kinds of problems with that car. One of the back windows wouldn't go up or down, the windshield wipers stopped working. Then little things like the inside door handle fell off: I felt that I had bought a lemon. I had been with Andrew for a year and a half and still was no fonder of him than I was when I first moved in. I would be 18 years old in less than a month. Monica had come over a handful of times to check on me. Andrew didn't give her a hard time, thankfully. Since I had left home, I only got to see Mom maybe twice for a short visit on the holidays. Andrew forbade me from seeing her. He even monitored my conversations with her. That meant I could only call mom when he was around. He made that clear. No one but him could answer the phone and that became his rule. I felt like I was living in a prison. However, I did get to go to church. Andrew was a regular in attending church. I never recalled him ever missing a Sunday. He would wash his Mercedes every Saturday to get it ready for Sunday's service. He attended a large Baptist church.

One morning I got up to go to work and was running late. I ran out of the house, leaving my lunch behind. Once I got to work, I noticed. My boss told me to clock in and take care of the line first and then I could run back home and grab it. I knew Andrew was off and he'd be there, but I didn't want to call him and wake him on his off day. So, just as my boss instructed, I helped with the line then I headed across the street to the apartment... Once I got back to the apartment, I took my key out and opened the door and, in the living, room was a lady in lingerie with rollers in her hair. Andrew had on underwear and nothing else. He said, "What are you doing back home?"

I said, "You don't worry about that, what are you doing with this woman in our apartment?"

He said, "It's my apartment. I can have anyone here I want."

"Yeah, you're right, my mistake." I got my lunch and went back to work. I had already started planning a permanent escape, but I needed just a little more time. I thought that the woman being there was no different than him watching those explicit movies or his little girlfriend at work who cooks him food and buys him clothes. I was really okay with it all, as long as it would help him keep his hands off of me.

Monica called me that afternoon and told me her mother had passed, and I told her I was going to come stay the weekend. She asked me if Andrew would allow me. I told her if he didn't, it didn't matter, I was going. When I got home from work, I told Andrew that I would be going to Monica's for the weekend to help her family with her mom's funeral. I was waiting for him to tell me I could not, but all he said was, "When are you going to come back?"

"Probably Sunday, Monday at the latest." He said it was fine. I left and went to Fort Worth, and Monica's entire family was there, even her baby sister and her husband from California. I had met them all a few times before, but it sure was strange not having her mother trying to be a hostess. We all sat around eating and listening to old stories about the family. No one had a problem with me being there, I felt like I was a part of the family. That Sunday I dreaded going back to that prison I knew as home. I really didn't understand why he wanted me there. He had a couple of women he messed around with and his porn that he was overly consumed with. Even though I was physical there with Monica and her family my mind could not help but to drift off into the situation that seemed to be so surreal and hopeless for me right now. I dared not bring it up to Monica how heavy my heart was in not wanting to return. I didn't want to appear to be selfish during Monica and her family's grieving time. One ray of light that continued to enter my spirit was the incident with Bill at the Gaylord when the Lord spoke to me instructing me to be watchful, stay focused and be diligent in looking for a way out. I was intentionally in that mindset but overwhelmingly feeling alone.

This chapter is proof that we can make a decision outside of God's will that we feel disconnected from His plan and lost from His presence. As humans it's not unusual that we make permanent decisions in a temporary situation. It can cause catastrophic changes to one's direction in life. God can use these situations as testimony to His goodness that He would be glorified. In my own words, it's not a setback that Satan inflicts upon us; but rather a setup for greater things done by Christ. God had been calling me since birth to walk in a life of sacrifice for Him alone. God is calling us out of our own will and into His will and plan. Satan knew that and put all types of distractions to derail men from God's plan. But God's word tells us clearly in *Jeremiah 29:11* the truth. ***Jeremiah 29:11 (NKJV), "For I know the thoughts that I think toward you, says the Lord, thoughts of peace and not of evil, to give you a future and a hope."*** Jeremiah surely tells you and I that God has nothing but good intentions for his people. The "Book of Proverbs" clearly states that no matter what sort of ambition drives us outside of God's will He'll use it to direct us to His greatness.

Proverb 16:9(NKJV), "A man's heart plans his way, But the Lord directs his steps."

Chapter 13
Disconnected from Happiness.

I RETURNED HOME ON SUNDAY NIGHT FROM SPENDING TIME with Monica's family after reliving the memories of her Mom. Like usual, there was never a word of fellowship between Andrew and me. We walked by each other in that one-bedroom apartment, saying nothing; not even greeting one another. Right before I got into bed, Andrew asked me if I was off on Monday. I told him I was but explained that I had class that evening. He said, "No worries, we'll be finished by then."

"Finished with what?" I asked.

"You'll see," he said. I had no clue what he was talking about. The next morning, Andrew woke up early and told me we had an appointment somewhere.

I asked him, "Where is this somewhere?" I felt maybe he could be making up for that woman being at the apartment the other day. It would really surprise me if Andrew did anything selfless with the intent to bless me. This would be something worth waiting to see. At this point, I was so finished with the relationship that I wanted to hop on a one-way train and never come back. All these thoughts of running away and never returning ran through my head, but when it came to putting them into action, I was paralyzed.

It hadn't been a full month of me living with Andrew when he had begun changing the way I dressed. Before I moved in with him, he was already buying me outfits that he expected me to wear when we went out together. Yet, after I moved in, it became obvious that his plan was to revamp my whole wardrobe. He started dictating what clothes I had to wear whenever I went anywhere with him, even if it was just to the corner store. The clothes that Andrew bought for me were pieces I would never buy for myself. Not only that but wearing them also made me uncomfortable most of the time. I felt like I was showing too much skin. Andrew was big on miniskirts, halter tops, tops that showed too much cleavage, and tight-fitting tops. I also had never been one to wear heels. Andrew required me to wear heels with all of my outfits, especially if I was wearing jeans and a t-shirt, to dress them up. However, I did complain when it came to the excessive heel wearing because I wasn't comfortable in the slightest. I never won any arguments, but this was one time Andrew would at least know how I feel. Even though I was nearly eighteen, I went around pouting like a little kid. I had always done my own hair in the past except when it came to perming it. I was a woman of many different hairstyles, but after moving in with Andrew, I could only wear one hairstyle. He made me keep my hair free and flowing; he never allowed me to wear any up-do styles. I would put on the clothes that he had laid out on the bed and left with him.

He was driving for about thirty minutes when I noticed the courthouse.

"Why are we going to the courthouse?" I asked.

"We're getting married today."

"I don't want to get married to you," I told him. "I won't do it!"

"Yes, you will, or you will die today."

"Why would I die today?" Andrew flashed his gun and told me if I tried to signal for help, whoever I involved would be shot first. Then he said he would shoot me and then kill himself. This sent me straight into shock. I covered my face and started praying for the rapture to come. I knew that would be the only thing that could save me. I asked the Lord to give me one opportunity to get away before he forced me to change my last name and be tied to him forever. After we parked and got out, I looked desperately for a sign. There was not one. Then I thought about all the opportunities that I let slip through my hands to get away from this mad man. Since the first day that I had met him he had a sign on his forehead saying, "Turn around and run the other way." But of course, I got caught up in the dollar signs of easy money; or so I thought. The money had been everything except easy. I had signed over my entire paycheck to him ever since I moved in. He stopped even giving me money or spending money on me ever since I had moved in. I also had been using my savings to pay for my classes and books at the Richland Community College for the last year or so. As we were entering the court building Andrew was able to get past security with his gun because he was a licensed officer. I was looking like a sad puppy in the face with red tearful eyes. He had to have been down here earlier to get all the paperwork pre-approved because I didn't have to fill anything out; just show my ID and sign. My eyes clocked every officer in uniform hoping they would stop and ask if I was alright. Not one said a word.

The constable who was signing the marriage license, said, "This is your big day!" I didn't respond. I looked down at the floor as though my life was over. He repeated what he had said louder and spoke directly to me. I didn't lift my head.

Suddenly, Andrew stepped on my toes and I said out loud, "Ow! That hurt!"

This caused Andrew to get in my face and he said, "I'm not playing with you. Straighten up." Andrew looked at the constable and told him, "Will you please hurry because we're in a rush." The constable replied that it was not a problem. He read Andrew his vows and asked him to repeat after him. Then the Constable read me my vows and asked me to repeat after him. I still didn't look up and I mumbled what he asked me to say.

He said, "Young lady I have to be able to hear you clearly so please speak louder."

Andrew said, "No I heard her fine, please let her sign the paper and let us go!"

The constable responded, "Well since you are in a hurry that will be fine. I hope that the rest of y'all's day gets better." Then Andrew grabbed the signed license as well as my arm, while walking off fast. It was the worst day of my life. I felt the little person inside of me was lost forever. I respected the seriousness of the marriage license, even if I didn't have any respect for the one whom I was forced to be connected to. That day I started praying every day for God to change my situation. I really believed I had it bad before we married, but after that day Andrew turned into an out of control, unbelievable maniac. He micromanaged everything in the house. A typically deep cleaning for your normal household chores was never good enough for him. Twenty-four-seven he was yelling for me to reclean something to meet his standards. He didn't just need things to be clean, but they needed to look brand new. He had Obsessive Compulsive Disorder (OCD) and he was always trying to get others to perform up to those standards. I had seen the way that Andrew had me arrange dishes in the kitchen cabinet and how I had to separate the utensils we ate with, from the ones we cooked with. He profiled people according to their appearance and financial status. It was easy for him to title people as being defiled. There was one time when the apartment maintenance guy came over to repair our washing machine and I offered him a glass of water. After he left, that glass had to be thrown out. There was another time when we had company over that accidentally walked on one of our rugs with their shoes. Andrew ordered me to throw the rug away: He felt it was defiled. You couldn't find a stain on it however it was something in his brain that marked it ruined. He never raised his hand to assist me in keeping things up to his standard. Andrew chooses to stand over me and instruct me to do what he felt that needed to be done. After I dusted or cleaned anything he would check for fingerprints or smudges. There were soap dishes that were placed in the corners of the bathtub that I was told to keep used soap in. One time I forgot, and he pulled me by my hair back into the bathroom and yelled for 30 minutes. He slapped my face for what he called insubordinate. That became a repeat response to everything that he asked me to do. Something as small as a water ring on the kitchen countertop would cause him to yell and hit me. He stopped calling me by my name and started calling me "Dude," "Dog," or "Man" to further downgrade my femininity. All of his dress shirts went to the dry cleaners and when they came back, they had special hangers that Andrew expected me to change them to. Then I had to button them up all the way from top to bottom after placing them on a special hanger in a certain way. All these dress shirts had to follow a certain color coordination in the closet too.

If even one shirt was out of color or pattern order, then he would slap me around and tell me how stupid I was to mess up something as simple as that. Andrew had a daily cleaning chore list that he would check off before the end of the night. That included dusting the ceiling fans, washing baseboards, walls, mopping behind the stove and refrigerator daily. Pine-Sol and bleach was the regular aroma in the apartment. Every time I cleaned the kitchen Andrew expected me to clean up under the eyes and beneath the stove. The life I had lived with Mom was nothing to complain about when I looked at what I had to deal with now. Andrew wasn't an alcoholic nor did he do any type of drugs. Matter of fact he called himself a vegetarian, but one who didn't eat a lot of vegetables but ate fish in replacement of meat. This was called pescatarian. I for one never cared to be turned into a vegetarian or a pescatarian. However, because Andrew didn't eat meat, he wouldn't allow me to cook meat when he was home and certain meats like pork could not be prepared in the apartment at all. He claimed that the smell of it lingered too long. Anything that Andrew allowed me to cook that was meat in the apartment required me to air the apartment out because spraying air freshener wasn't good enough for him. He was so dramatic about everything. I started having problems with a nervous stomach. I was a size 3 petite when I had first moved in with him and now, I was a 0. That's pretty small for someone at my height of 5 feet and 8 inches. I looked malnourished. I was more of his housekeeper and cook than anything else. I didn't have to be a sex slave anymore thankfully. He got his fulfilment from porn and his outside girlfriends. I was very okay with that. The first four years living with Andrew, he went out clubbing every Friday night and most Saturday nights. This was the time that I used to be comfortable at home by myself. I never stayed up waiting on him or used any of my time thinking about him or who he was with. This was an opportunity for me not to worry about him getting in the bed trying to fool with me. Every now and then he'd force me to have sex with him if he wasn't getting it out. I believe it turned him off because I wasn't into it. He'd get offended during intercourse with my face or the way my body was posed in a lifeless manner as to say please hurry up and get finished. Any time we were in the bed together I slept on the very edge of the bed because I didn't want him to touch me and not even by accident.

He allowed me to attend Monica's mom's funeral, and I was so glad that he let me go by myself. None of Monica's family liked him. The funeral was very sad; however, I enjoyed not being micromanaged for that day. The family allowed me to sit with the immediate family members which was an honor. Before I came back to Dallas, Monica gave me her word to check on me more often. I never faulted her for staying away when she did. She had her own life plus I had gotten myself into this mess. Monica called me once a week and visited once or twice a month. It was the only time I smiled. I was faithful when it came to going to the community college until my money ran out. I had been in community college full time for two years; however, I didn't have an associate degree as of yet because I took reading, writing, and math pre-college courses to help me bring up my IQ to college level. My savings had become scarce and the hours I worked only covered my car note, car insurance, and the bills that Andrew had me pay. I started going to school part time because that's all I was able to afford now. Andrew wouldn't help me with a dime. My major was computer science. Plus, when we went to church, I was very adamant about paying my tithes. Every time I would fill out my offering envelopes Andrew would snatch it out my hand and take half of the tithes out and put it in his pocket. It was very disturbing. I felt if you don't want to pay your tithes that's on you, but to steal mines was wickness on a whole nother level that could only come from the Devil himself. I believe that I had married the devil. He looked, acted, and sounded like the Devil. I prayed for God to change my situation daily for a year and a half. Then, I started noticing Andrew would fill out credit applications in my name and keep the credit cards for himself. I started noticing everywhere he went he was charging them up. I told him, "You don't have permission to mess my credit up."

He told me, "I don't need your permission for anything. I can do whatever I choose to do." I had never seen such a naturally evil person like himself. I knew one day I would be free from him; I just had to pray it would be in this lifetime.

The check cashing place was going out of business and I was looking to find another job. I started looking at different banking institutes. There was a bank near downtown Dallas that was 30 minutes away from our apartment that I applied for. It would be a $2.50 pay increase; much more than I'd ever made at any time. I would have to put school on hold for a while because the hours were long and the commute to school was too far away. I was 20 years old and had been married to Andrew for approximately 2 years when I started working at First City Bank as a teller. I had noticed that he was buying $400 to $500 suits, and shoes for $800. It was as though he believed he was Mr. President himself. He had a credit card from every major store in my name. It made me sick to my stomach because I felt that it was ridiculous how he lived and spent above his means. As soon as I got the job at the bank, he started looking for penthouses to live in. He told me he'd never buy a house while he was married to me because he didn't want me to divorce him and take it. I never understood the logic of throwing money away than investing into something that will one day be yours or passed down to a loved one. Even if I were to have taken the house in a divorce proceeding you would still be able to see where your money went to. There was no logic in his mind. We paid $1,300 a month for a one bedroom, "upscale" apartment in the year 1990!

I also immediately ran into some problems at my new job: My immediate supervisor started acting racist. She would make comments behind my back to other tellers concerning me in referencing that I thought I was better than other people. I wondered why she would say something like that. I knew right from the beginning I had to be careful what I say and how I say things because of the possibility of it being twisted around or taken out of content. My immediate supervisor's name was "Terry", and she didn't have anything to do with hiring me. However, I had to work with her all the time. I was well liked by my customers so much that they didn't want anyone outside of me helping them when they came to the bank. Terry would be mad about that. When my teller line would get long, she would go to each customer pleading for them to go to the other tellers; or herself. Their response would always be, "We don't mind waiting, we want Mrs. Karen to wait on us." Terry hated to see Andrew drive his Mercedes Benz to my job. I keep my personal problems under wrap and never shared them with anyone I worked with. The last thing I needed was my business to be put out there for Terry to stick her nose in it. One of my customers told me about a modeling assignment that would come around every three months that was down the street from the bank at the Market Center. They told me it would be a weekend job and I could make up to$400 a day. I went to the Market Center to get details, that way I could take off from work during those weekends that they needed models. I keep my mouth shut about the modeling job. I knew Terry would be trying to block me from taking off to make extra money. During my first weekend working as a model, it was awesome. There were all types of models needed and they were paying us all cash. They needed runway models, showroom models. Over one thousand companies had designers represented there. They had formal wear, casual wear, teen wear, swimwear, evening wear, and more. Every clothing line that was represented there had been created for the next season of fashion from all over the United States. Designers came together to sell to commercial businesses. The designers that were interested in me as their model were selling formal wear and evening wear. I was hired to model for showrooms that held thousands of companies who were prospective buyers. My first weekend I worked Friday and Saturday for a total of 14 hours and made $650 for both days. I was told I could've made more if I was experienced. However, I was good with the $325 a day they gave me. For the next year and half, I was able to make up to $800 per event working only Fridays and Saturdays. I only stopped because of the different attitudes that came from some of the models I worked with. I realized that I didn't fit into that line of work. Most of the girls were snobbish and uppity like my husband. Andrew fought with me about staying with them for the money. He didn't care how I felt about any of it; he wanted what he called "easy money". I was still a person of genuine compassion for others and had a heart filled with love. I didn't feel I had to force myself to be around those who were the opposite outside of Andrew. No amount of money would ever change me. So, I quit! Any time I went out to eat dinner with Andrew he was rude to the waiters. He was short with them and spoke in a way that demanded total control. It was very embarrassing to me. Andrew made a scene if the meals took too long, and he expected prompt service on anything he asked the waiter for anything. He had no problem asking the manager to compensate for his inconvenience. Whenever we went to the grocery store or pharmacy Andrew would bring attention to himself to prove dominance. Other rude customers that were like himself, he would challenge verbally. I, on the other hand, would walk behind him or try to sneak off because I didn't want to be seen in the middle of that nonsense.

I had noticed Andrew's work schedule had become free and he was no longer going to work for the police dept. He never shared any information with me concerning a lay off or him being fired. He was doing contract work for himself still. He had two buildings that he was doing security work for and I noticed him doing paralegal work for certain law firms. All of a sudden, he told me he was going into the Army. I was glad because it meant I wouldn't have to put up with him as much. I was curious on how in the world he would make it through because he was not one to be controlled or to follow rules. I was still at the bank at this time, and it had been a year and a half. Every three months we were given a performance evaluation for a pay increase by our immediate supervisor. Every time my evaluation came up, Terry would tell me she didn't think I worked hard enough for a raise and she didn't put one in for me. I missed 6 raises, not because I was told anything that I needed to correct, but because Terry felt I could have been working harder. My attendance was perfect, I was always on time for work, and I balanced my cash drawer down to the penny daily. My customers were always leaving good remarks concerning my good customer service skills. Never once did I get a customer complaint, but my raise increase was left up to a lady trying to hold me back in every way she could. I could've gone over her head, but the 10 to 30 cent raises weren't worth the dispute. I had a hidden desire to work for the post office at that time anyway, and I hadn't shared it with anyone. The year I graduated from high school I took the postal exam and failed it and told myself once I had some more schooling, I would retake it.

Andrew went and took the test to enter into the military and was set to enlist in a month. I had a friend named "Sharron" that used to work with me at the check cashing place needed a place to stay. I was trying to see if Andrew would allow her to come stay with me for a few months to help with bills while he was at basic camp training. He didn't have much resistance to the idea. Off went Andrew and in came Sharron. Sharron was a very pretty young black girl, around my age, and she was now working at a pawn shop in the Oak Cliff area. She had been staying with her mother, but they had lots of conflict in their relationship. The only problem was Andrew's dog that was very moody. He was a male Chow breed. This dog respected Andrew but with me he had no respect. Many times, when I told that dog to do something he would raise his head up and look at me as to ignore me and lay his head back down. When I would get angry and become serious at the dog he would respond slowly as to say I wish you would leave me alone. I love animals but this one had an attitude problem that was too unpredictable. I caught him growling at me a couple of times when I was preparing its food. I didn't like the way he stared at anyone that came to our apartment. He was an inside house dog. When any company enters our apartment, this dog would stare viciously and follow them until they sit down. Then he wouldn't allow the company to move once they were seated.

Right after Andrew went off to boot camp, it was confirmed that I was two months pregnant. Andrew was happy but I had a problem with bringing a child into our relationship. Not only because Andrew wasn't the type of father that I wanted for my children, but also, I didn't want any of his personality traits or his physical appearance to be imparted onto my child. As I started showing, Andrew's dog became very hard to control. I started worrying he was going to bite someone. I had been asking Andrew about getting rid of him but that was his dog, and he loved that animal dearly. The first person he bit was Sharron. She didn't have health insurance and he bit her bad enough where she had to go to the hospital. Sharron asked me to pay for the bill. She had every right; however, I didn't have a dime to my name. This caused us to fall out of friendship. Sharron moved out right after the incident. Which meant I couldn't afford to pay all of our bills on my salary alone. It would be at least two and half more months at least before Andrew came. I went to Mom to see how she would feel about me coming to stay with her until Andrew got back.

Mom said, "Well it'll just be me and you." I don't have a problem with that. I told mom I would pay half of all of her bills and she could use this time to put some money in her savings. Mom said that sounded great and I moved right away. She also let me bring Andrew's dog. The dog seemed to have more respect for Mom, maybe it was because she talked to it with authority and never in a playful way.

I could see that dog thinking, "*Well, I don't want to get on her bad side.*" She obviously doesn't like me. Mom was still working for Dart the City Bus in Dallas. She had leased a condo down the street from the bus barn. Kaleb, my brother had moved back to South Carlina to get to know his real father. Tina was living in East Dallas with her boyfriend who was a maintenance man at the property they rented from. I never asked for details on what had happened to Mom's relationship with Mr. Lee and his boys. I do know even after their falling out mom stayed connected to Richard, Mr. Lee's oldest son. Mom seemed totally different after I moved in. It had been a little over five and a half years since I had originally left home. She was like a roommate now. I had a room upstairs and hers was downstairs. I kept my area clean, and Mom did the same in hers. Most of the time we would fend for ourselves when it came to cooking. Mom cursed but nothing like she used to. She still drank but was very functional, and I had no problems with that. She had two or three best friends now that worked with her. She looked at them as family. They were the Brown sisters who also drove buses like Mom, and there was a Dart bus mechanic named "Joe" that would do anything for Mom. They came to visit randomly, or Mom would go to the Brown sisters' house to hangout. The sisters roomed together. I was glad because Mom needed friends. Every now and then she would close up in her room but nothing like she use to do. Andrew's dog ended up biting one of Mom's friends from work. I started to seriously consider having him put to sleep. I knew Andrew would never agree to it but if it was done before he got back it wouldn't be much he could do and at least the dog would be dealt with before the baby comes. I had just finished my shower and the dog was in my room laying on the floor by my bed. He appeared to be sleeping. I sat on the bed then reached down to pet him and he bit me. It was so hard that I started hitting the dog back and he bit me again. That was it; I had decided that dog would not be around any baby of mine. I had a child on the way and that dog wasn't fit to be around a family. I asked mom if she would take him to the pound for me to have him put to sleep. As bad as the dog needed to be put to sleep, I didn't have the heart to do it myself. The dog gave Mom no problems. She said he went without a fight. This was something I waited to tell Andrew until he came home.

When Andrew finished his boot camp training, he was assigned to a National Guard Unit. We got an apartment and I left mom again but this time with no animosity. Mom and I had enjoyed the few months of being roommates. Andrew would have guard duty every other weekend. After boot camp, he was a time bomb always ready to go off. Living with him was like walking in a field full of landmines. Andrew's patience with me was zero to none. Nothing positive ever came out his mouth. He was in a totally bad mood all the time. The first week back from boot camp he had been home all day waiting for me to get off from work to cook. I was 6 months pregnant now and my feet were swollen because of the extra weight I picked up. When I walked in the house Andrew said, "You need to hurry up and fix my dinner because I'm hungry." I told him to give me 15 minutes to get out my shoes and clothes. He responded, "No, I want my dinner fixed now. Your comfort is not my concern." Normally I would have just fixed it just to keep things from escalating, however, my entire body was aching from being on my feet all day. So, I did not respond to him and I continued taking my shoes off. He grabbed my hair and dragged me out of the bedroom and into the kitchen. I was trying to get his hands open and out of my hair. He had pulled out half my hair on the floor and slapped my face twice. Then I hit him, and he hit me back. I was able to get to the phone and call 911. I told them my husband was betting on me and before I could tell them my location. Andrew had taken the phone out my hand and through it and I just started to scream. Then he started choking me to where I could not breathe so I would stop screaming. He said, "I'll let you go if you go do what I told you to do." I was still crying but I told him, "Okay, let me go." As soon as he let me go the doorbell rang and I tried to run to it, but he grabbed me around my throat once again. I nodded my head in defeat and went into the kitchen as the beating on the door got louder. A voice behind the door was saying, "Police, open up!" Andrew opened the door and the officer recognized him saying, "Officer Drew, you live here?"

Andrew said, "Yes. Yes, I do." The officer went on to explain how they were responding to a call from a female asking for help at this address. Then he asked, "Is she alright?"

Andrew said we were having a disagreement and she's fine.

Andrew said, "Right, honey?" I didn't respond. I was looking at them from the entrance of the kitchen. It was obvious that there had been a struggle, but they overlooked that and my appearance. They apologized for the interruption and told us to have a good evening. That was one out of many times that I had called the police on Andrew. This happened repeatedly because they realized him as a fellow officer.

Faithful church-going Andrew would go to church simply because it was another place he could dress up and look like he had money. Obviously, he never paid attention to any messages other than the one about wife submitting to their husbands. Every day he would quote this scripture to me any time I wasn't doing anything fast enough. He would only quote half of it and take it out of context, calling himself preaching to me.

One Sunday after church he started yelling at me because I told him I didn't want to go out to eat. I knew we had no money, and he was running my credits into the ground using credit unnecessarily. I told him, "I just went grocery shopping, it makes no sense to go out to eat." Immediately he started driving on the freeway erratically. Then he pulled into the far-right lane which was considered the slower lane. He started telling me to get out of his car while it was still moving. He pushed my shoulder and told me to open the car door and jump out. When I didn't do it, he grabbed the handle of the inside car door and swung the door open while the car was going at least 55 mph on a 5-lane freeway and pushed me out. I fell out on my side, shielding the front part of my stomach, trying all that I could to pre-vent the baby from getting injured. Thank God I had on pants that belonged to him. I can't image what I would have looked like with my dress up in the air and underwear showing while hitting that concrete. Andrew would never allow me to spend money on maternity clothes. I did not understand the logic in it when he shopped fervently for himself. I would've been okay going to a consignment store knowing that I would only use the clothes for a short season. However, he wouldn't be caught dead in one and since I was his wife it looked bad on him, so I wasn't allowed. I wore his shirts and pants. He had made it clear that he didn't care about me being pregnant and I was just "fat" in his eyes. Andrew said, "he wouldn't allow me to waste money on maternity clothes that would only be used for a few months." After that car incident I decided that the car is not a place to engage in an argument on the freeway with Andrew behind the wheel. This man had no boundaries. My prayer had changed from asking God to change my situation to God please change this man. Maybe I should've prayed both at the same time. Neither prayer seemed to be working. I knew God could change things, but I didn't understand why he wasn't. I didn't give up praying, I was going to believe in God for a change and not stop praying until something happened.

I was still working as a teller at that bank. I went in one morning and everything was like a normal day until lunch time came around and I saw two plain-clothes officers walk into the bank. They went straight to the bank president's office and then I saw them coming towards Terry. They said a few words to her, and she pointed to me. Terry said, "Karen come away from your cash drawer and give me the keys to it!" I had been at that bank for two years now and I was being treated as a thief. I did as I was instructed without any suspicious movements.

The officer said, "Are you Karen Marie?"

I said, "Yes I am."

Then they said, "We have a warrant for your arrest for check fraud." I looked around at all the customers and employees in the bank and everyone had totally stopped their business and every eye was on me. Every other person was whispering.

I heard Terry say, "I told y'all she couldn't be trusted. People's messes always catch up with them." They read me my rights and put cuffs on me in the middle of the bank room floor and walked me out. I was totally shocked, and I didn't know why or how this had happened. Once I got downtown to the jail I was fingerprinted. I was made to take off all of my clothes in front of two female jailers with my big pregnant stomach and cough as though I would be hiding a weapon in my more private regions. I had to put on inmate clothes and be locked up in a room with 5 other female prisoners.

There was a phone in the cell, which I used to call Mom and she said, "Honey I can't help you, call your husband." So, I hung up and called Andrew. I finally got a hold of him and he said, "I'll have you out before tonight." Two of the women in the cell talked bad about me. They said I was "Miss. Goody Two Shoes". I ignored them and kept my silence. I refused to indulge into further discussion about the comment. Within two hours Andrew had me brought out of the cell into the office of a judge and had me sign an affidavit stating my checks and ID had been stolen. The picture of the checks the Judge had showed us had Sharron's signature in place of my name. There were a couple of liquor stores and department stores she had written checks to on my closed account. I couldn't believe I was set up by her, but this was one time I thanked God for Andrew and his connection with law enforcement and judges. I was told by inmates and the jailor that no one gets bailed out that quickly ever. I was able to go home right after I signed the affidavits in the judge's chambers. That night I had to overcome a personal pride issue and return to work the next morning. If I didn't have Andrew pushing me to return to work, I might not have. After the scene Terry put on in front of all the employees and customers was very downgrading. The next day I reported to work as I normally did and played it off as though nothing had happened. I did not feel privileged to share the truth with Terry. When she asked, I just told her it was a mix up. I didn't take offense to Mom's response of not trying to be helpful as she knew I was pregnant and in jail. I didn't feel a need to call her back and let her know everything was fine. However, I felt in my heart to start reaching out to her more often just to say, "I love you and I'm just checking to see how you're doing." Tina had been to my house a handful of times for just a few minutes just to see how I was doing and to give me updates on herself and family. That was God working through Tina. This chapter has demonstrated the fruit of the title **"He Kept Me"** more than any other chapter in my book. Now that I'm older and mature in God's word, I can walk in His truth. I am here today sharing my testimony. When I look back, I can see why man can overlook God's greatness. Even when you read my story, you may ask yourself, why did God allow such a heinous situation of captivity and imprisonment? The truth is that these types of things are always happening all over the world. In broad daylight many walk past it or live next door to it and may not realize that it's even going on. Then there are also some deeper darker webs of sex trafficking and child work slaves all around us. God's truth about this is: This is not His plan nor will for man. We've discussed God's plan in regard to man in previous chapters, and in the book of **Jeremiah 29:11** God's plan is for good and not for evil. We've also covered in previous chapters the love of our Heavenly Father giving his children free will to choose and make decisions that could take them out of God's will and plan.

John 1:12-13 (NKJV), "But as many as received Him, to them He gave the right to become children of God, to those who believe in His name: who were born, not of blood, nor of the will of the flesh nor of the will of man, but of God." Now I would like to share the good that comes out of man's bad decisions brought on by man's will and not God's will. First, keep in mind that no matter what horrible situation you're faced with, God is an all-present God meaning even in the midst of tragic circumstances God is still with you; it may just be hard to see or perceive Him. **Psalm 46** tells us that God is our refuge and strength. **Deuteronomy 31:6** tells us for the Lord your God, He is the One who goes with you. He will not leave you nor forsake you. The second thing that you need to remember is that God is all powerful; this means His authority and power is unlimited. **Matthew 19:26** states that with God all things are possible! He is able to turn all things around for your good so that he may be glorified. At any time, God can choose to take you out of a bad situation or not; empower you to go through it. You will become stronger and wiser by being drawn to Him. It also positions you to be able to be a testimony for someone else.

Revelation 12:11 (NKJV), "And they overcame him by the blood of the Lamb and by the word of their testimony; and they loved not their lives unto the death."

2 Cor 4:7-10 will encourage you, if you are not there yet, to be able to see there's good that can come from all bad situations.

2 Corinthians 4:7-10 (NKJV), "But we have this treasure in earthen vessels, that the excellence of the power may be of God and not of us. We are hard-pressed on every side, yet not crushed; we are perplexed, but not in despair; persecuted, but not forsaken; struck down, but not destroyed always carrying about in the body the dying of the Lord Jesus, that the life of Jesus also may be manifested in our body."

Chapter 14
My First Ray of Hope

ANDREW RECEIVED ORDERS FOR DEPLOYMENT TO GO TO Desert Storm. He was to be flown to Saudi Arabia. He would be leaving to go overseas in 2 months. Our first child was due in 9 weeks. He said that in 30 days he would have to leave for a training camp at the Fort Hood Killeen Army Base, which was 3 hours away, and then be sent overseas. The time came quickly, and my stomach was too big to fit behind the steering wheel of my car to drive to see him off. I called Monica and she came and picked me up and took me to visit him on the last day he was supposed to be in the States. On the way down there, I started to feel short labor pains, and the closer to Killeen we got the more intense the contractions came. I couldn't believe I was going to go into labor a week early on the army base. We found Andrew and he took me  to the Killeen Military Hospital, and I was in hard labor for 10 hours straight with no medicine. Andrew's superiors postponed his deployment to Saudi Arabia for one day. After the birth of our daughter, he was airlifted to his platoon. He was to be gone for 9 months. I was so grateful to Monica for always being someone I could count on. I only took off from work for 6 weeks with Little K. I found a daycare which was walking distance from the bank and enrolled her there. It was now just me and Little K. God had truly blessed me, she was my little look alike. She was the cutest baby you have ever wanted to see. Even Monica said we needed to thank God that this baby didn't look anything like her daddy. I Amen that. I went out to buy her all kinds of precious outfits. The nursery said that the entire staff would come out to the nursery just to see what outfit "Little K" was dressed in. I also enrolled her in a Gerber Baby Pageant, and she won first place out of one-hundred-fifty finalists. The babies had to smile and have a charming personality and character. Their outfits and hair were graded. I was not surprised Little K placed first place. It didn't take much to get her smiling and engaged. I was also able to take her to let her bond with my mom while Andrew was away. Mom said that she was a very peaceful and playful baby. She never cried unless she was hungry or wet. She was always alert and amazed by her surroundings.

I had struggled with migraines since adolescence. They had gotten worse since being involved with Andrew. It got to the point where I needed to see a neurologist and start taking medicine. My head would hurt me 28 days out of the month. With the medicine they gave me, every three to four days it would be a bad headache which was more tolerable than usual but still painful. I had eventually pinpointed everything that would set off a headache. Stress, certain smells, certain food, too much sleep, not enough sleep, fatigue, and additional respiratory sicknesses. You would think that during the nine years of suffering with migraines I would have a plan of action that helped me, but no, I still became totally incapacitated for days at a time with these tormenting headaches. During my 9 months of freedom, with just me and the little one, I started to see God answering my prayers to change me to be stronger and more mature in Him. For the first time, I started to understand the Bible by myself. The church we were attending at the time was a Mega Baptist Church. It was primarily African American that attended there. We had been there for at least five years and had not connected to a single soul on a personal level. Even while there was three months where Andrew was in the choir. I would notice they would preach one sermon and I took great note to study it, but then two weeks later the same verse would be taught by a different preacher and sound just as good but had a totally different message. However, that message seemed to line up with scripture, just as the others did also. I would find myself at home crying out for God to reveal his truth of that scripture to me and not just man's revelations. I started hearing the scripture in *Matthew 7:15.*

Matthew 7:15 (NKJV), "Beware of false prophets, who come to you in sheep's clothing, but inwardly they are ravenous wolves."

Right after my daughter was born, I knew God was with me. That precious little life he had entrusted to me was proof enough for me. I knew I wasn't living the life he'd called me to however, I hoped and believed that would change one day. God was showing me that it was easy to be deceived in this world when you're following man and not Him. I still didn't understand the whole magnitude of what God was trying to reveal to me. I was still going to seek him out in a more earnest manner and not be so gullible to man's enticing speeches. I started seeing God talk to me about the smallest things such as a sun shining day, going into stores when there's no lines, having food to eat, no headache days, and every time I got a paycheck. I could now see these things as a blessing. I started feeling God pouring the joy back into my heart; He loved me. Not that He had ever stopped, just that it's easy to allow the world to become a blind to the presence of God. That's what I allowed Andrew to do, was blind me from God's love and His presence. I felt my new mindset demanded me to focus on God's greatness and to stop worrying that I wasn't where I wanted to be; in God's perfect timing I'd get there.

Philippians 1:6 (NKJV), "Being confident of this very thing, that He who has begun a good work in you will complete it until the day of Jesus Christ."

I know this new mindset would be harder to keep up when Andrew came back home, but it gave me light at the end of the tunnel. Andrew was not from Texas he was from originally Missouri as he claims it's the show me state. I had met his mom and grandmother briefly over a weekend trip and they seemed to be very pleasant, as with his little sister who was much younger than him; she was still in grade school. His mom was a single parent and a nurse that raised two boys by herself with the help of her family and was now raising a daughter. I could never make any sense of what had taken place in Andrew's life to make him the way he was. He showed all sorts of respect to his mother and grandmother, however there was a disconnect from him to have any reverence for other women outside of his immediate family. He had told me that he disowned his biological father because of a disagreement between them. I didn't ask any more questions concerning that because knowing Andrew it really didn't take much to get on his bad side. Andrew went to college in Missouri and had a best friend that I also met who was a banking officer. Their personalities were nothing alike, but they seemed to connect well. His name was Arnold. He would be the only person that could stay connected with Andrew and not step on his toes or make him feel offended. Arnold, unlike Andrew, lived his life with an honor code when it came to the opposite sex. I had not ever seen him dishonor or disrespect a woman, even if she deserved it. He would shut down first, then entertain a combative conversation. The other reason why being around Arnold was pleasant was because of his willingness to always look for an opening to defend me without attacking Andrew's character or making it seem as though he was choosing sides. He was the voice of reason that Andrew respected. Because of the work Arnold did in the banking industry his employer would pay him to travel to different states and take training classes so he could bring back the information he'd learned and teach it to the crew beneath him. This meant he had been able to come see Andrew and I during one of his paid work trips. During one of his trips to Texas he met my friend Monica and fell for her; they'd committed to a long-distance relationship ever since. Anytime he was in town we would all do something together.

I was 23 years old when Andrew returned from Saudi Arabia. Little K was 10 months old, and she was going to be able to spend time with her father for the first time. I didn't know what to think about it. Everything in me wanted to protect my precious daughter from him. She and I met him at the airport. He took hold of her like she was everything. I was surprised to see how cautious he was acting with her. Once we got home, he had all types of gifts from overseas he had brought back for her. One thing that topped all of them was a ring set he'd bought. It was connected to a bracelet. It was 24 carat gold with the inscription reading, "For my baby girl." She never took it off until her little wrist grew out of it. Andrew spent hours entertaining his daughter. I didn't care one bit that I wasn't getting any attention. I felt no attention was better than negative attention. It started to look like Little K would calm him down some. He was eager to get back to working a regular job. Andrew went and applied at UPS as a driver and was hired on. I started to think maybe it was time for me to study for the postal exam. The bank that I worked for had been taken over twice in the 5 years that I had been there; and I'd never received a raise. Within months of Andrew being hired at UPS, I was told that my bank was going through another buyout. This time it was looking like we'd all be laid off unless we were in upper management. Within 6 months, I was given a severance package of 3 months' pay and let go. Andrew said he didn't want me to look for a job right away because he wanted me to stay home with Little K and homeschool her to be above her level. I would have embraced this opportunity, however, this meant I would never be able to have a life outside of his control. I stayed with Little K for three months and poured into her as much as she would allow me to. Then I began to feel morning sickness once again, and I took a pregnancy test which came back positive: I was devastated. I wasn't working and I was pregnant; something that neither of us wanted at the time. I looked for a good time to share it with Andrew, but it never came. All of a sudden he said, "Why are you always sick? You better not be pregnant again because I'm not paying child support for two kids."

I told him, "Yes I am pregnant, and I was waiting for a good time to let you know."

Andrew responded, "Well, we're not having any more kids. On my next off day, I'm taking you to the abortion clinic." I didn't say one word in response to his decision. I felt when the time came, he'd calm down, especially as much as he loved his daughter. On Sunday night Andrew tells me he's dropping me off at the Planned Parenthood Clinic in the morning. He gave me $150 to have an abortion. I was still quite; not sure if I had any choice in the matter. That morning he dropped me off after we took Little K to a drop in childcare facility.

I walked in and the lady asked me, "May I help you." I told her I wasn't sure. She said, "Well what is your need?"

"My husband dropped me off to get an abortion and I wasn't sure what my options were."

She said, "Well you're in the right place, fill out this paperwork and I'll get someone to speak to you." As I was filling out the forms, I felt overwhelmed with sadness to think that I would even consider aborting the little one inside of me. I completed the first page and then I stopped. I thought about this baby's voice forever being silenced by a decision I allowed because of the selfishness of its father.

Then a nurse walked up to me and said, "Follow me." She continued by saying, "I couldn't help but to notice you looked puzzled. I'm here to answer any concerns you may have." I explained that I was married and that he didn't want this baby to be born and gave me an ultimatum to terminate the pregnancy. The nurse said, "First of all this is your body not his. It doesn't matter that he's your husband or your baby's father. You are the only one that can make a choice to terminate the pregnancy or not. How do you feel personally about the baby?" I told her I had a lot of mixed emotions about bringing the baby into my house as it was. However, now that the baby was here, I didn't believe I could just terminate its life just because of the technicalities. She said, "Well there's your answer and you don't need to finish filling out this paperwork." When Andrew picked me up, he asked if it was done. I told him I didn't go through with it, and. he started yelling at me. He said, "If you don't abort the baby then I'm going to kick you out. You don't have a job nor any place to go." My eyes were red, but I didn't cry.

We made it to the daycare and picked up Little K. I saw her and all the other little ones; I knew that the life inside of me had to be protected. I picked up Little K and hugged her as though it was our first and last hug. When we got back to the apartment, Andrew told me to get my chores out of the way and to sit down with Little K and do her curriculum. I did as I was told. When it was time to work with Little K, I started working with flashcards in her room on the floor. I heard Andrew yelling that I had only half cleaned her highchair. So, I stopped, and went to reclean the highchair. I didn't see anything wrong with it, so I went back to doing flash cards with Little K. The next thing I knew, Andrew had come into the baby's room and hit me in the face. I started crying and Little K started crying too. He then grabbed my arm and pulled me into the dining room where the highchair was. I don't know which hurt more, the way he grabbed my arm or how he was pulling me. I was crying, "You're hurting me, you hurt me!" Once he got me in the dining room where the highchair was, he grabbed my hair and pulled it.

Then pushed my face down to one of the legs of the highchair telling me, "Do you see that mess on the leg of the highchair?" It was a smudge from the baby, where her hands had touched when she pulled herself up. Then he yanked my hair again and dragged me into the kitchen. I started hitting his hand away from my head. The baby had crawled into the kitchen and was trying to hit Andrew and was crying for me. He took his hand behind my head and pushed my face into one of the bottom cabinets. He was telling me that I didn't clean the kitchen because if I did there wouldn't be food on the outside of one of the cabinets. Once again, it was another place that I had forgotten to wash down because of the baby's dirty fingers. I wiped it down and told Andrew to keep his hands off of me. That night I slept in my baby girl's room with her, in her bed, which I would do regularly if I was angry at Andrew. I started to entertain the thought of an abortion just because I didn't want another baby in the middle of the mess. The next week, Andrew took me back up to the Planned Parenthood Clinic. This time he told me I better not leave that clinic if I hadn't aborted the baby. I got out and went back into the clinic this time, I didn't even bother to grab the paperwork or sign in. I just sat down in the waiting room area. An hour went by, then two hours, then three. Eventually a nurse came out and asked me if I was waiting on someone. I told her no.

She asked, "Is there something I can help you with?" I told her no.

Then another hour passed by and the nurse I had counseled with before remembered me and said, "Come here let me talk to you." I went with her and she asked me to have a seat. "How long have you been here?"

"My husband dropped me off this morning when y'all first opened up, I've been in the waiting room ever since."

"I'm not even going to ask if you've had a change of heart. Do you know why?" I told her no. "We have a policy that if any of our patients seem to be unsure or show signs of uncertainty, then we refuse them service. Even if you had come in today and told me you've thought about it and now have a change of heart. You've still had too many signs of uncertainty by your words and actions since you first came in last week. We would highly advise against an abortion in your case. Many women have nervous breakdowns because of the guilt, and they can't live with it. Please go home and ignore your husband and have your baby." I called Monica to come and pick me up from the clinic. She came and got me, and I shared with her what I was dealing with. She told me if Andrew didn't come to his senses about the pregnancy, then Little K and I could come stay with her, at her parents' house, until I could get back on my feet. She dropped me off at the apartment and Andrew was there with Little K waiting on me. Little K was hungry and needed to be changed so she was whining and was a little tired from being at the childcare center all day.

So, I took her and started changing her, and Andrew asked, "Did you get it done?"

I said, "What?"

He said, "You know what I'm talking about. Is the abortion finished?"

"No. I decided that's not what I want for my child."

"It's my child too. I told you to go have it done, this isn't up for debate."

I said, "Well I'm sorry you feel that way, but this is my body and I'm not putting my baby and myself through that." Then Andrew grabbed my hair again and told me that I was going to do whatever he tells me to do. I told him to stop because he was hurting me.

He went on to say, "I'm calling in from work tomorrow and we are going to the clinic together; you will have the abortion done. Now go fix my dinner.". I told him, "Give me 15 minutes to feed Little K and lay her down."

"No. I want my dinner now."

"Wow Andrew, the baby is screaming at the top of her lungs! Please let me take care of her?" He turned and started hitting Little K on her legs for crying. Then I screamed, "Stop hitting her! Do not touch my baby!" We started struggling but by this time her bottle had been fixed. I told Andrew to leave her alone and I would get her to stop crying. He said you have 5 minutes and I want my dinner in the next 10. I ended up sleeping with Little K that night and the next morning I got up before either of them. This gave me enough time to pack a bag of clothes for Little K and I in case we ended up at Monica's after the clinic visit. I made sure that everything Little K needed was packed. Then I showered and put on a pair of jeans and t-shirt. I waited until Andrew was in the shower to grab some fresh changes of clothes and undergarments to potentially take to Monica's. I fed Little

K and prayed myself into a peaceful spirit. God knew my heart and my intentions, so I believed he would fight for me without me getting hurt. This time Little K came to the clinic with us. She was such a quiet baby that you would never know she was there. We arrived at the clinic 15 minutes before it was open and sat out in the parking lot. Andrew loved Rap/R&B music and I couldn't stand listening to it ever. I was more into classical music. He would not only play the rap but blast it. He refused to listen to anything else. Meaning anytime that he had vexed my spirit I would turn the radio off. It became so frequent that every other time I was in his car with him I would turn the radio off. Once the clinic opened, we all got out and I placed the baby and I's bags into Little K's stroller.

When we went into the building the receptionist looked at me and then said to Andrew, "Yes sir how may I help you?"

Andrew said, "My wife is here to have an abortion."

She said, "Well sir, we told her yesterday that we couldn't do it."

Then Andrew said, "Listen I want to see the doctor now! Y'all will be doing this abortion!" I took the stroller and went to sit down in the waiting area. Andrew stayed standing with his hands and arms folded in front of the receptionist desk. The nurse that had spoken to me the last two times came to the front and saw me and I pointed to Andrew.

She walked up to Andrew and said, "Hello sir. How may I assist you?" Andrew went on to say, "I need you to abort our baby."

She responded by saying, "Well, this clinic is in support of women and I have interviewed your wife twice and she's clearly not a candidate for our abortion procedure. We will not be able to help you here unfortunately."

Andrew said in an authoritative voice," We are not leaving until y'all do what we came here for you to do! I want to speak to the doctor." Within 5min the doctor came out and asked Andrew to leave the facility immediately.

He said, "I am the doctor, and I will not have you here upsetting my staff or my patients. You can leave now, or I'll call the police on you."

Andrew said, "I'm a paying customer and I demand you do what I'm paying you for."

"Your money is not accepted here and there's no service we'll be willing to provide for you!" I got up and walked out with Little K and her stroller, while Andrew was busy cursing at the doctor. Finally, Andrew came out of the clinic and started going off on me because I walked out.

I told Andrew, "I do not have to be told twice to leave a facility."

Andrew said, "You don't leave nor go anywhere without my permission." I told him fine.

Then he said, "You need to figure out where you're going because you can't come back to my apartment." I told him that was fine too. I went back into the clinic and apologized for Andrew's behavior. They said it was no problem; it is what it is. I then asked if I could use their phone to call for a ride? They allowed me to use their phone. I called Monica to come pick us up. I started back on my way outside and the receptionist said, "You can wait in here if you'd like."

I said, "Okay thank you." As I looked outside, I noticed that Andrew was gone; I felt a sense of relief. Monica was there within an hour to pick Little K and myself. She took us to lunch, and we sat and talked. Monica shared with me that she was eight weeks pregnant and that we would be having our babies around the same time. She also started pointing out some other positive things. There was a guest house which was separated from their main house that Little K and I were welcome to stay in; it had a half shower and bathroom built into it. It made me feel better that I wouldn't be making anyone in the main house feel put out. We left and Monica gave us a tour around Fort Worth. Then she wanted me to meet her baby's daddy. Monica had already told me that he was a deadbeat; just someone to kick it with a couple of times. I thought to myself, *"My sister, Monica, is becoming a little soft."* Monica had another young man that we both liked a lot, but he was all about making money and multiplying it. This young fellow name was "Christopher". He had an on and off relationship with Monica for years. He worked as a technician for the hospital in the imaging department. Many times, he experienced Monica's wrath, but he loved her as long as he didn't have to commit.

During the next three months, Little K and I made our home there with Monica. We spent a lot of time together and I didn't worry about getting a job. I had thought long and hard about it, but it would mean that I would have to pay for childcare. One thing I remembered was that childcare was so expensive that you could work, and your entire paycheck would go towards that. Monica convinced me to go to the Attorney General and put Andrew on child support. I also filled for W.I.C.K. and Food Stamps; these items really were immediate help. I didn't hear or see Andrew during that time. Monica worked part-time at a gas station around this time. She used her check towards gas money and even contributed and helped me buy diapers for Little K. She also took me to see my mom at least twice and she was looking good. She told us that she had fallen out with Mr. Lee because of his youngest son being rebellious. I thought to myself, "*Who would've known after all of us moved out Jeremiah and Mom had problems.*"

A voice in my head knew that Mom would've said, "*You made that bed and now you have to lay in it.*"

Monica and I were 6months pregnant and both were showing. This was Monica's first baby, and she had all kinds of cravings. I didn't have any appetite. I started going to the library to study for the postal exam and had put in to take the test again. The library had all types of post office guides for me to study with. I applied myself and committed to making an 80 or above on the exam. When I reached 7 months, Little K and I had both grown content that Andrew had made his decision and we had made ours. Monica had just found out she was having a boy, and I was going to my gynecologist to have an ultrasound.

I had an excellent report. My doctor told me that all my previous screenings for problems with the baby was ruled out and everything was looking good. In reality that was the only news I needed to hear; but I got an extra good report. I too was having a baby boy. Monica and I would be celebrating our boys together for the rest of our lives. A few days after I found out about this good report, Andrew showed up at Monica's house saying, "It's time for y'all to come home."

I told Andrew, "We are home. Little K and my baby are doing fine without you." Andrew told me he was wrong in what he did.

I said, "You think so?"

"Yes, I'm sorry, can we be a family again?" This was the first time Andrew ever apologized to us or anyone that I knew of. He asked where Little K was, and I told him that she was asleep. He said, "How could you just leave her alone?"

I said, "Really Andrew? Maybe you need to be asking yourself that. You've been M.I.A. for 4 months now." I couldn't believe I was speaking so freely to him. I thanked God for some of the survival skills and boldness I had picked up from Monica. However, I realized that there were going to be many needs for my baby boy and for right now I wouldn't be able to do it on my own. I still had a plan to become totally independent once I got on with the post office.

We went back home and then I shared with Andrew that we were having a baby boy. He wanted to name the baby "Junior".

I said, "Not over my dead body. You don't have a right to name my baby anything after you had almost cost him his life." I didn't hear any more from Andrew pertaining to that subject. I secretly forgave him and was going to wait until after the baby was born to let Andrew choose his middle name. I didn't want his humble spirit to be short lived. Unlike my first pregnancy, this baby was so active. I don't think he'd ever sleep. My stomach looked as though I had twins. I didn't gain weight anywhere but my stomach in both pregnancies. I thanked God for Little K. She was an angel baby. I knew she would be an awesome big sister. She never got on my nerves or did anything intentional to get in trouble which I thought was weird because she was already three by that time. Little K had passed the terrible two stages into the threes and showed no signs of rebelliousness. On the contrary, she had started walking at 9 months; and at 12months she was potty trained. She loved learning and was ever so easy to work with.

I had seven days before I was set to take the postal exam. I was excited and nervous all in one. I had learned a handful of things to keep me from wasting time practicing things that could be counted against me. I also spent time getting familiar with looking at different residence addresses. I could always use more time to study but why put off things for the future when I could do them today. With this attitude I walked into the testing center of the main post office on testing day with confidence. It was a large classroom of mostly men. I sat down and did the section that I was familiar with and applied myself the best I knew how to in the areas of unfamiliarity. I couldn't believe it; I was finished before they called, "Times up." I was relieved to know the test was behind me and now I just had to wait on my results. I knew anything below a 75 would put me in a position to not be hired or to be put on a waiting list.

It was October and my "Little Prince" was due to be born in a week. Monica had already had little "Zachariah" two weeks prior on September 25th, 1993. Now my Little Prince was fighting to get out my stomach; I thought by the way he kicked and bowed my stomach with every part of his body, it would be a quick delivery. October 6th came, and I started feeling strong contractions when I got out of bed. I felt that the baby was just a little more active than normal, but as the day went on, I told Andrew that I needed to go home and lay down and put my feet up: We had been out all day picking up last minute items so I could pack my bags in case I went into labor. Andrew around this time started being a little more helpful with Little K. He had warmed her food up and put her in the highchair. As I was getting into my PJ's my water broke.

I told Andrew, "My water broke!"

He said, "Why didn't you tell me you were in labor?"

I said "Honestly, I couldn't tell the difference between the normal pain and the labor pain; it's been bad all day. Anyways, it's time to go to the hospital." Once we were in the car. I started reminiscing on the contractions I had with Little K in Killeen when she was born. I recalled the same severity; but not as fast. When we got to the hospital and saw a doctor; he said, "Well it's going to be a while you're only 4 centimeters dilated." The joke was on me. The pain was worse, and the baby was obviously bigger. The nurse said that the baby would drop down faster if I got up and walked around. I thought she must be out of her mind. I could barely stand because of the severity of the contractions. The doctor had us admitted and rolled me into a room. For 24 hours Little P had only dilated to 8 centimeters. The doctor said, "We can't do anything until you dilate completely to 10." The pain was so severe that something within me disconnected from that baby. I did not want it anymore. I did not care if it died, or I died but I needed the pain to go away immediately.

Monica came into the room and said, "Sister it's going to be okay."

I said, "Listen, that's easy for you to say. You've already had Zachariah." I had all kinds of mean thoughts. I felt like the baby was taking out all his anger on me because he was not happy that I allowed Andrew to treat him less than human. Then I thought about the many times my stomach was upset because of stress and I didn't feed him. There wasn't a thing that didn't run across my mind that day. When I finally hit 10 centimeters the doctor said it was time to push.

I told him, "I have no energy left after fighting with this baby all day and night! If he doesn't come out on his own, he might not be coming out." I felt the two nurses pushing my back for me. Andrew was right there with the doctor looking crazy. Once the baby was out, they cleaned him up and measured him. Little Prince weighed 10 pounds and 6 ounces, and he was 22 inches long. The doctor and nurse asked me if I wanted to hold my baby. I said, "Get that baby out of this room. I don't want to hold him or hear him or see him!"

The nurse said, "Is that normal?"

The doctor said, "No, not usually. We need to give her some time to rest." Thirty minutes later the nurse came in to check on me. She asked if I was ready to see my baby and I said, "No and you better not bring him in here!" She asks Andrew if he wanted to see him, and he follows the nurse to go meet his baby boy. For an entire day, I wouldn't allow them to bring the Little Prince in my room. Finally, the next day came and Andrew said, "When are you going to meet the baby?"

I said, "What for? You're here! Why do I need to see or hear that baby? I've been through enough with you both."

The nurse came in and said, "Your baby is waiting for you."

I said, "I do not want to see a baby; not now or later!"

Then the doctor came in and said, "I heard you haven't seen your baby yet? It's not normal for a mother to not want to see her newborn baby."

"Well, it's not normal that I had to go through what I did to have this baby. He has a father that can walk into the nursery to see him."

Then the doctor said, "Can I please have your permission to let the baby sit in your room while your husband is here, so he can feed him?" I told the doctor it was fine. The nurse brought Little Prince into my room and Andrew jumped up to get him and I still could not stand to look at either of them.

Andrew said, "Are you sure you don't want to peek at the baby?"

I said, "You and that baby need to leave me alone." By the end of the day, I started to look at Andrew with the baby. I thought to myself, *"He's all about that baby now, but a few months ago he was so adamant on the abortion clinic. How ironic."* Little K finally came back with Monica. She wanted to hold the baby and for the first time I saw the baby's face when she grabbed him. Poor Little Prince, He looked just like Andrew! That was his twin. I said, "Oh my goodness, poor thing." Maybe the baby was mad when he was coming out because he'd already known he had his daddy's face. My heart broke and I felt compassion for the little thing. What came to mind in that moment is that he didn't need to have a mom that hated him. I thought he'd have enough push back in school from his peers. I took my baby and showed him a true mothers love. From that day forward, I bonded with Little Prince. He became so attached to me; he didn't allow no one to hold him outside of me and Little K. There was this odd thing about Little Prince, I never saw him smile once. Even when I showed him love and affection the most, I would get from him was these big glossy eyes look of curiosity. Outside of that, Little Prince had always carried this expression on his face as though he was angry or constipated. I had never seen an infant look like they were mad at being in the world. I've heard people say that your mood can impact the baby when you're pregnant. My son was a true example of that. As he became more aware of his surroundings, he would not connect with or trust anything that was fiction.

I recall when he first saw Santa Claus he said, "No mommy. Bad!" When he saw Chuck E. Cheese he said, "No mommy! He's bad!" Any Disney Character in the mall, he would say "Bad!" and start to cry loudly. I had never seen anything like that. It wasn't long before Andrew exposed his true character. Little Prince started refusing to be around him without me. Any time Andrew tried to pick him up or take him somewhere he'd start screaming as though to say: "I don't like you, and I'll never trust you!" Every time I brought Little Prince over to Mom's, he'd never let me put him down without crying; so, I just carried him. Mom said, "You really got that baby spoiled." Deep inside I knew it was more than that: Little Prince was intertwined with my heart. He knew the years of pain I had experienced and could connect with me. This smothering effect had him pushing people away; especially those who I still had problems with. By the time that Little Prince could walk, by holding on to things, he started trying to keep Andrew and I out of the same room. Andrew was always fussing at me about something. Little Prince would do everything he knew how, to become a distraction; by crying or hitting me to get my attention to come away from Andrew. Little Prince spent his entire infant and toddler years trying to protect me the best way he knew how. He would cry and scream anytime I was out of his sight, especially at home. If I was in the kitchen he'd be in the kitchen. If I were cleaning in the living room, he'd be in the living room. Little Prince watched me like a hawk. That angry frown of an expression on his face did not improve until he was 3 years old. He would be much older when he would learn to smile. Andrew was very mad that his son didn't want him to hold him. He was even angrier that I was shielding him. I wonder if Andrew thought that this was a curse placed on him for trying to abort Little Prince. I truly don't believe that. However, I do believe that the baby was closer to my heart.

It was another sight to see how Little K protected Little Prince. She would always make sure he had his bottle and had his blanket; just like Linus from "Charlie Brown". She didn't allow anyone to get in his face except for me. She was quick to say, "My brother doesn't like to be touched!" Little Prince looked at Little K as his personal protector when I wasn't around. I never saw a baby rely on another baby for security like those two did. Little Prince was grounded when it came to his own feelings; but when he wasn't sure, he would quickly attach himself to whatever feeling, or emotion Little K displayed and trusted her instincts.

In this chapter I feel the Lord was speaking to me from *2 Corinthians 4:18.*

2 Corinthians 4:18 (NKJV), *"While we look not at the things which are seen, but at the things which are not seen: for the things which are seen are temporary, but the things which are not seen are eternal."* Change is not possible outside of God's word. God's word is constant, and we need to center our focus on His word. My subconsciousness and consciousness both eagerly waited for a change for God in my life. I was always anticipating God to show up in my life and rescue me and the kids. My encouragement to whomever may encounter similar circumstances or worse is: Don't keep God in a box by believing that if He doesn't come through for you the way you expected, then he doesn't care or is not going to. Be open to however and whenever he wants to make a change. Many times, we have given up on God or even shut the door to dreaming again, but we need to remember God's word.

Isaiah 55:8,9 (NIV), "For my thoughts are not your thoughts, neither are your ways my ways, declares the Lord. As the heavens are higher than the earth, so are my ways higher than your ways and my thoughts than your thoughts."

Chapter 15
Ask God and He Will Answer!

LITTLE PRINCE WAS BORN ON OCT 6, 1993 AND IN DECEMBER I started working a seasonal position at the post office as a clerk. I had both of the kids kept in childcare during the days I had to work. When I was hired, I was told the ending date for that job was on January 16th. I would be let go unless they offered me another temporary position. When January came around, they told me that I would be laid off for one week, but they wanted to bring me back as a casual mail handler for a 3-month term. I finally received my test scores during that time, I had scored surprisingly higher than I thought I would. I received an 88 for the letter carrier test and an 86 for the clerk position. After speaking

with other career employees, they told me that more times than not, a good score would lead to a permanent position before the temporary assignment was finished. The one thing I had to think about were the two positions and their suitability for me. The carrier position would offer me more money hourly and daytime hours for me to spend the evenings with my kids. I had heard that it was the most physical of the two jobs: I figured I'm still young and very teachable. I was still struggling with those unbearable migraines though, so I needed to get my health in order so that when I start working, I wouldn't have any distractions. I went to my neurologist and he went over all the medicine that he had tried previously on me. He said, "Karen we are running out of stuff to try. There may be other options if we look at it from a different angle. A Lot of the medications you've tried have two uses. They are used to treat people with depression or other mood disorders as well as severe headaches. Would you be willing to try something that is strictly classified as an antidepressant? At the time I was willing to try anything. The neurologist said he was ordering a few tests to be done, a CAT-scan and an MRI, to make sure there's no physical obstructions around my brain. As soon as I started the medication, I started feeling better. On top of that he had prescribed me a medication called "Imitrex". It was an injection that I was meant to use when I was having a chronic migraine. I was very fearful at first, but once that pain hit me in my head; I quickly overcame the fear of giving myself shots. Oh, how it hurt. Then I would get a brain freeze right after the shot. The whole process took a total of 10 minutes but then it was as if I had never had a migraine to begin with.

Within a week, I was offered a letter carrier position from the post office. I had only been a mail handler for two weeks at that time. In the letter containing a job offer there was also a place for me to walk-in to take a drug test. The doctor had just put me on a lot of new drugs, and now I had to take a drug test. Thanks to prayers, I knew if God opened the door, and he would allow me to walk through it. I didn't have to take a detour to go to a special postal facility to take the drug test: There was a medical unit in the same building I was working in. I took that as a sign of God's favor. On my lunch break I went to the medical unit and took my drug test. They took urine and a hair sample from me. I brought all of my prescriptions in advance to go ahead to clear me from illegal drug usage. A month later, I was sent a letter of ineligibility to be hired for the letter carrier position, due to the negative drug test I had taken. Andrew read the letter and right away he started talking about an appeal letter that he was going to write for me. I had no disputes with that; but first I wanted to take my letter to the Post Office and ask the medical unit for advice. Later that day the neurologist office called and said that the doctor wanted to set up an appointment as soon as possible to review the test results on my brain scan. The nurse said it was urgent that they saw me this week.

I thought, "Wow y'all are really making a big deal out of some test." I went on to schedule the office visit right after work on Friday. I had no worries or fears. I felt it was time to fix the root of my pain. The next day I went to work, I took my letter with me to the post office. On my lunch break I went to talk to the nurse in the medical unit. I showed her my letter. She said the post office is known to send out these medical denial letters. She went on to say they do it to wean out people who may be a financial risk later on. I asked the nurse if there was something I could do.

She said, "Sure, have your doctor write a letter of medical necessity for those prescriptions you take and resubmit that letter with another letter of your personal reasons why the post office should reconsider you as an employee. They are not allowed to discriminate, so they will reconsider." I was relieved to hear that. I knew it was God answering my prayer. I had been praying for God to change me and he had. I had become wiser and stronger. I was no longer acting as a victim but one who had God on their side; I was proud of myself. I kept in touch with Mom weekly now, it didn't bother me anymore when I called her, and she had a lot of negative things to highlight in her life during our calls. I knew she was still drinking and was depressed but I never said a word about it.

What I would say to her was, "I'm sorry that your life seems to be so overwhelming. Things will get better one day; never forgot God loves you and so do I. Then I would let her know that I was praying for her. She might have taken that religiously, but I truly prayed for mom and I loved mom. What I had been through with Andrew made me appreciate Mom on a new level. I realized she had experienced pain that I wouldn't ever be able to relate to and her drinking was not by choice; it was a sickness.

Friday came fast and I was excited to see what the doctor was going to say about my tests. I left work an hour early with my supervisor's permission. I didn't want to run into any problems getting the kids on time after my doctor's visit. By the time I got there, signed in and paid my co-payment the nurse took me straight back. They had the original films of my MRI already set up in my exam room. The nurse turned to me and said, "Have a seat. Dr. Norman would be right in."

"How's your day been?" he said as he entered the room and shut the door.

I told him, "It's nothing to complain about. I must say it's good to have a job."

He said, "That's great to hear, and I wish I had good news to tell you to go with it. Unfortunately, there is a brain tumor the size of a golf ball that showed up on your MRI. It's located near your pituitary gland; we can't remove it because the surgical procedure is an incredibly high risk one. If it were to be removed there would be a 50-50 chance of survival. It is terminal though, and depending on the growth rate of it, you may have two years left to live." I felt like the information he was releasing did not belong to me, so as Dr. Norman spoke, I was totally disconnected from having any kind of thoughts pertaining to what had been said. I knew God had promised me deliverance and freedom, not death. Even though I wasn't strong in the word at the time, I knew God had called me. Dr. Norman went on to say there's no option for chemo or any other type of treatments in this circumstance. The only plan at this point would be to monitor the growth rate. "Every 3 months I'm going to order a new x-ray and compare it with the previous one. If the growth of this tumor surpasses my expectations then the first thing it will affect is your vision, then your hearing, then your nervous system will be compromised, and you'll go down pretty fast from there. Do you have any questions for me?"

I said, "About what?"

He said, "Everything I just told you."

I said, "I'm sorry doctor, I was listening, but I refuse to believe any of that to be something that I will have to deal with. I feel that there has been a mix up."

He said, "I understand, but let me tell you this: You have two small babies. Do not live naïvely. Please come in and let me do my part in following up with an MRI every three months."

I told Dr. Norman, "I hear you." I left his office and I put up a wall of positive thoughts of why that information was not intended for me and I kept it up. What I had to think about was the selective few that I would share the information within case of emergency. The first person I would need to tell is Mom. My concerns with that would be her taking it literally. Mom was already struggling with depression and the past lost in her life, so this would make things compounded. The other person that I felt needed to know was Andrew. I could actually see him being happy about knowing, because he wouldn't have to continue to deal with me and I couldn't ever go off and be happy with someone else. Andrew's least concerns would be our children losing their mother early on in life. He would easily replace me; at least he likely believed so. The only other person I planned to share it with would be Monica. She was my children's godmother and would be the only one who would be a positive encouragement through it all. If worse came to worst, I knew she would keep my memory alive for my kids as they came of age. On my way home I looked at both of my children and began to encourage myself further. I thought about how good our Heavenly Father was to entrust me with these two precious babies. I could see in both of their eye's that God was going to use them in a mighty way for His kingdom. At that point, I made up my mind to teach my children the things I knew about God. Prayer being first on the list. I started praying with them every night. Little K was like a sponge, and Little Prince would stare as to say I'm not sure, however, I'm not going to turn my back on it just yet. I had this new attitude. Something deep inside of me was anticipating that God was going to do some great things in my life. I opened my Bible and read these three scriptures and kept them with me any time the Devil tried to bring anything Dr. Norman said into my head.

Psalm 118:17, "I will not die but live and proclaim the works of my God."

Ephesians 3:20 (KJV), "Now unto him that is able to do exceedingly abundantly above all that we ask or think, according to the power that worketh in us."

Jeremiah 32:17 (KJV), "Ah Lord God! Behold, thou hast made the heaven and the earth by thy great power and stretched out arm, and there is nothing too hard for thee." I had not met anyone who had received a miracle from God, but I saw myself as a survivor as one who God was going to do miracles with and through. I had never been taught that in any of the churches that I had attended but I had read Jesus' miracles in the Bible. The God that was in the Bible was the same God I served. He's the same yesterday, today, and forever. That's where my faith was.

At the time I did not know there was a scripture to support that, so I can say that the Holy Spirit spoke that into my consciousness.

Hebrews 13:8 (NKJV), "Jesus Christ is the same yesterday, today, and forever." After I began to think in this way, nothing anyone could say to me could discourage me. I looked for confirmation signs from God everywhere. He made Himself known around me in every aspect of life. A week after I sent my dispute letter to the post office, they were scheduling me for orientation for career employment as a city letter carrier. Right after that, I was going through their driver's training and safety classes. Andrew had become very sloppy with dating women outside of the house. I had different people telling me that they saw a woman driving his vehicle during times when he claimed to be at work. I never sought out the information; it just came to me. There was one day when I drove by a private school by our house and saw Andrew's car parked there. I believe the Lord was setting things up for me to run into her. Andrew had never denied anything. Confirmation coming from him sounded like, "If you were a better wife you wouldn't have to worry about me cheating." What he didn't know was that I wasn't worried. I was preparing for God to open a door for me to have a permanent exit. One evening I was on the way to get the kids, but I needed to stop at the grocery store first. I did so and took a back road to avoid traffic. I was not thinking about passing that private school, but I rolled right past it. I saw a woman a little older than myself getting into Andrew's car. I did a quick U-Turn and went back. I pulled into the driveway and blocked the car from pulling out the parking space. I got out and walked up to her window.

My first question was, "What is your name?"

She said, "Why?"

I said, "Is that the way you answer a person's question with a question?"

She responded, "Why?" once again.

I said, "Well I'll take that as a yes. I want you to know that I'm Andrew's wife and you're driving my car."

She said, "No, this is Andrew's car and you're in your car."

I said, "Hun, you put a lot of play into your words, are you a teacher here?""Why?"

I said, "Because I don't believe this private school would keep a teacher who teaches improper English."

She said, "If you don't move, I'll run you over."

I said, "What? You're going to run me over? In my own car? Let me tell you something: I can have you arrested right here, right now if I call the police and tell them you stole my car. Then you won't have to worry about your boss firing you for your improper English. But no, I won't do that. I'm Christian, and the Bible teaches that if you have an offense then you are to come to Him and work it out. This is your warning. I'm going to allow this to slide."

She said, "You're not going to allow me anything, because Andrew and I have been together for over six years and I'm not going anywhere."

"What are you saying? Are you married to him also? Have you gone and married Andrew? If so, then you're right. I am sorry and I digress in that case. He is not worth fighting for honey! You can definitely have him!"

In response she said, "No I haven't married him. We have an open-door policy in our relationship. I'm sorry you're in the middle of it. Will you please let me go now?"

"I will this time however, I can guarantee the police will be involved if I catch you in my car again." I got back in my car and left to get my kids. For sure I thought I would be late to pick them up, but I arrived with three minutes to spare. I knew it was a favor of God to not have to pay a late fee. I also thought that God was constantly revealing a door for me to get out of this marriage. I knew it had to be much bigger than just Andrew's adultery; he had been living 8 years of our marriage as a church hypocrite, and a heathen. God knew I needed something more. I didn't know what God would give me, so that peace and confirmation be poured out for me to get a divorce. In my mind I had not been married to Andrew, but to God and His covenant.

Later on, that night after, the kids were fed, bathed, and put to sleep, Andrew came in. He had a way of attacking me and making me out to be the guilty one when in fact he was the culprit. He could be caught red handed and still yelling at me because I wasn't the ideal wife that he wanted. I started a long time ago shutting down quickly because our arguments would go nowhere. He wasn't denying anything on the contrary; he was saying, yeah, it's all true but it's your fault. He came straight out and asked me, "What do you think you were doing putting my friend on the spot like that while she's at work?" He said, "My friend hasn't done anything to you. Why were you there making a scene?"

I responded, "First of all, Andrew, why are you allowing a woman to drive around in your car, bringing dishonor to me? If you want to discuss something, let us discuss the six-year open door policy relationship you have with this woman."

Andrew responded, "Our relationship has nothing to do with you. So, you need to stay out of it!"

I told Andrew, "You know what, you're right! I need to disconnect with you completely. That way: nobody you're fooling around with and nothing that you've been doing will have any bearing on me."

After that conversation, Andrew started to be gone during his days off, and would get home from work really late in the evening. I looked at it in a positive way: He always brought a bad presence into the atmosphere of our apartment. When he wasn't there the kids and I would be at peace. There were things I was still having problems with, though. Andrew was taking my entire paycheck, claiming to be paying the bills, and was leaving me with no gas money or emergency money. He would hand me $50, then tell me I better make it work for the next two weeks for groceries. He would never fill my gas tank up. It stayed on a quarter of a tank most days. He would tell me that I wasn't allowed to go anywhere but to work, to pick the kids at daycare, and back home. He'd figured out the mileage from our apartment to my job, to the daycare, and then back home. On days I needed to get groceries he figured out the mileage to get to the store and back too. It wasn't because we didn't have the money for gas or food either. Andrew had just bought a brand-new SUV, "Ford Explorer", for the family and got rid of the lemon car I had. He had sold his Mercedes Benz-CLS and was now driving a newly pimped out "BMW-1, series-M" racing car. He was all about controlling me. It seemed like Andrew would check my miles every day to make sure I hadn't made any extra stops anywhere else. How a person could be diligent; I would never know. Andrew also made it his business to be the only one to check the mail. I never considered he would be hiding anything. He'd been transparent and bold in the midst of his self-absorbed righteousness. I started taking notice after he brought the mail in the apartment: he would somewhat guard it or immediately dispose of it, never leaving a letter laying out. I had no intention of snooping to see if there was something going on. At this point, nothing surprised me when it came to that man. However, I came home one day and was cleaning when I saw a letter creased inside one of his magazines. It was a collection letter with my name on it from an apartment complex I had never heard of. I knew he had credit cards placed in my name, but who could be using my social security number for an apartment. I wrote the information down so that I could call later.

I had finished the orientation and training for the city letter carrier position. The post office had great benefits a 401k thrift savings plan that they matched for those who wanted to participate. I put my maximum effort into that program and got all of the extra insurance that was offered to me, such as dental, vision, life, and short-term disability. The only thing that I opted out of was health insurance because Andrew's insurance had already covered us... I was assigned to a post office which was 15 minutes away from our apartment. The first full paycheck I received was the largest one I had ever gotten outside of my modeling check. I know I would never miss that little extra money if I started taking it out right at the beginning. I had decided I was going to stop him from controlling my paycheck.

My first week I carried mail, brought back memories to me of the Oklahoma Military Boot Camp that I had gone to with Jr-ROTC. That was the last time I had walked over 10 miles in a single day. The majority of the routes for that postal station were walking routes. When walking you had to keep a quick pace to be able to complete your mail route on time. My first month, all I could do was to pray that God would continually strengthen me every day. I weighed barely 100 pounds at the time and was meant to carry around a 45-pound mail bag for the entire day. As time went on, I gained muscle and learned from senior carriers the best routines to further improve my work ethic. Regardless of how much I loved my job, my heart desired to transfer to a post office that had less walking involved. This was added to my prayer list. One thing I liked about working out of the neighborhood mail station was that they changed management regularly: every 3 to 4 months. They had some supervisors that were called "2O4B" which were regular carriers who filled in or helped out doing supervisors' jobs. They could relate to the carriers very well and were easier to work under because they knew our job. I loved my work schedule. I would be off most days by 3:30 and on heavy days it would be 4:30 which gave me an hour's worth of overtime and plenty of down time before I picked up the kids. It was rare that I worked after 5:00 p.m. unless it was during a holiday. Either way I didn't have to pick the kids up until 6.

I finally got an opportunity to call the property that had a collect letter in my name. I was told that there was a man and woman who showed ID proving to be Mr. and Mrs. Blankied. They said that they present Social Security Cards for both names and credit cards as further proof. The apartment complex went on to say that after the third month of the lease the woman said her husband left and she wasn't able to pay her rent. The property said they owe them $4400 for breaking their lease and for property damages. I was devastated. Here I was thinking about Andrew messing up my credit with credit cards years back. Now I'm finding he's using my name as identity fraud for his adulterous life. It made me sick to my stomach. The townhomes we were living in right now didn't even have my name on the lease. I thought it was because Andrew wanted to control this unit so I couldn't put him out; now I believe it was so that he could destroy my credit. I didn't go home and act like a madwoman. I didn't even bring it up. I thought about what I could do now that it happened, which turned out to be nothing. So, what would be the purpose of bringing it up? I drained myself just thinking about having any type of conversations with him about it.

It was time for me to have my follow up with Dr. Norman for another MRI. I had made up my mind that I was going to treat this visit like a wellness check-up. I would expect only good news. I haven't thought about it since I spoke last to Mom. She was good at reminding me about it every time we spoke. She believed she was encouraging me, not knowing bringing up the subject did the complete opposite. Mom had also shared it with everyone I had ever known, including my entire family. So, much for my little secret. I couldn't be mad at her. I know how mothers can unintentionally cause hurt. Dr. Norman had an imaging facility connected to his office and after I took my MRI, I waited 15 minutes for the film to be printed, and then I was able to go next door for my office appointment. It wasn't long before I was called back to the examining room. Dr. Norman walked in with another surgeon and said, "How's my favorite patient today?"

I said, "Thanks for asking. I'm doing wonderful. It's been a beautiful day.""This is Dr. Chang and he's a neurosurgeon. He's come to give me a second opinion on your MRI."

"Okay Dr. Norman, that's fine with me." They both were silent for 5 minutes as they compared the MRIs.

"Just as I expected, there has been growth."

Dr. Chang said, "It's around 2 centimeters worth, and that's more than what we would like to see in a 3-month period."

Then Dr. Norman said, "We will continue to do our 3 months follow ups and hope for the best." I left the office and didn't speak to anyone concerning my follow up visit.

Andrew had responded, "Why are you telling me that's your body, and your problem?" I wasn't surprised, but I didn't care. I went on to get my two bundles of joy from the daycare. Little K was a little chatterbox. There was never a quiet moment with her. She was 5 now and asking about the sun, moon, and stars. She would ask why everything was the color it was, why certain things are shaped the way they are, why the tree's leaves fall to the ground, why we can't see the air, and any other questions that would come from her. She never ran out of questions. You could never ask her to do anything without her asking why. I never met a toddler that asked so many questions.

I would start responding to her, "Tell me what you think?" That worked for a while because she always had some ideas on every subject. Little Prince was the opposite, he would be quiet as a little mouse and listen and watch Little K. After I picked the kids up, we went straight home. I keep the kids on a schedule during the week so that they wouldn't give me a hard time getting up as early as we had to. It was rare that I had to put anyone in time out. It is funny how kids and pets can discern stress in adults and in most cases, they tend to be more nurturing. I would stand back sometimes and watch them play. They played well together. I saw Little Prince tell Little K, "No!" and hit her hand. I corrected him right away. He did it again, and Little K started telling me that he'd hit her or was pulling her hair. I was very concerned about this because he had very clearly seen his daddy do it to me on several occasions. I decided to start spanking him for it.

When I got to work on Monday, we had a new supervisor. Her name was Carol, and she was a pleasure to work under. She was an older African American female. Unlike any of the other supervisors I had met, she built relationships and tried to become friendly with everyone. There were only four women working at this post office. One being her, another me, and then there was one white carrier and one clerk. We worked with around 55 men carriers in total. Carol would always ask me how things were going. I would tell her that I was doing well. She started asking me if I like carrying walking routes and I told her not particularly, but I couldn't put in for a transfer until I was vested. I came in to work like normal one morning. I had heard a handful of carriers talk about a storm that was going to be in the area. Everyone, including myself, was rushing to get our mail in deliveries in order and to get out of the office. Carol made an announcement that this storm looked like a bad one. Her instruction was to never be caught out in the open and to find shelter if it gets really bad to stay away from your vehicles. That day I was assigned an unfamiliar route, so I didn't have any customers that I was friends with yet whose houses I could take refuge at. My only plan of action was to deliver as much mail as possible and as fast as I could before the weather got too bad and I had to stop. After getting my route together and loading the vehicle; the winds had already started picking up. I drove to my delivery street and parked in front of the house where I was to start my deliveries and immediately the sky got dark. The wind and rain started blowing hard. I sat in the vehicle looking to find a place for shelter. I was in an all-residential area. The street that I was on had 6 wooden houses which were sitting on brink stilt which was used to keep houses from flooding or to prevent foundational damage. I started seeing trees being unrooted, and my vehicle was sliding backwards by itself. But debris was flying everywhere in the atmosphere from customers yards. I did not see one person waving at me to come in. I knew I had to get out and away from the vehicle to take shelter but at that time, even with the vehicle sliding with the emergency brake on, it seemed to be the safer place for me. I started praying that God would still the winds for a moment so I could find some shelter. And in an instant the winds were still, like when Jesus spoke to the wind the disciples were in the midst of the storm in a boat. I left everything in the postal truck, locked up, and looked at the houses around me. The one I was parked in front had garden tools such as rakes and flowerpots and landscaping bricks everywhere, and this was the house that had the uprooted tree. The next house had kid's toys everywhere, so I ran to the opposite side of the house; they had a tree I thought about holding on to, but the Holy Spirit spoke and said, "Get under that porch and hold on to that brink stilt." As I ran to it, I noticed a medium size dog who was tied up to a tree barking at the wind. He was at the house next to the one I was at. I got on my knees and under the corner of the porch and grabbed onto the stilt: The wind and rain picked up again. This time it was worse than before. Within seconds, I saw that little dog being lifted up and taken off by the wind. Then up came the tree I was going to hold on to. All sorts of stuff had been lifted up in the wind and was flying around again. I struggled to keep under the porch and connected to the stilt. I could hear windows breaking and debris hitting up against people's houses. I stopped trying to see anything anymore because the debris was getting into my eyes. I began to pray for God to save me. I told him that I was sorry for putting the blame of hardship on everyone in my life except myself. I told God that I took responsibility for everything, including my marriage. I told Him that if he saved me from this storm, from the doctor's diagnosis, and from my marriage I would dedicate my life and my kid's life fully to Him. Right after that prayer, that storm left as quickly as it came, and the skies lightened up. I walked around looking for that little dog and didn't see him anywhere. I prayed and believed that he had gotten caught in another tree and was safe. My vehicle was in the middle of the street two houses down from where I'd parked it. I walked over to it, got in and reparked, and resumed my deliveries. That day the Lord heard and answered my prayers. I knew that was confirmation that God was removing my tumor and getting me out of my marriage.

Two weeks later, Carol called me into the office, and she sat me down to talk. She said, "Karen I don't know your story; but I like your character and you're a hard worker. I know you have young children and the type of routes we have here are very physical and the terrain is bad. I would like to pull some strings on your behalf; to have you be a swing carrier between this station and another

North Dallas station. I know you will like this station: They have more business and apartment routes and a few of their residential routes are driving deliveries where you don't even have to walk. Though there is a catch: the mail volume is twice at this station because it's closer to the Galleria area and those people have new money and growth."

I said, "Yes ma'am, that would be a blessing."

She said, "Then it's final. You're officially still assigned here but any time they can use you I will allow you to work out there." I knew this was a blessing and an answered prayer because I had at least another year and half or longer before I could transfer out.

Isaiah 45:1 (KNJV), "Thus says the Lord to His anointed, To Cyrus, whose right hand I have held To subdue nations before him and loose the armor of kings, To open before him the double doors, So that the gates will not be shut."

In this chapter, the Lord was telling me that my life was in a period of change and I was coming out of the darkness into the light; I knew He would be there with me. That word lines up with *Isaiah 45:1*. Isaiah was told by God that He would hold his people upon his right hand, and He would go before them. God's done that for me. I knew because it was not normal for any carriers with as little seniority as I had to be transferred before their appointed time. This move alone opened the door for me to be positioned for more of God's blessings.

Chapter 16
Trail of Fire

I REPORTED TO THE GALLERIA STATION THAT SAME DAY AND it was only 10 minutes away from our townhome and close enough that I didn't have to get on the freeway to get there. It was a hub station for carriers only, meaning there was no window service. I had never seen mail in such large quan-

tities like I had seen on some of those routes. I was nervous and I knew I needed to stay focused. There was also a more diverse mix of people at this station; more women and people of all races too... This station had well over 150 employees and at least 100 mail routes. It was intimidating and overwhelming at first because of how heavy the mail volume was and because of the variety of routes. Every day I carried a different type of route: apartments, drive-outs, residents, malls, shopping centers and businesses. Having to learn the different techniques of delivery was very intense for me. I was being moved around constantly in this large station. However, I made friends fast and most of the regular carriers I came into contact with liked me. They would volunteer their help in the station and out on the street. In time, an older, black gentleman who was a seasoned carrier approached me with words of encouragement. He said at first it can be overwhelming but like anything else you learn the ropes and it becomes a piece of cake. His name was Tim, and he was a T-6. That meant he was the regular relief carrier for 6 routes. Tim routes were considered to be the top "senior" routes in the station. He had been there a very long time and a union representative that was well liked. From what I'd heard, he had saved several carriers' jobs; even carriers who should've been fired. It was obvious that he was very friendly to me. I was not bothered by it. I was drawn to his wisdom and he had a wealth of knowledge about the postal law. Tim was familiar with just about every route in the station. At first, he started coming to my route daily to check on me. He would finish his route quickly to come help me finish on time. He would also be my rescue when I was turned around on a route or lost. Other male carriers stopped coming to check on me because they would see Tim. They respected him. It was pretty obvious that he liked me. He was in my face every morning like clockwork with no shame. I knew he was married, and I had no intention of having an affair. However, I just enjoyed the attention. After ten years of abuse, I was broken. Tim looked a lot younger than he truly was and was in excellent shape. It was nice having a gentleman in my life who cared and treated me with respect. He started teaching me the ropes in caring mail and the bylaws, so I knew my rights as a carrier. It took less than 30 days for me to start working at Galleria Station permanently because of him. Tim showed me how to put temporary bids on down routes and how to watch the vacation schedule for senior carriers whose leave of absence was coming up; so, I could place temporary bids on their routes for the time they were off. That way I could be placed on good seniority routes weeks at a time, and not be tossed around the station to unfamiliar routes, and bad routes at the mercy of the supervisor. One day at work I had finished my route. I went to load up my postal truck and there was a tall, middle-aged, black postal mechanic checking out the vehicle assigned to the route I was carrying. He told me that the regular carrier had put a work order in because it was leaking oil. He asked me if I minded exchanging vehicles with him, so that he could take the one with the problem back to their shop. He seemed to be very friendly and outgoing. I told him as long as the truck he is leaving me is up to par, it would be fine.

He smiled and said, "What is your name?" I told him and he said, "Well, it's nice to meet you, Karen. My name is Keith and I'm a son of God. I try to be up right in all of my ways."

I said, "Okay 'Son of God' let's make this exchange." I loaded the replacement vehicle and stopped to get gas in it. Then I took off to my route halfway the vehicle started choking as though it was running out of gas. I called the station to let them know my vehicle had stopped on me.

Jim, my supervisor, said, "We don't have any extra vehicles right now; however, the postal mechanic is still here. I'll send him your way." Within 15 minutes Keith came with this big smile. He got out of the vehicle and said, "What have you done to my vehicle? It was perfectly fine when I gave it to you."

I said, "Look here Mr. Son of God, the 'up right one', how dare you?"

Keith said, "I'm sorry. Let me take a look."

As he was checking out the vehicle, he asked me, "What church do you attend?" I told him that my husband had been taking us to First Baptist Church for a while now; but I've been praying to find a church in this area that had discipleship classes. He said, "Have you heard of Pastor Mike Hayes?" I hadn't. Keith went on to say, "It's an awesome ministry, very family oriented. If you want a deeper walk with God you definitely want to check it out... Anyways, let me try your vehicle and see if it works properly now." The vehicle cranked right up.

I asked him, "What was wrong with it?"

He said, "All I did was wipe some things off."

"Are you kidding me?"

"Yes, for real!"

"Well, thanks for getting it started again for me." Keith said it was no problem. He went on to say, "Go check that church out. The name of it is: 'Covenant in Carrollton' and it teaches the full gospel. I guarantee you'll love it." I told him thanks for everything. I was back in business and on my way to my route again. The route that I was doing was an apartment route. I had planned to knockout the smaller units first. I got there and parked the postal truck and unloaded my vehicle. There wasn't a soul around. I was relieved so that I could put the mail in quickly and head to the next apartment. I had my headset on and was listening to a sermon on family life ministry. I didn't notice someone had walked up behind me and was waiting. When I finished, I closed and locked the mailbox door. I was startled by the person watching me. I told the man that I was sorry I hadn't seen him before. I told the customer that I would have given him his mail, but I didn't realize he was there. The customer responded, "That's no problem. I wasn't here to pick up mail. I just have a word for you." I got quiet and my eyes got big because I had seen words given to people, but I've never received one before. He went on to say, "God has a calling on your life. You will walk in it. You will counsel and help many people in God's word." Then the man walked off. He didn't attempt to check his mailbox. I wasn't the normal carrier: I wondered how he knew I was going to be there. The regular carrier delivers this apartment complex later on in the day at the end of his route. I accepted it as a word from the Lord. I had never seen that man before nor have I again. I knew three things had to happen in order for that word to be for filled: First I needed to be healed from this brain tumor. Secondly, healed in my heart and third to have learned the deeper things in God's word. I knew God was going to do them all. I believed the postal mechanic as well as this stranger were sent to me by God. They were no coincidence.

I believe Andrew started noticing a change in my personality after I had been working in this Galleria Station a few months. I was more confident and less tolerating of his foolishness. God had been restoring my self-esteem and self-worth.

One Saturday night I told Andrew I wasn't going to our church anymore and that there was another church down the street that I wanted to visit. He started yelling and hitting the wall and furniture asking are you seeing someone at that post office because it sounds like someone has been instructing you to say and do certain things. I told him, "I will never be the person you've been to me". He slapped me twice.

Then Little Prince grabbed my legs and started screaming, "Let's go Mom; No daddy, no hurt mommy!" Then Andrew pushed Little Prince. Little K said, "Y'all stop fighting!" She picked Little Prince up to console him. Then I told Andrew that I was eventually going to get away from him. Then he started choking me.

Little K said, "Stop daddy stop, stop!" Both the kids started hitting Andrew right as I was blacking out. I felt my body lifted up. Andrew tossed me on the glass coffee table: my body impacted it, and it broke completely. I remember just laying there and I couldn't get up. Andrew left right after and I remember both kids crying. Little Prince screamed until his little chocolate face had turned red. I told Little K to go get a pillow and a blanket for me. When she brought it back, I rolled myself off the broken coffee table to the rug and laid there. They both went to get their pillows and blankets and laid next to me. I told Little Prince, "Mommy's okay now you can stop crying." He wasn't screaming any more, but he was still whining. K and I pat him until he was asleep. I got up the next morning and Andrew still hadn't returned. I was so glad; the kids were still shaken up. I didn't know what injuries I had sustained but it hurt to move. I had the kids help me pick up the piece of broken table. The rest of that day I loved on the kids and they loved on me. I continued to apologize to them for Daddy and Mommy's fighting. I took a hot Epsom salt bath and took two Tylenol and put icepacks on my ribs, side, and back. Calling in for work isn't something that I could afford to do. I never went back into our bedroom. I stayed in the kid's bedroom and rested and seeked the Lord for strength and direction. That night Andrew came home long enough to grab some things and leave. We didn't say anything to him, nor did he say anything to us. I spent the night in the kids' room. I had an open vision dream that night. I dreamed that Andrew came and picked me and both of the kids up. I kept asking him where he was taking us. He wouldn't respond. The only thing he said is that we'd see once we got there. We got to this big bridge and Andrew stopped right in the middle of it.

I asked him why are you stopping?

He said I want you out of my car and I want all of you to jump off this bridge.

I told Andrew, "We'll get out of your car, but we're not jumping off this bridge!"

Andrew said, "Really?" He pointed a gun at me and asked me, "How about now?"

I got out of his car and Little Prince was saying, "No mommy don't listen to daddy."

K was saying, "Daddy why are you doing this; don't you love us anymore?"

Andrew said, "Who told you that I loved you? You need to hurry up and get out of my car with your mother." I had never seen K cry in the way she was crying. Normally Little Prince was the one who would cry dramatically. I picked K up on the opposite side of my body, that Little Prince wasn't on, and held them both. I looked at Little Prince as he was saying, "Mommy he's not our daddy! You don't have to listen to him!"

I said, "What do you mean? He's not your daddy?"

Then the Holy Spirit said, "Your son is right. Don't make the wrong decision again, next time it'll be too late." When I woke up, I was overwhelmed. I remembered every detail and I knew what the dream was saying to me. It was the confirmation that I had been waiting for: God revealed to me that it was in his will for the divorce to go forward: now I had total peace about going forward with divorcing Andrew. It had been nine long hard years married to him. I knew time wasn't on my side. Time would be vital. We had valuable art that was worth a lot of money hanging in the apartment. In our savings we had at least 40 thousand dollars from selling some of that art and recently both of our vehicles had been sold. I needed to get an undefeated attorney to draw up the paperwork to freeze our accounts before Andrew liquidated them. I also needed a protective order against him while I was filing the divorce. Everything had to be done before Andrew knew that I was even thinking about this course of action. I know this would need an intervention by God. Andrew was a paralegal and an ex-police officer and knew how to get around the law and court proceedings. He was still connected to several judges that would be on his side. I dropped the kids off and went to work and while I was at work I networked among the carriers. One of them gave me an attorney that was known for no nonsense. When I got on the street to deliver my mail, I called her. She did a phone consultation and told me that she normally requires money as a down payment, but she would put in the paperwork and make him pay for the divorce. That was the first sign of God intervening. She asked me if I could come in and sign a contract to retain her. This black female attorney was already typing up protective orders and getting the things that were needed to jump start the proceedings. That day, I finished my route early and high-tailed it to the attorney's office. It was right down the street from my old post office. I met her and as wonderful as she sounded on the phone, she looked even more professional and sharper than I visioned. Dee sat down with me and showed me five documents that she had prepared for my case after speaking to me that morning. She said she would be filing them with the court in the morning and would subpoena Andrew. I signed the attorney and client contract, a protective order, a motion of discovery and research, a motion for the court to freeze all assets, and a divorce proceeding. Mrs. Dee proved herself to be on top of everything. I thanked her and left right away to pick up my kids. When I got home there were still no signs of Andrew's. The house seemed to still be in tack as though Andrew had never been there. I was excited that things went so well with the attorney and that by tomorrow Andrew would be legally prevented from putting his hands on me and liquidating our assets. I was still sleeping in my kids' room just in case he came home. I wanted to be able to avoid any more confrontation between him and I.

The next day, I was scheduled to do a follow up MRI. I looked forward to being given a clean bill of health. The next morning, I dropped my kids off at the daycare, got to work on time, and rushed to get my mail ready and out on the street to deliver. Tim had been working with me daily on the street. I would help him with his route, and he would help me with mine. We enjoyed working together and he became a person I told everything to. The other benefit was that I got off on time every day to take care of my business.

I left work on time to go to my appointment to see Dr. Norman. After taking a new MRI, I waited for them to call me back in for results. It wasn't long before they put me in an exam-room. Dr. Norman walked in, once again asking, "How's my favorite patient?"

"I responded never better. I believe you have some good news today for me?"

Dr. Norman smiled and said, "Why is that?"

"My instincts had been anticipating a miracle healing, and I believe this is my time."

He said, "Well, wouldn't that be nice." I agreed. He went on to say," Let's have a look at what things are looking like." For 10 minutes Dr. Norman looked at all the films and compared them three times and said, "Karen before I say anything, let me get a second opinion."

He left the exam room and came back with Dr. Chang. Dr. Chang said, "Hello Karen, do you remember me?"

I said, "Yes sir, you're the neurosurgeon."

He said, "Yes I am. I'm going to check your MRI and see what your progress looks like." He looked at all the film and said, "Karen have you been experiencing any abnormal symptoms of any kind?"

I said, "No, why? What's going on?"

He said, "The growth of this tumor seems to double every time we check it. At this rate, we have to think about exploring other options."

I said, "Like what? I'm not having no surgery. Dr. Norman already said that surgery is high risk. Plus, I am believing in a miracle. You'll see." The doctors looked at each other and then Dr. Norman thanked me for coming in and said that they'd continue our three months follow up. I left that doctor office telling God that he'd missed another opportunity to show his glory. I said, "God you promised to take sickness and disease from the midst of me. I told the Lord you're not a man that would ever lie and your word propels you to manifest your glory. I reject that tumor, it's a lie from the devil." Then I went to get my kids.

Once I got to the daycare the owner was approaching all the parents telling us that this was their last day open until the health inspector allowed them to reopen. They wouldn't tell us why; other than there had been some unforeseen circumstances with safety. That was a major, unexpected shock to me. I was quiet the entire way home. K asked me if everything was okay. I said, "Yes sweetheart, I'm just tired and need to lay down." We were home within 10 minutes and I still didn't see Andrew's car. I was glad that he was anywhere except here. I got the kids out of the car and into the apartment and it looked as though we walked into the wrong apartment. It was completely empty. Andrew had taken the living room, dining room, and master bedroom furniture. I ran up the stairs to see if he bothered the kids' room: No, it was still intact. I went back down the stairs and all the expensive oil paintings were gone. Andrew had cleaned out the entire townhome except for the kid's room. I went into the kitchen and all my dishes and pots and pans were gone. There were 3 plates, 3 spoons ,3 forks and 3 cups left; everything else was taken. Yes, these things were unfortunate, but I couldn't be moved from my place of peace, even with no furniture. I was finally free from Andrew. If I had nothing and I didn't have to deal with Andrew, then I had everything. If I had everything and had to deal with Andrew, then I had nothing. So, I felt richer than I had ever been. I still had to figure out what I would do with the kids while I was at work tomorrow. Then something came over me saying, "You got to trust God in everything." All of a sudden, I felt that I was supposed to get dressed for work and get the kids ready as though they were going to daycare. Then I would leave and take them to work with me. It was settled! As I got ready to shower, I thought about it. All my undergarments were gone and jewelry and most of my outfits. I decided I'd just hang my undergarments out to dry after washing them in the sink. The kids ate T.V. Dinners that night. We all slept peacefully. Bright and early the next morning the kids and I got up. I packed all their things as though I was taking them to the daycare, and I got them some extra things to play with in the truck so that they wouldn't become too bored. As far as I knew, my plans would be to leave them in the truck while I got my route ready and sneak them into my postal truck. I prayed I wouldn't have to do that, but at this point I was just trusting God. When I got to work, I parked close to the dock where the loading zone was. I knew many carriers took smoke breaks back there and I wouldn't look strange coming back there a few times to check on the kids. I wasn't as concerned with K as I was with Little Prince. He was only three and sometimes would get out of control with Little K. I could depend on K if she were by herself because she was quite advanced for a 6-year-old. I knew if management caught the kids in the vehicle it could mean my job, or even worse. I clocked in and went to my mail case to start putting up my route. I felt consumed with thoughts of what ifs. Then all of a sudden, I heard this squeaky high-pitched voice and from my corner view there she was: Mrs. Williams, the Postmaster. On all the days to visit our station she had to pick today. Man! There was nothing I liked about that little petite blonde haired white lady, and I mean nothing. Any time she came to our station she seemed to be looking for things to complain about. Mrs. Williams was big on micro-managing and being seen. I felt if I left my case other than getting more mail or taking my morning break It would be noticed by her. She had a thing for black men, but she hated women. I had a very close male friend named "Mr. Chan". He was a kindhearted guy. Every morning he'd make a point to speak and ask me how things were. Anytime I wasn't smiling, he would say, "Are you okay? Is there anything that I can help you with?" Not once did I ever confess to having any problems. I loved how kind and how peaceful he was. When we were loading our postal trucks next to each other our conversation would surround our children. He had two girls close to K's age. I waited until I thought Mrs. Williams was in the manager's office to run out and check on them. I couldn't be sure outside of her squeak voice and her little heels clucking around. You could look around at the carriers and tell if they were engaged into a relaxed conversation. You could be sure that if she was anywhere close most of them would not talk freely. Mrs. Williams was one to scream about time wasting practices. I rushed out the side door as soon as I thought it was safe to check on the kids. It had only been 15 minutes since I had clocked in. I looked in the truck and K smiled and unlocked the door for me. low and behold Little Prince was crying.

K said, "Mommy I told him not to cry and that you would be back soon, but he didn't listen."

I said, "Thank you K. You did a good job."

I said, "Little man, what's wrong? You're a big boy. Big boys don't cry. Please stop crying. Come give mommy a hug." He gave me a hug and I said, "Wow you need a diaper change. Come here and let mommy take care of you." I changed his diaper and gave him some graham crackers and he seemed to have calmed down. I went back inside and heard Mrs. Williams raising her voice at the supervisor for something. I was praying that I wasn't spotted. All of the carriers had scattered morning breaks according to their routes they were on. I had made up my mind that I was going to work through my break so I could get caught up from the time I lost when I checked on the kids. As I was casing my mail, I thought about Little Prince crying. I was moved to run and peek on him again. I had to be sure the way was clear. There were at least 3 employees who worked close to me that I shared what was going on with me. I did this for the cover and protection of the kids. One person was our maintenance man. He was walking around on the dock making sure the kids didn't get out of the vehicle to go wander off. I went back outside and peeked in the truck. This time it had been 20 minutes and Little Prince said, ``Mommy I want to go.''

I told him, "You'll be able to go soon, but right now I need you to be a big kid like your sister." He looked at K like he was mad at her. I was trying to get him to sit and play with his toys, but he wanted to be with me. I told them both I had to go back to work, and I would be back soon. I looked at Little Prince and he had looked as though he wanted to cry again. I told him, "You better not! I mean it! Your sister wants to go, I want to go; but everyone is doing what they have to do right now!" Little Prince pulled it together and gave me a different look. His expression was more like fine mommy. I went back into the station highly frustrated. I begin to case my route again. As I cased my route, I was also trying to figure out what I was going to do? I said a quiet prayer: "Lord, you know I need my job. Please help me?"

Within 5 minutes of that prayer Mr. Chan walked over to my case and said, "Good morning Karen, are you okay?" I shook my head no and stretched my eyes. He said, "What can I help you with?"

I said, "Mr. Chan, It's a long story but my two kids are outside in my truck. I didn't have a sitter today and I have been to the truck twice since I clocked in. The three-year-old is losing patience with me."

Mr. Chan asked, "Has your break time passed?" It hadn't. He said, "On your break take them across the street to that Methodist Church. They have childcare and they are very nice people. The church is on Montfort Road hidden behind the 7-Eleven; you won't miss it. I know you know where that 7-Eleven is. The one right there on the corner, where most of us get gas. Mr. Chan said don't worry." As I thought about what he had said, I had 5 minutes before my break so this might work. I put up as much mail as I could in that five minutes and then ran out of there. I jumped in my truck and went straight to the church. I hadn't noticed it before but just like Chang said, it was there. I got the kids out of the car and left their stuff. As I walked into the church there was a heavy set older black man coming down one of the hallways. I walked up to him and introduced myself and explained my situation. He said, "Mrs. Karen God is good all the time and all the time God is good. He said we got these babies, so you don't need to worry."

I said, "I do sir. It'll be two weeks before I can get another paycheck to pay anything."

He said, "My name is Pastor Robinson. I'm the pastor at this church. We don't turn anyone in need down; so long as we can help them. I normally don't come in this early, but I had a burden and needed to walk these hallways and pray. The Lord is good all the time and all the time the Lord is good. The toddler room is two doors down on the right."

I said, "Sir, I don't want to lose my job. Please can I come back in an hour and give the ladies all the information they need?"

Pastor Robinson smiled and picked Little Prince up and said, "Man we're going to be good buddies." Pastor Robinson looked at me and said, "Mommy we'll talk to you later." I smiled and ran out of the church and drove back across the street to the post office. I parked and ran in. I pulled all my mail that the clerks had sorted and started back to my case.

My supervisor Jim stopped me and said, "I need to see you at my desk after you drop your mail at your case." I went to my case and dropped off my mail and walked to Jim's desk which was located in the middle of the workroom floor. Jim said, "Karen, I'm not harassing you, but Mrs. Williams said she noticed you away from your case at least two times and neither were during your break. She is on a rampage today. I normally don't let people stress me; however, she's telling me to write you guys up and put you off the clock. Please hurry and get your route cased and get out of here... By the way, is everything alright with you?" I told him all was well. He went on to say, "You know that you're not allowed to leave this post office in the morning after you clock in; outside of going to your route, that's grounds for immediate termination." I told him I had no idea... He said, "Well, now you know now."

I said "Yes sir. Thank you." And off I went to finish casing my route and I then started to load my postal truck up.

Mr. Chan came up to me and said, "How's everything going now?"

I said, "You saved my job. Thank you so much."

He went on to say, "I deliver mail to that church. It's a stop on my route. Every time I come in there, without fail, they are always very friendly. Don't worry, that's one place that I would trust with my girls."

I said, "Okay Mr. Chan, thank you again." I finished loading my postal truck and went straight to check on the kids. The door was locked now, and they had a bell to ring for someone to let you in. An older black lady opened the door and asked me if she could help me. I told her that I was there to check on my kids and to fill out enrollment paperwork.

She asked, "Is your name Mrs. Karen?"

I said, "Yes ma'am."

She said, "Please come right in. My name is Debra. I'm the first lady. My husband told me about you and your little ones. I'll let you peep at them and drop their stuff off. Then I'll get you the paperwork to enroll them." The first room we went to was the 3-year old's room. Little Prince was sitting at a table with the other 3year old's having a morning snack and watching an educational program. His teacher was Miss Sheila; she appeared to be very experienced and much older than myself. I had preferred a teacher such as her that wasn't passive. I was very shocked when Little Prince didn't start crying for me to pick him up. I gave Miss Sheila his diaper bag and then I kneeled down and kissed him. I told Little Prince that I would be back after work.

He said, "Bye mommy." I could feel the love of God at that very moment. I felt so blessed. I left and Mrs. Debra took me down a different hallway. I could tell the church was very clean. When we got to K's classroom her teacher had them all sitting on the floor having story time. She was older also and I was very pleased by that. I put K's backpack on the children's coat rack. K got up and ran to hug me. I told her that I loved her and would be back later to get her.

She said, "I love you too Mommy, that's fine. See you later." I left there with so much peace.

I stopped at 7-Eleven and gassed my postal vehicle and made a quick phone call to the attorney, Mrs. Dee. I told her what Andrew had taken and she said she couldn't believe it. She said, "If he's willing to do that; I would put it past him to break the temporary order that I subpoenaed him with. He was not to touch any joint property, including your accounts. We already have a hearing set in three weeks; however, I need to see if I can get it moved to this week. Please call me before we close for the afternoon, we have to get Andrew in front of a judge so he can be held in contempt of the court." I went to my route and later on, Tim stopped by. I told him about all that was going on.

He said, "Girl God got you." He helped me to finish my route and we went to lunch at a Kentucky Fried Chicken and there were 3 other male carriers there having lunch. We sat with them. Then Tim and I noticed Andrew sitting outside, stalking me. Tim went outside and said something to him, and whatever it was got Andrew to leave. Right after I went back into the station, I clocked out and started walking to my personal truck: there Andrew was standing outside by it; waiting for me.

He said, "I need to talk to you." I told him that he wasn't allowed to be 300 feet near me because of the protection order.

I said, "If you want to talk to someone, talk to my attorney." Andrew grabbed my arm real forcefully and Tim came running out of the post office and got up in Andrew's face.

He said, "Man I told you, leave her alone!"

Andrew said, "Oh, and who are you? Her boyfriend?"

Tim said, "No man I'm your worst nightmare; alive and in the flesh!"

My supervisor Jim, pulled up in his vehicle and said, "Is everything okay Tim?"

Tim said, "This man is trespassing on Post Office Property and there is a protected order covering Karen from this dude." Jim jumped out of his truck and walked up to Andrew. He was a big white guy, of around six foot six inches and weighed 370 pounds.

He said, "Is that right?" Andrew looked at him and walked to his car and left the postal parking lot.

Jim said, "Karen are you okay?" And then volunteered to follow me home.

Tim said, "Man that's nice of you to offer. But I'll do it."

Jim said, "You sure, I really don't mind?"

Tim said, "Yeah man, but you'll have to get the postal police involved. This guy has no boundaries. He's showing up on Karen's route and threatening her."

Jim asked, "Is this so Karen?" and I told him it was true." You should have told me. We're family here and we look after our own."

I said, "Well thank you Jim." Jim said I'm on it first thing tomorrow. I'm writing a report and getting the Postal Inspectors involved. Tim followed me to pick the kids up and then to my apartment. He helped me get the kids out and into the apartment. We saw Andrew was there sitting in his car, waiting. Tim said, "You just take the kids in the house and call 911." I did as he said. I called the police and then Jim, my supervisor. I didn't want Tim to be by himself dealing with Andrew.

Jim said, "I'm right down the street, I'll be there in 5 minutes or less. Don't worry, Tim is a smart man, and you have the police on their way." Within 15 minutes there was a knock on the door. It was a police officer who asked me to come out and speak to them. Tim and Jim had already spoken to the police. Tim explained again that when Jim pulled up and got out of his truck Andrew jumped into his car and left again. The officer looked at my protected order and said, "You did the right thing in staying in the apartment and locking the door. You have two nice guys that obviously care about your safety. The only thing we advise is that if you see his car at your apartment again and you're alone, do not get out of your vehicle. Go back to the post office or to the closest police station which is right there on Preston Road. 5min's away. Then the police turned to Tim and Jim and said thank you both, please watch your backs."

I went back into the apartment and called Mrs. Dee to tell her what had happened. She said, "Girl, you're married to a madman. You make sure you have that protected order wherever you go. I do have some good news for you. They're going to work us in on Thursday. so, make sure when you go to work tomorrow let your supervisor know you'll need time off that morning. Andrew will be subpoenaed in the morning at his job. Have a good night and watch your back." I hung up from talking to her and I felt so overwhelmingly blessed. I had an awesome attorney and coworkers who were like family. Now that I look back at this story it clearly showed how God turned it around for me. At one point it was Andrew and his police officers' colleagues' shoulder to shoulder against me. But God raised up a support system for me and the kids.

There had been a notice left on the front door by the property manager. It read, please stop by or call the office at your earliest convenience. I called to speak to the property manager right away. I was told that the renewal of the lease was next month. I explained to her that Andrew and I just separated two weeks ago and were going through a divorce and he was no longer here. The property manager informed me that I wasn't on the lease and to be able to keep the apartment I would have to fill out an application and get approved or move in thirty days. At the time I told myself this was something else I would be trusting to God for.

I started back sleeping in the master bedroom. I made a place on the floor and was at peace. That night I was awakened a few times with sounds of someone outside of my building: I believe Andrew was outside stalking me trying to make sure I didn't have anyone here. The next morning the kids and I were up and out of the house on time. As I started the truck it started choking as if it wasn't getting gas. I cut it off and tried to crank it again, but it would not turn over to run again. I took the kids back in the house and called my job. Jim allowed Tim to come and get us. Tim said he knew someone who had a mechanic shop on one of his routes with a tow truck. He said he'd have them pick up the truck and work on it while we're delivering mail. Tim and I went to check on the truck after we finished our routes. The mechanic said that someone had put sugar in my tank. He had to drop the whole tank to clean, and it cost me $200 dollars. I didn't have any proof, but Tim and I knew it was Andrew's doing. What I didn't understand was how a man could put his own kids out to get back at his wife. Tim blessed me and paid for the repairs of my truck. I told him I would give him the money back on payday, but he said "No, I have it to give. You take care of those babies."

After that I picked the kids up and went to the rent office to fill out an application in hopes it would be approved. I was rushing because I had been invited to the carrier's union meeting by Tim. It was a once-a-month meeting for all City Carriers of Dallas and Ft. Worth region. So, after I finished putting the application in, I got the kids feed and got them ready to go with me to the union meeting. I met a lot of carriers from other stations and learned how the union operates. I enjoyed it so much, I decided to start coming every month.

Thursday had come fast and today was the day I had court. Mrs. Dee told me to be there at 8:30 am and I arrived 20 minutes early. She was there early reviewing the paperwork on the case. I told Mrs. Dee what Andrew had done to the truck. She said, "If you had proof I could have him put in jail. We can get a statement from your coworkers of him violating the protective older, and there's no dispute that he took everything out of the apartment." After we saw the judge, she told Andrew that if he violated any more court order that he would be jailed.

She went on to say, "Since you can be so heartless to take your kids furniture away to punish your wife: I'm ordering you to pay her $1000 to replace the stuff. I want you to give the money to her attorney because I don't want you near her job nor residency." Mrs.Dee and I were smiling after that hearing.

In every chapter of this book God has manifested Himself in divine ways. During our lifetime we go through many obstacles not realizing God is in the midst of us. That alone tells us how good Father God is to be with us through the storm. One thing I learned personally was that anything that doesn't kill you should make you wiser and stronger. Biblically speaking, as a Christian, it should be a priority to grow your relationship and faith in God.

James 1:17 (NKJV), "Every good gift and every perfect gift is from above, and comes down from the Father of lights, with whom there is no variation or shadow of turning." I'm here as a testimony to God's greatness; you can find good in every bad thing. You have to allow your mind to always be seeking out those precious blessings of the Father. The more you focus on the positive things, the more they will be highlighted to you.

Chapter 17
Existing in my Own Identity.

I HAD TO GET BACK TO WORK QUICKLY AFTER THE COURT PRO-ceedings. I knew my supervisor had a whole route waiting for me to go out and deliver at. I went to work, and I was feeling blessed and highly favored; until I made a phone call. I had got a page on my beeper before I left the post office. I called the number, and it was our apartment manager. She told me that I would not be able to renew my lease at the apartment because of my credit. She apologized and said, "You have 30 days until you have to be out." I asked her if I could stop by and get a copy of my credit report. She said, "We normally don't do that, but I know you're going through a lot right now, if you stop by, I'll print it for you."

Now I had to find a place to move. On my way to deliver my route; I stopped by Tim's route to share with him about the court proceedings that morning. He had a big smile on his face and said, "I told you God has got you." As I was talking to Tim, he asked me what church I went to. I told him I was in between churches at the moment. He said, "Girl you got to get yourself and those babies into a church." I asked him if he knew of any in particular. He told me about this young guy that was a high school teacher at Skyline High. He said he just started a church in Pleasant Grove. He said overnight this man congregation grew fast with young people and families. Tim said that he had been a few times and the man brought the word of the Lord. I told him we would check it out. I couldn't wait.

I picked the kids up and stopped by the rental office to get my credit report. The manager gave it to me, and I asked her for an extra key for the mailbox. She made me one and I got all the mail. Once I was in the house, I started looking through it and saw something from "Aetna", Andrew's health insurance. I opened it up and started reading it, they said as of two weeks ago I was officially no longer covered by Andrew health insurance. I couldn't believe that man took me off the health insurance so quickly knowing I had a brain tumor which is a pre-existing condition that may hinder me being able to sign up for health insurance with my job. He had to have done it that first week we fell out. My check was barely enough to pay for childcare and rent. Now I'm going to get even less in my take home pay because I had to take out health insurance. I was floored and could see the true evil in Andrew. I had to keep it together. I knew the Lord would provide and at least I had health insurance that I could sign up for. It would take me at least a month to activate it if there weren't any problems. So, I would have to put the MRI testing on hold for a month or two.

As I looked at my credit report, I saw that it was a 430 score. It had me owning two apartment properties that had evictions that I had never even applied for and 4 credit cards that were closed in a write off. On top of 4 others that were maxed out and in collection. I was devastated. Andrew had really messed my credit up. I would not be able to get an apartment in my name with my credit report being like that. I felt like this repeated feeling of helplessness was pulling me in a direction of continuing trusting in God. I knew that God wanted me to depend totally on him, not myself or man. However, I wasn't used to operating in the unknown.

After, I prayed and slept on everything; I felt compelled to call Mom and ask for guidance. I shared about my credit and the apartment. Mom said, "Well you and the kids really need to have your own apartment. I don't mind taking you in for a little while but there may be another option. I have been in this apartment for two years now and never late on my rent. The manger here is down to earth and is around my age. I feel like I could call her my friend. Give me a couple of days to catch up with her and see if she'll be willing to rent you a place with me vouching for you. I will explain everything to her, so she knows right off the top why your credit looks like it does. If worst comes to worst, you'll put your stuff in storage and stay with me until you get your credit straightened out." I knew Mom didn't want the little ones to invade her space. She'd always make it known that her living room was off limits for the kids to go in whenever we'd visit. If they were in the dining room, they had to be sitting not touching anything. She didn't want them in the kitchen either. I understood all of that. Mom had a beautiful, white, antique-looking living room set and she had a chest filled with collectible crystals and a China cabinet in the dining room along with a glass dining room table. Mom's apartment was not the place for a 3- and 6-year-old to live. Whatever adjustment I had to make then that is what I would do.

The kids and I went to "The Inspiring Body of Christ Church" in Pleasant Grove that Sunday. We were very impressed. Tim was right, it was a family-oriented Bible church. The pastor was young and not much older than me. What was impressive to me was that I'd never seen so many young men fellowshipping in one church. Plus, it was the first full gospel church I've ever been to. He really taught the word and had compassion for God's people. I strongly believe God was calling me to walk in a deeper measure pertaining to His word. We attended for a while but because they were newly getting started; they didn't have a children's ministry yet. The Lord brought it back to mind when the postal mechanic had told me about the Covenant Church in Carrollton. He said it was a family oriented, and full gospel ministry. The kids and I had to go visit. I knew I could not settle on not having ministry for my kids, especially at this time in their life. They needed the word just as badly as I did. We finally visited Covenant and it was everything Keith said it was. This church had members from all nationalities from all around the world. It was a very mixed congregation of black and white Americans. The Senior Pastor and his wife were white and in their 40s. The whole church seemed to be 3,000 people estimated. They were mostly young members with families such as me. They were well established so they had classes for each one of my kids. Both Little Prince and K loved it, so we joined and jumped right into everything that would help us grow spiritually. They always had something going on for the children during the time I was taking classes. I even signed the kids and myself up for personal healing and deliverance. I didn't realize at the time that Covenant had a couple that were African American Pastors over their deliverance ministry. This is so profound to me that the church was the first place I noticed the breakthrough of spiritual oppression between the black and white community. Now I was actually worshipping and seeking God next to an ethic group different than my own.

After that we started building relationships with other Christian families. Covenant had what they called small groups. A small group were 5 to 15 families with similar interests that would meet outside of the church sometimes in members' homes or at an outing event like the park or bowling alley. The purpose was to build close net relationships in a large church. There was no limit to how many groups you could be a part of. I took advantage of that to build a strong support system with other Christians. The children ministry was on fire for God. My daughter was the first one to get the gift of speaking in tongues. I was extremely excited and a little jealous. I worked hard on trying to have it happen to me, but I believe I was complicating things. Then on a Wednesday night the spirit fell, and I was speaking in the Heavenly language. I couldn't be happier. I started volunteering in the children's ministry to give back to all I continued to receive.

One Sunday Andrew followed us there and I acted as though I did not see him. I said a silent prayer; I told the Lord that I wasn't going to miss out on His word while being worried about Andrew and his foolishness. He sat two rows behind me. I started praying immediately that he would be saved or be led to leave if he had bad intentions. God is so faithful, because within 45 minutes Andrew got up and left the service. I would pray all the time concerning the fear I had of his revengeful self. Sometimes I would find myself looking over my shoulder for that dark chocolate, bald head and beady eyes Andrew. There had been times I spotted him and walked out of stores and left everything behind. It took years for me to get delivered from that fear. But God did it just as I knew he would. After stalking me for 3 years following our divorce. God placed people in my life to help me come to terms with the authority God had given me.

God has kept me in the right mind since that dream. It's important to know that time heals no wounds; God is the healer. You can have an offense become dormant because it was never healed. As soon as a related memory comes to you that wound will reactivate, producing fear, hurt, pain, and sadness that can lead to depression. Thank God for His spirit and word.

Philippians 2:5, "Let this mind be in you which was also in Christ Jesus."

Colossians 3:10 (NKJV), "And have put on the new man who is renewed in knowledge according to the image of Him who created him." Paul, the Apostle, is telling us in Colossians 3:10 that the new man is being formed by the word of God. He tells us furthermore to be more like Christ. This requires the knowledge of God's word being mediated (study) by us. This endured giving us the character of the new man.

Psalm 107:20 (NKJV), "He sent His word, and healed them, And delivered them from their destructions." I can't express enough the importance of God's word for all His people. Healing and deliverance comes from God's word. Equipping, strengthening, and growing comes from God's word. We need God's word!

Ephesians 4:12-14 (NKJV), "For the equipping of the saints for the work of ministry, for the edifying of the body of Christ, till we all come to the unity of the faith and of the knowledge of the Son of God, to a perfect man, to the measure of the stature of the fullness of Christ."

Mom called me the following week saying she had spoken with the property manager and she was very moved by my story. Mom went on to say that she agreed to allow Mom to cosign for me for six months. Then she said she would allow me to be on the lease by myself to rebuild me credit after that trial period. Once again, I was truly blessed and feeling thankful that the kids and I didn't have to be homeless. I had only been over to Mom's 3 times since she'd begun living there. I recalled that Mom was living in the very front of the property. I hadn't ever gotten a real good look at the property; I just know it was very large. My drive would be 30 minutes away from the post office I worked at. Though, I had driven further in the past, so I didn't think this was too bad. I came by to fill out all my paperwork and pick out an apartment. The manager was saying that she had 3 floors and the top floor was the least expensive. I told her I didn't want to go up three flights of stairs with two small children or live on the 1st floor because I didn't want an apartment that was too easy to break into. She found something in the middle. Before I moved in, I was able to get living and dining room furniture, and a bed for myself.

I had two of the guys I worked with help me move in. As we were moving the furniture in, I started seeing brown roaches, not just in the kitchen but in the bathroom and living room and bedroom. I called Mom and told her that roaches are in every room.

She said, "Why did you let them continue to bring your furniture in?"

I said, "Mom, the U-Haul had to be returned and I had to be out of the other apartment. I really didn't have a choice. Little Prince won't let me put him down and K is hollering that there's a bug on her bed."

Mom said, "Don't pull out any more of your clothes to bring into that apartment. Make sure you have enough changes of clothes for the kids and work and come stay with me until we fumigate a few times. Stop at the manager's office and have them spray as soon as possible and I'll go buy some bombs and have Mr. Charles set them off today." The kids never went back into the apartment, but I stopped by the next day after work and the roaches were worse. The ones that had been killed were on every piece of furniture I owned. The tan carpet looked like it had chocolate chips spread all throughout it. I couldn't believe there were roaches still walking around in the light as though they hadn't come in contact with any chemicals. Mom bought more bombs and came and helped me sweep up the dead roaches. She called her coworker, Charles, again to do another fumigation of the entire apartment. Mom had Asthma so she could not be in the apartment for too long with those chemicals. After the third bombing I waited until the end of the next day. The beige carpet had no white showing. The entire carpet was covered with dead roaches and I could see from a distance still a roach crawling on the wall.

This time, I could not stand to enter the apartment all the way. Mom could not come into the apartment at all because the fumes were too strong. Poor Charles cleaned all the dead roaches up and convinced Mom and I to wait two days and bomb again.

He said, "These roaches are German roaches, and their nature is to adapt to chemicals or leave and go to the apartments around you and wait for the chemicals to die down then they come back." When I heard that I was sickened. Charles said that the chemicals that the apartments were using the roaches had adapted already, but you could still let them spray at least a couple of times and it would mix with our stuff and those roaches would die. The manager couldn't get anyone out here for a week. That was totally unbelievable to me. It seemed to me someone should be spraying weekly or even daily. Even though this situation grossed me out, I didn't act ungrateful. I was blessed that I had a place of my own. The roaches would eventually all die out. And they did after 3 weeks of treating them.

I received a call from Mrs. Dee and she said, "As soon as you can I need you to get over to my office. I believe Andrew has been pulling a fast one on the two of us with your savings account."

Right then I said, "Yes ma'am, I'll see you after work." All day I was concerned about money and taking care of my babies. I wasn't receiving child support as of yet. I had not been able to make one note payment on my truck. I always believed in paying priority. Every time I looked at the bills, I looked at them as though they were going to disappear somehow. They were all priorities. The rent and child-care were two bills that I considered non-negotiable. Then I had electricity, water, phone, gas, food, and toiletries. I played around with them and rotated them as much as possible.

I finally got off from work and high-tailed it to the attorney's office to see what she was talking about.

When I saw Mrs. Dee, she shook her head and gave me this look of defeat. I went into her office, sat down and looked over all the bank statements Andrew had given her. I didn't see any of our 40 thousand dollars in the account. He disclosed that he only had $20 and no other assets. I knew that we had two accounts, but I had not been allowed to observe them myself the entire time we were married. He had hid the mail, so I was not sure if this account was an account he just opened and lied about the other. All I could be sure about is the amount of money we had together because I was there when we sold both cars and I saw the invoice and check written for the oil paintings.

Mrs. Dee said, "Karen I have to be honest with you. Because you do not even know the bank information of the account, he was keeping the money in then it's your word against his word. This money might as well be useless at this point. I will try to catch him in a lie in front of the judge but even so, it'll prove nothing but what we know him to be already: a liar and a cheat. What I will demand from Andrew on top of him paying all my fees will be a request for him to pay the truck note and the insurance for the kids on top of his child support." I told Mrs. Dee that it is what it is. I was feeling disturbed at the time: I would be lying if I said I wasn't. The fact of the matter was I wasn't surprised. I knew before I hired Mrs. Dee that Andrew was capable of this.

There would be plenty more obstacles to overcome throughout the years of raising two kids as a single parent: but I am here as a testimony to God's greatness. **He kept me!** Through Andrew having the truck fall into repossession after being ordered to pay it by the courts, **God made a way**. Years of not paying child support **God made a way**. Years of Andrew refusing to build a relationship with his kids and stay connected to them; **God kept them!** Through God's promise to restore me. I was able to clean my credit and three year after my divorce I bought my first 4-bedroom single family home and raised my children there. This is where I still reside to this day. **He is a keeping God.**

Chapter 18

His promises will always come true.

IT HAD BEEN 4 MONTHS AFTER ANDREW FIRST MOVED OUT that I was finally able to go back to see Dr. Norman, my neurologist. I took another MRI and waited for him to enter the examining room. I didn't know if there had been a problem because Dr. Norman never kept me waiting, but this time he did. He walked in the room with Dr. Chang and said, "Karen I almost gave up on you. I hadn't seen you in a while."

I smiled at him and said, "I've been going through a little bit."

He said, "Is everything alright?"

I said," Everything is great. I'm officially divorced."

"Oh, I'm sorry to hear that."

I told him, "It's not a loss here; all is well."

He said "Well then great! I'm sorry to have kept you waiting for so long, Dr. Chang and myself were trying to verify this new MRI you took today to make sure it was accurate."

I said, "Why?" Dr. Norman looked at Dr. Chang.

Dr. Chang said, "The tumor is gone!"

Dr. Norman said, "It's definitely your film; but you don't have a brain tumor anymore."

I said, "Man I told y'all God was going to heal me."

"You've said that since the first visit" Dr. Norman said, "But I thought you were just being optimistic."

I said, "No sir! I serve a healing God. Now you're a testimony to His work." Dr. Chang laughed and looked at Dr. Norman.

Dr. Norman said, "Yes we are. If everything else is okay with your migraine medicine, then just let me know when you need a refill." As I share this testimony **Isaiah 25:8** comes to mind.

Isaiah 25:8 (NKJV), "He will swallow up death forever, And the Lord God will wipe away tears from all faces; The rebuke of His people He will take away from all the earth; For the Lord has spoken."

The Author's Closing Remarks

I WANT TO REALIGN YOUR VIEWPOINT TO WHAT THE FATHER is saying concerning it all. The following Psalm speaks loud in pertaining to all that I went through.

Psalm 34:19 (KJV), "Many are the afflictions of the righteous: but the Lord delivereth him out of them all." I lived in Mom's apartment complex for a year. It was long enough to get a track record of good rental history. After that, Mom and I went our separate ways, but we always stayed in contact by phone. We both have had other struggles that we have endured but God's word was clearly seen in both Mom's life and my own.

Psalm 30:5 (KJV), "For his anger endureth but a moment; in his favor is life: weeping may endure for a night, but joy cometh in the morning." Mom is now living a peaceful Christian life and has been saved, delivered, and set free from her affliction. We are good friends now and talk daily. Even though she lives a few hours away, there are times I just pack up and go see her to be a blessing. I never miss a holiday to show her how much I love her. I'm a Pastor,

Evangelist, Chaplin, and now an Author. In this scripture, God has promised me restitution which I see manifesting daily.

Joel 2:25 (KJV), "And I will restore to you the years that the locust hath eaten, the cankerworm, and the caterpillar, and the palmerworm, my great army which I sent among you."

I remarried 22 years later after my divorce, to a true man of God. He is an Apostle, Pastor, and Evangelist. I now live in the true purpose and meaning of marriage by God's definition: God is being glorified and the fruit of His word is being reflected in every area of our lives. I kept my promise to God when he saved me in that hurricane that I would raise my children in His word and way. Both of my children love the Lord with all their hearts and honor me for teaching them strength, wisdom, and God's word. My son still seeks to go deeper in his relationship with God and to walk in his calling. My daughter is ministering to millions of women all around the world and she has an eight-year-old son; my only grandchild and he wants to be a teacher and preacher of God's word. God has given me and my entire house a promise from *Haggai 2:9.*

Haggai 2:9 (KJV), "The glory of this latter house shall be greater than of the former, saith the Lord of Hosts: and in this place will I give peace, saith the Lord of Hosts." God has been faithful to manifest His fruits of the word of God daily in every area of our life.

He Kept Me
Prayer guide for your
darkest moments

Prayers that will ensure that God will keep you.

I have generated these prayers for all of my readers no matter what season you may be in. I encourage you to use them as needed and share them as you are led to do so. God hears and answers all prayers. Be encouraged His word will never return void: it is "Yes" and "Amen!"

Psalm 34:19 (NKJV), "Many are the afflictions of the righteous, But the Lord delivers him out of them all."

Prayer of Salvation

"Dear Heavenly Father, thank You for sending Jesus to die on the cross for my sins. I acknowledge that I have sinned and that I cannot save myself. I believe that Jesus came to give me life, and by faith I now choose to receive Jesus into my heart and life as my Lord and Savior. Thank You for saving me Jesus. Amen."

Prayer to be filled with the Holy Spirit

"Dear Heavenly Father, you are present in this room and in my life. You alone are all-knowing, all-powerful, and everywhere present. I worship You alone. I declare my dependency on You, for apart from You I can do nothing. I ask you to fill me with Your Holy Spirit and empower me to do your will on a daily basis. I ask all this in the name of Jesus, I pray. Amen."

Prayer of Forgiveness (for others)

"Lord Jesus, I confess that I have been holding offense toward; name the person or position (teacher. Coach, school official, employers, ex-husband or husband, ex-wife or wife, church leaders, God, parent, stepparent, legal guardians) because of wrong doings against me by them. I release them now from all judgment. I choose to forgive them and allow you to be my vindicator, redeemer, restorer and one who brings restitution into my life. Amen."

"Lord Jesus, I choose not to hold on to resentment. I relinquish the right to seek revenge and ask You to heal my damaged emotions. Thank You for setting me free from the bondage of unforgiveness and bitterness. I thank You for Your word in **John 8:36(NIV).** So, if the Son sets you free, you are free indeed. I ask You to bless those who have hurt me. In Jesus's name. Amen."

Prayer of Forgiveness (for self-deception).

"Lord Jesus, I renounce the spirit of self-deception. I confess that I have wrongly defended myself by; saying I have no sin, thinking I am something and I am not. I can be truly religious and not bridle my tongue, thinking that God is the source of my problems, thinking I can live my life without the help of anyone else, being a hearer of God's word but not doing what it says. I pray that the work you have

begun in me you will perfect and complete it until the day of Christ Jesus' return. I pray all these things in the name of Jesus. Amen." (**Phil 1:6(Amp)**)

Many people don't realize how deep-rooted fear can be in one's life. The spirit of fear is a demonic strongman. What is a strongman? It is one who has a deep root with many other roots extending from it. It is important to me that I expose the truth about this spirit. It is nothing to be dismissed or minimized. Any sight of the spirit of fear can look to be natural or normal but it is everything except that. God's word tells only through faith can we know Him and serve Him.

Hebrews 11:6 (NKJV), "But without faith it is impossible to please Him, for he comes to God must believe that He is, and that He is a rewarder of those who diligently seek Him." Hebrews is telling us that faith is the key to walking in our relationship with God. If we operate in doubt or unbelief, we hinder our relationship with Christ. That's why spirits such as stress and worry spring up from the strongman fear.

Romans 1:17 (NKJV), "For in it the righteousness of God is revealed from faith to faith; as it is written, The just shall live by faith." Romans tell us that faith should always be growing and to grow it has to be rooted in the word of God which is the righteousness of Jesus that we should all be walking in. Many things we encounter cause us to veer from faith to fear. To prevent this from happening we should be rooted in God's word and be operating by His Spirit; which is the Holy Spirit."

Prayers to Overcome Fear

"Dear Heavenly Father, I confess that I have allowed fear to control me, and that lack of faith is sin. Thank You for Your forgiveness. I recognize that You have not given me a spirit of fear, but of power, love, and sound mind. Amen." **2 Timothy 1:7(NKJV).**

These are some examples of fear that we should not excuse or minimize: Fear of death, never being loved, Satan, embarrassment, failure, being victimized, rejection, marriage, disapproval, divorce, going crazy, debt, illness, never getting married, the future, death of a loved one, confrontation, not being loved by God, losing your salvation, and any individual. Renounce and reject any spirits of fear operating in your life. Ask God to reveal any and all controlling fears in your life and the lies behind them. Pray: "Dear Heavenly Father I desire to live by faith in God and in the power of the Holy Spirit. I curse the root of all spirit of fear and release the fire of God's word to burn up every seed and residual turning it to ashes and confine it to the pit of hell never to be active in my life again. In the Mighty Jesus name, I pray. Amen."

Prayers that will Deliver you from Generational Curses.

"I renounce, reject and break all generational curses of pride, lust, perversion, rebellion, witchcraft, idolatry, poverty, abandonment, rejection, fear, failure, lack, debt, confusion, addiction, death, grave, and destruction in the mighty name of Jesus. Anything that has been used to hinder the Holy Spirit or the word of God in my life be silenced and destroyed. In Jesus mighty name. Amen."

"I command all generational spirits that came into my life during conception in the womb, in the birth canal, and through the umbilical cord to come out in the mighty name of Jesus and let their activities in my life be burnt up by fire. In Jesus mighty name. Amen."

"I reject, renounce and cancel all spoken curses and negative words that someone else or I have spoken over my life in the name of Jesus. Let all flaming arrows sent against me and evil altars built to curse my life; be burnt up by fire. In Jesus mighty name. Amen."

"I break the legal right of all generational spirits operating behind a curse in the mighty name of Jesus. I reject and renounce your activity in my life by fire and by force in the name of Jesus. I cancel any curses through my mother and father blood line in the name of Jesus. I sever all ties to any legal right that the demonic realm has been given through my parents and forefathers choices made in their past life. In the mighty name of Jesus. Amen."

Prayers of Protection

"My Lord, my God send Your angels from heaven with flaming swords of fire to fight my battles in the Heavenly realms and release Your word on fire and burn up the works of darkness in my life. Thank You that your angels encamp round about me and they deliver me. In the mighty name of Jesus. Amen." (**Psalms 34:7**)

"My Father my God let your righteousness be revealed in my life and may you be glorified in every area of my life. In the mighty name of Jesus. Amen."

"Father God activate in me Your discernment, revelation, and wisdom so that I will know my purpose and destiny that You have for my life and equip me through your spirit. In the mighty name of Jesus', I ask. Amen."

"My Father my God defends me from those who unjustly rise up against me and deliver me from the hands of the evil man. May their evil plans for me boomerang back to their house seven-fold and let their works of evil be silenced forever. let the fire of God surround me and protect my life from destruction. Father keep me in all my ways. Order your angels to help me complete the assignment you have for me. In the name of Jesus. Amen." (**Psalms 91:11**)

"My Father, my God refrain my feet from every evil way so that I will keep your word. I pray for the heart and mind of the Father that I would love the things

He loves and hate the things He hates. Holy Spirit teach me to always seek the kingdom of God first. In Jesus's name. Amen." (**Matt 6:33**)

"My Father, my God I reject, renounce and sever all assignments of the enemy against my finances, my family, my life and my ministry. I release the fire of God to consume the root of the attack. I resist the enemy and he flee from me. In the mighty name of Jesus. Amen." (**James 4:7**)

Prayers of Prosperity

"My Father my God let peace be within my walls and prosperity be within my palace. Open the floodgates of heaven and overflow in my life, so that I can receive more than I have room to store. So that I may be a blessing to your kingdom. In Jesus's mighty name. Amen." (**Mal 3:10**)

"My Father my God make all grace abound towards me; that I will have sufficiency in all things and abound to every good work. allow your favor to follow me wherever I go; that way I can receive your blessing and be a blessing in all things. In Jesus's name. Amen." (**2Cor 9:8**)

"My Father my God give me a hunger for your word, that I may meditate on it day and night. Allow your word to be alive to me and tangible to my touch; that I would always be grateful, and I will glorify you by praising you with thanksgiving all the days of my life. In Jesus's mighty name. Amen." (**Psalms 1:2**)

"My Father, my God I ask you to bless my life financially, so that all my needs may be met according to your riches in Christ Jesus. I decree that the blessings of the Lord makes me rich and adds no sorrow to it. In Jesus's name. Amen." (**Prov 10:22**)

Prayer for Healing

"My Father, my God I thank you that by the stripes of Jesus I am healed. You sent your word to heal us and deliver us from every (name whatever the sickness you're dealing with) destruction. Thank you for divine healing and divine health. In Jesus mighty name. Amen." (**1Pet2:24, Psalms 107:20**)

"My Father, my God You healed me O Lord and I will be healed, You save me O Lord and I will be saved. For You are the one that I praise. Thank You Lord that my soul prospers and that I am in good health. In Jesus name. Amen." (**Jer 17:14, 3 John 2**)

"My Father, my God I thank You for healing my broken heart and binding up my wounds. I decree and declare that every organ in my body comes to divine alignment with the word of God and functions in the proper condition that God created it to function. In Jesus mighty name. Amen." (**Psalms 147:3**)

"My Father, my God I decree, and I declare that every physical, mental, and emotional sickness the devil is bringing against me and my house is broken and destroyed. I fortify my walls and doors with the word of God and blood of Jesus. I decree that the enemy cannot come near my dwelling. In Jesus mighty name. Amen." (**Isaiah 10:27, Job 22:28**)

Acknowledgements:

I FIRST WANT TO RECOGNIZE THE INSPIRATION THAT WAS imparted into me by the Holy Spirit. This manuscript would not have been completed if it weren't for Him.

I would also like to thank and honor my husband, Pastor James Izekor. His words of wisdom and intercessory brought me guidance throughout this entire process. I'm overwhelmed with gratitude. In many of my chapters in this book; I asked him to put on his "Pastor Hat" to give me a grade on the words that were given to me by the Lord and the scripture God had placed in my spirit. To make sure they aligned with the word of the Lord and the scripture God had placed in my spirit. Words can't express how much I love and appreciate this anointed man of God.

I would like to express my highest appreciation to my daughter Ca 'Drain C. Blanks. She drove me to aim for a higher level of excellence. There were many things we viewed in different lights, but because of that I was able to open my book up to a larger audience. In the last few chapters, she literally had nothing but good to say. This was relieving after the constructive criticism I'd receive on earlier parts. I also accredit her for helping me come up with some of my chapter titles.

My best friend and ministry partner, Tami Schnars. I'm genuinely thankful and grateful for this Might Women of God in many different ways. After the third time I lost the entire manuscript, due to computer issues and thumb drive glitches, Tami constantly encouraged me not to give up. On every off day she was waiting on me hand and foot, and that shut out a lot of distractions. On top of all of that, she was excited to listen to any portions of the book that I had time to share.

I recognize with high honors Latoya Ogidan my Pastor friend and ministry partner. This amazing woman of God has been a true blazing fire in my life for the kingdom of God. She's been both my accountability partner and ministry partner. I was 5-chapters from finishing after losing my manuscript once again, and Mrs. Ogidan went out and bought me a new computer just to ensure that this book would be written. I'm forever indebted to her for her support and kindness.

In addition to I would like to thank my editor of this book, Haley Willens. The first day working with Haley I knew she was God sent. She was very thorough in proofreading and correcting this book. I had never met Miss. Haley in person; but I could discern she was soft-spoken and kind as she could be. This being my first book, I felt most of my publishing knowledge was obsolete. Miss Haley educated me on what publishers were looking for and what I should expect from them. She started promptly on my manuscript and finished on time for her projected date, which was very impressive considering the many changes she encountered last minute with no extra charge to me. I owe Miss Haley a thousand thank for a job of excellence.

I would like to thank my 11-year-old niece Samaya Harrison for posing as my cover girl model for this book. You were a joy to work with. You are a gifted and talented young lady that God will use mightily in His Kingdom. May you continue to blossom and flourish in Christ. Also, I would like to recognition Samaya's father Xavian Harrison. My stepbrother who part was played in Chapter 7. of this book as 5-year-old Zaiden.

My love and appreciation go to my spiritual son and daughter Devin and Taylor Young. Devin shot all pictures of my nice and me in prayer poses and the inside photos of this book. Taylor is my hair stylist. Devin's contact Information ProsperityPhotos,prosperityphotos20@gmail.com. Taylor's contact information Facebook.com/reedhair

I give credit and pay tribute to De Jai Moore for taking great pictures for the Author Bio, Author Closing and Front Cover of this book. His company name is Moore Exceptional Photography. dj.moore214@yahoo.com.

9 781662 814778